Fodor's InFocus

YOSEMITE, SEQUOIA & KINGS CANYON
NATIONAL PARKS

1st Edition

**Where to Stay and Eat
for All Budgets**

**Must-See Sights
and Local Secrets**

Ratings You Can Trust

Fodor's Travel Publications New York, Toronto, London, Sydney, Auckland
www.fodors.com

FODOR'S IN FOCUS YOSEMITE, SEQUOIA & KINGS CANYON NATIONAL PARKS

Series Editor: Douglas Stallings
Editor: Douglas Stallings
Writer: Reed Parsell

Editorial Production: Evangelos Vasilakis
Maps & Illustrations: Mark Stroud, *cartographer*; Bob Blake and Rebecca Baer, *map editors*
Design: Fabrizio LaRocca, *creative director*; Guido Caroti, *art director*; Ann McBride, *designer*; Melanie Marin, *senior picture editor*
Cover Photo: El Capitan & the Merced River, Yosemite Valley: Chris Falkenstein/Yosemite Stock
Production/Manufacturing: Amanda Bullock

COPYRIGHT

1st Edition

ISBN 978–1–4000–0374–7

ISSN 1946–2336

SPECIAL SALES

AN IMPORTANT TIP & AN INVITATION

Although all prices, opening times, and other details in this book are based on information supplied to us at press time, changes occur all the time in the travel world, and Fodor's cannot accept responsibility for facts that become outdated or for inadvertent errors or omissions. **So always confirm information when it matters,** especially if you're making a detour to visit a specific place. Your experiences—positive and negative—matter to us. If we have missed or misstated something, **please write to us.** We follow up on all suggestions. Contact the Yosemite, Sequoia & Kings Canyon editor at editors@fodors.com or c/o Fodor's at 1745 Broadway, New York, NY 10019.

PRINTED IN THE UNITED STATES OF AMERICA

10 9 8 7 6 5 4 3 2 1

Be a Fodor's Correspondent

Your opinion matters. It matters to us. It matters to your fellow Fodor's travelers, too. And we'd like to hear it. In fact, we *need* to hear it. When you share your experiences and opinions, you become an active member of the Fodor's community. Here's how you can help improve Fodor's for all of us.

Tell us when we're right. We rely on local writers to give you an insider's perspective. But our writers and staff editors also depend on you. Your positive feedback is a vote to renew our recommendations for the next edition.

Tell us when we're wrong. We update most of our guides every year. But things change. If any of our descriptions are inaccurate or inadequate, we'll incorporate your changes in the next edition and will correct factual errors at fodors.com *immediately*.

Tell us what to include. You probably have had fantastic travel experiences that aren't yet in Fodor's. Why not share them with a community of like-minded travelers? Share your discoveries and experiences with everyone directly at fodors.com. Your input may lead us to add a new listing or a higher recommendation.

Give us your opinion instantly at our feedback center at www.fodors.com/feedback. You may also e-mail editors@fodors.com with the subject line "Yosemite, Sequoia & Kings Canyon Editor." Or send your nominations, comments, and complaints by mail to Yosemite, Sequoia & Kings Canyon Editor, Fodor's, 1745 Broadway, New York, NY 10019.

Happy Traveling!

Tim Jarrell, Publisher

CONTENTS

ABOUT
THIS BOOK

Our Ratings

We wouldn't recommend a place that wasn't worth your time, but sometimes a place is so experiential that superlatives don't do it justice: you just have to be there to know. These sights, properties, and experiences get our highest rating, **Fodor's Choice**, indicated by orange stars throughout this book. Black stars highlight sights and properties we deem **Highly Recommended**, places that our writers, editors, and readers praise again and again for consistency and excellence.

Credit Cards

Want to pay with plastic? **AE, D, DC, MC, V** after restaurant and hotel listings indicate whether American Express, Discover, Diners Club, MasterCard, and Visa are accepted.

Restaurants

Unless we state otherwise, restaurants are open for lunch and dinner daily. We mention dress only when there's a specific requirement and reservations only when they're essential or not accepted—it's always best to book ahead.

Hotels

Unless we tell you otherwise, you can assume that the hotels have private bath, phone, TV, and air-conditioning. We always list facilities but not whether you'll be charged an extra fee to use them, so when pricing accommodations, find out what's included.

Many Listings
- ★ Fodor's Choice
- ★ Highly recommended
- ⊠ Physical address
- ↔ Directions
- ⊕ Mailing address
- ☎ Telephone
- 🖷 Fax
- ⊕ On the Web
- ✎ E-mail
- 🎫 Admission fee
- ⊙ Open/closed times
- Ⓜ Metro stations
- ▭ Credit cards

Hotels & Restaurants
- 🏨 Hotel
- ⟵ Number of rooms
- ⟀ Facilities
- ⦿ Meal plans
- ✕ Restaurant
- ⟁ Reservations
- ⦦ Smoking
- 🍺 BYOB
- ✕🏨 Hotel with restaurant that warrants a visit

Outdoors
- ⛳ Golf
- ⛺ Camping

Other
- ☺ Family-friendly
- ⇨ See also
- ⊠ Branch address
- ☞ Take note

WHEN TO GO

Yosemite National Park has different appeals depending on the time of year. For a potential "winter wonderland" feel, make reservations to stay in the Valley sometime between Thanksgiving and late March. If you want to see waterfalls at their fullest, visit in late spring or early summer. If you want to stroll about Tuolumne Meadow and take hikes off Tioga Road—and if you want access to all the park's amenities and ranger programs—go in the summer. If you want to avoid crowds to the greatest extent possible, visit Yosemite in October (when waterfalls will be at their least-impressive) or February.

Most people visit Sequoia and Kings Canyon National Parks in the summer, when everything is open and accessible. Generals Highway (Rte. 198), which connects the two parks, is open year-round but may impose chain requirements during snowstorms and their aftermath. The parks' two significant secondary roads (Kings Canyon Scenic Byway [Rte. 180 between Grant Grove Village and Cedar Grove Village] and Mineral King Road [which branches off Rte. 198 at Three Rivers]), both about 30 mi long, are closed from mid- to late October through May, typically, due to snow accumulation and rockslide dangers.

Make lodging and campground reservations for Yosemite Valley and Sequoia National Park's Giant Forest area as far in advance as you can.

Climate

Yosemite receives most of its precipitation, which averages 37 inches a year, from November through April. Summer rainfall is rare. The average high and low temperatures in the Valley are 49 and 26 in January, 65 and 35 in April, 90 and 54 in July, and 74 and 39 in October.

Sequoia and Kings Canyon weather is similar, with slightly less precipitation overall but with a bit more chance of occasional summer showers. The average high and low temperatures at elevations from 4,000 to 7,000 feet are 42 and 24 in January, 51 and 30 in April, 76 and 51 in July, and 61 and 38 in October.

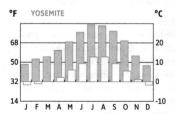

Welcome to the Parks

WORD OF MOUTH

"The views will leave you speechless. Yosemite Valley is flat so riding a bike isn't strenuous. This is a great way to get many different views of the Valley as well as seeing some wildlife. We also made our way up to Glacier Point—by car. So worth the trip!"

—ScarletandGray

By Reed
Parsell

STAND ALMOST ANYWHERE IN YOSEMITE VALLEY and
turn slowly in a circle. In a minute, you will see more natural wonders than you could in a full day in almost any
other national park. Half Dome, Yosemite Falls, El Capitan,
Bridalveil Falls, the meadows, Sentinel Dome, the Merced
River, white-flowering dogwood trees, and perhaps even
bears ripping into the bark of fallen trees or sticking their
snouts into beehives—all that is in the Valley. Elsewhere
in the park, which is about the size of Rhode Island, you
can examine some of the world's biggest trees, take hikes
along some of the country's most scenic trails, and hang
out in two of California's best indoor spaces, the Ahwahnee
Hotel's Great Lounge and its iconic Dining Room.

To the south, Sequoia and Kings Canyon national parks
beckon with their own set of awesome visuals. Stand amid
a dozen tightly grouped mature sequoias—all more than
1,500 years old and more than 200 feet tall—and contemplate the significance (or insignificance) of your fast-paced,
high-tech life as a human being in the 21st century. Drive
through Kings River Canyon, on the way to Kings Canyon
National Park, and look up at granite cliffsides that are
taller than those found in Arizona's Grand Canyon.

None of the quintessential California experiences—strolling
the hilly streets of San Francisco, driving along the dramatic
rocky north coast, going for a sail off San Diego, wondering
at the adaptive life forms at Death Valley, being dazzled
by the delights at Disneyland—is likely to last longer in
your memory than what you will see and do in Yosemite,
Sequoia, and Kings Canyon national parks. Granted, you
will need a few hours to reach the parks, which are 200
to 300 mi from greater Los Angeles or the Bay Area, not
to mention a solid 60-minute drive from the nearest airport, Fresno International. And the crowds, especially in
Yosemite Valley, can be a downer. But the sights will more
than make up for that.

Ideally, if this is your first visit, try to allot at least a week
to explore the three parks. You could get by with a shorter
trip, of course, as long as you take mental notes on what
you will do upon your return. Been here already, have
you? Well, perhaps this is your chance to finally make the
heroic trek up Half Dome, pulling yourself up by a steel
cable the final 400 feet. Or maybe you could leave all your
troubles behind for a few days and disappear into the vast
High Sierra wilderness of Kings Canyon National Park.

Another delicious possibility: pitch your tent under massive Sierra redwoods in Sequoia's Atwell Mill campground and spend your days hiking to high-altitude lakes in Mineral King, and your evenings chatting around the campfire with family and friends.

HISTORY OF THE PARKS

YOSEMITE

As many as 8,000 years ago, people began living in what now is called the Yosemite Valley. No one can say when exactly they arrived, or where precisely they came from, but historians agree that Southern Sierra Miwoks eventually laid claim to the region. The tribe's long-standing Valley culture was one of song and spirituality, of hunting animals for basic necessities rather than for sport, of harvesting the acorns of black oak trees, and—evidence suggests—of regularly burning the underbrush to promote the landscape's future health. The Miwoks also established a trading partnership with the Mono Lake Paiutes of the Eastern Sierra.

The California Gold Rush triggered a series of upheavals that spelled trouble, if not outright doom, for most of the native peoples in northern California. On March 27, 1851, barely three years after James Marshall's discovery of gold in the foothills 50 mi east of Sacramento, the Mariposa Battalion arrived at Yosemite Valley. These state-sanctioned troops, who waged war against the Indians, represented the first group of non-natives to record their entry into the Valley. Four years later, the first tourists arrived. By the end of the century, most of the Indians were long gone, having been killed, overcome by newly introduced diseases, or relocated to distant camps.

The Valley's special geologic qualities, as well as the giant sequoias of Mariposa Grove 30 mi to the south, so impressed a group of influential Californians that they persuaded President Abraham Lincoln to grant those two areas to the state for protection. Lincoln's signing of the Yosemite Grant on June 30, 1864, while the Civil War raged on, was the first step toward preservation efforts that continue today. Eight years later, in 1872, Yellowstone became the country's first national park, and on October 1, 1890—thanks largely to lobbying efforts by naturalist John Muir and Robert Underwood Johnson, the editor of

Century Magazine—Congress set aside 1,500 square mi for Yosemite National Park.

For the next 16 years, the state continued to oversee protection of the Valley and Mariposa Grove, while federal soldiers managed the national park's vast wilderness areas. African-American troops, known as the Buffalo Soldiers of the Sierra Nevada, were stationed at Army headquarters in Wawona for several of those years. In 1906, three years after Theodore Roosevelt and John Muir famously gave the president's protectors the slip and went camping on their own in the Valley, the two state-operated areas were ceded to become part of Yosemite National Park. In 1914, civilian rangers took over control of the park from the military.

Muir had first seen the Yosemite Valley in 1868. He was still on the scene 45 years later as he lobbied against the damming of the Tuolumne River in Hetch Hetchy Valley, north of Yosemite Valley. That effort failed in 1913, when Congress approved construction of the O'Shaughnessy Dam. Muir died a year later, and controversy over the reservoir—which supplies water to nearly 2.5 million people in the Bay Area—still simmers today.

Visitation to the park rose significantly once the Yosemite Valley Railroad, which ran along the north banks of the Merced River from Merced to El Portal, opened in 1907. Six years later, automobiles were allowed into the park. In 1954, for the first time, more than a million people visited Yosemite. More than 4 million people were coming annually by the mid-1990s, although in more recent years that number has been in the 3.3 million to 3.7 million range.

SEQUOIA/KINGS CANYON

It may surprise you to know that Sequoia National Park is older than Yosemite National Park, though only by a week. On September 25, 1890, President Benjamin Harrison signed the bill that created Sequoia. On October 1, when Yosemite was born, Congress not only tripled the size of Sequoia but also created General Grant National Park. (That's the area that today constitutes Grant Grove Village and the grove itself.)

For many millennia before that flurry of preservation efforts, native peoples lived in the region, just as they did in the region that is now Yosemite. The Monache, a Paiute tribe

CLOSE UP

John Muir

1

Although he was born a continent and an ocean away, in Dunbar, Scotland, John Muir was one of the most influential figures of the American West. Largely because of his popular writings and impassioned lobbying efforts, Yosemite National Park was established and eventually expanded. He also co-founded the Sierra Club, the nation's oldest grass-roots environmental organization.

When he was 11, in 1849, he and his large family (Muir had seven siblings) immigrated to Wisconsin. By the time he made his way to San Francisco 19 years later, Muir already was an established naturalist, having walked from Florida to Indiana after a factory accident nearly cost him his sight and prompted his embrace of nature.

"No temple made with hands can compare with Yosemite," he wrote about seeing the Valley for the first time, in March 1868. Soon he returned for many extended stays, one time to herd domestic sheep, animals he later famously referred to as "hoofed locusts."

Muir went on to conduct several extensive studies about geology and ecology of the High Sierra, before taking a break in the 1880s to devote himself to his new marriage and to the new family home in Martinez, east of San Francisco. Then he led the way to have Yosemite Valley and Mariposa Grove designated as a national park in 1890. In 1903, Muir personally lobbied President Theodore Roosevelt on a camping excursion in and around the Valley. Roosevelt was so impressed by Yosemite—and Muir—that in 1905 he helped orchestra California's surrender of the rest of present-day Yosemite National Park to federal control.

The last lobbying effort of Muir's life was unsuccessful, as despite his impassioned pleas for conservation, President Woodrow Wilson in December 1913 authorized that the Tuolumne River be dammed in Hetch Hetchy. Muir died one year and five days later, on Christmas Eve 1914. His spirit lives on in today's "Restore Hetch Hetchy" movement, and his name adorns many a public school and building in California; Theodore Roosevelt published an appreciation letter three weeks after his death.

---

also known as the Western Monos, spent warm months in the mountains and valleys. They traded with Paiutes on the other side of the mountain range, lugging goods to and fro over the 11,823-foot-high Kearsarge Pass. In winter they migrated to the foothills, where Yokut tribes lived year-round. Today, 265 archaeological sites and 69 historic sites are protected in Sequoia and Kings Canyon national parks as a tribute to the Indians, who by the 1870s no longer lived within those areas.

European Americans came onto the scene in the early 19th century, first looking to establish missions, but eventually to hunt, trap, and skin animals. In the years following Marshall's gold discovery and the massive migration it inspired from the east, ranching gained a foothold in mountains east of Visalia and Fresno, as did logging operations. Thanks to the persistence and persuasive abilities of John Muir (who first visited Kings Canyon in 1873) and George Stewart, the editor of Visalia's *Delta* newspaper, a bill to protect the region's sequoia groves was presented to Congress in 1881. That effort failed, and although Muir afterward turned his full attention to Yosemite, others rallied to the cause of a Sequoia National Park, and that latter effort succeeded nine years later.

In 1926, Kern Canyon and Mount Whitney were added to Sequoia National Park. On March 4, 1940, Kings Canyon National Park was created and incorporated what had been General Grant National Park, which became its smaller, western portion. The valley region around Mineral King was added to Sequoia National Park in 1978.

By the way, there is a historical reason why no apostrophe appears in Kings Canyon. When Spanish-speaking missionaries first saw the river valley in 1806, they christened it "El Rio de los Santos Reyes"—the river of the holy kings, a reference to the three wise men of Christian lore. Of course, students of English punctuation might object that the story fails to explain why there is no apostrophe *after* the "s."

GEOLOGY OF THE PARKS

Until 200 million years ago, you could have gone sailing over what's now the Sierra Nevada region. At some point after that, magma started bubbling up through the sea and creating points of land. Inside those new formations, lava hardened into granite. By 25 million years ago, the sea was long gone, volcanic activity was winding down, and erosion had largely stripped overlying volcanic rocks to expose the granite. Then something even more dramatic began to happen.

CLOSE UP

Park Passes

1

For Yosemite, admission fee is $20 per car and is valid for seven days; for the combination of Sequoia and Kings Canyon, the fee is also $20 per car. Individuals arriving by bus or on foot, bicycle, motorcycle, or horseback pay $10 for a seven-day pass. A one-year pass for Yosemite is $40, while one for Sequoia and Kings Canyon is $30. A 12-month "America the

Beautiful–National Parks and Federal Recreational Lands Pass" is $80 and gets you (and your family) into all federal recreation sites that charge entrance fees. Seniors (age 62 and older) can purchase the annual pass for $10. People with lifetime disabilities are entitled to an "Access Pass," which is free.

Ever so slowly, the eastern part of what became the Sierra Nevada began to rise. By 3 million years ago, its basic shape was in place: about 400 mi long and from 40 mi to 80 mi wide. On the western side, the slope is gradual, starting from what's basically sea level in the Central Valley, up through the foothills, and on into the 8,000- to 10,000-foot mountains and peaks that are in the western portions of all three national parks. But the parks' highest points are farther east, where they tower dramatically over valleys that extend into what is now the state of Nevada. (You can see this geological feature for yourself by driving on Highway 395.)

The Yosemite Valley and Kings River Canyon were made increasingly deep by the rivers that flowed from the higher eastern Sierra on down toward the Central Valley. Then, about 3 million years ago, ice began to play a major role. Glaciers up to 3,000 feet deep nearly filled Yosemite Valley several times, breaking off huge portions of granite formations such as Half Dome, and depositing them on streambeds to the west. The ice movements also polished what granite was left behind. Both Yosemite Valley and Kings River Canyon, which had even larger glaciers, were carved to the shape of a "U." (A "V" shape indicates rivers alone formed a canyon.)

When the last glacier receded in Yosemite, about 15,000 years ago, it left a "terminal moraine"—basically a dam of huge rocks that the glacier had scraped off the mountains—on the Valley's western side. That created a lake, which eventually became swamps and after that the meadows that exist today. As you head into Yosemite Valley, 6 mi inside the Arch Rock entrance and a few hundred yards past Pohono Bridge, you can see the terminal moraine's outline. Not surprisingly, it resembles a modern-day levee.

FLORA & FAUNA

National parks are sanctuaries for plants and animals, and in these three extraordinary California regions there are many species to protect. The parks are large—Yosemite encompasses 1,169 square mi, while Sequoia and Kings Canyon together cover a combined 1,350 square mi—and that expanse supports a wide variety of plant and animal life. The parks' great variations in altitude—in Sequoia's case from 1,700 feet to 14,494 feet—create conditions for a great diversity of life. As you venture from foothills to the High Sierra, the landscape changes dramatically, as do the creatures who call these various "life zones" home.

Remember when you visit these parks that you are here to observe, not participate. The automobiles and noises that we bring into nature's intricate mix of other life forms is disruptive, for sure, but limit your impact to whatever extent you can. Don't leave your car's engine idling when you are parked. Leave pine cones on the ground and flowers on their stems. Keep your food in "bear boxes" or inside other authorized, secure locations. Dispose of your trash properly, including by using the omnipresent recycling bins. If you are a smoker, limit it to the extent you can and never toss cigarette stubs on the ground. Do not approach wildlife, do not talk to or shout at wildlife, and do not feed wildlife. Enjoy them by using cameras and binoculars, and by taking pictures with your mind's eye.

FLORA

Due to the parks' wide range of elevations, lots of different things take root in this vast region. In Yosemite alone, you'll find 35 types of native trees and nearly 1,500 wildflower species. The undisputed plant star in all three parks is the mature sequoia, which you simply must see to believe. In addition to what's listed below, keep a lookout for dogwoods, which grow throughout Yosemite Valley and reportedly were John Muir's favorite tree.

California Black Oak (*quercus kelloggii*). Native Americans preferred this deciduous tree, common in the foothills regions of Sequoia National Park and prominent in Yosemite Valley, as a source for their acorn meal. The bark is dark, as is suggested in the tree's colloquial name, and leaves are a yellowish green. This is California's most prolific hardwood species.

Ferns (*petridophyta*). These luscious plants, of which there are more than 20,000 varieties worldwide, grace many a trail in all three parks. Famed photographer Ansel Adams took some lovely black-and-white images of what in Kodachrome color is a gorgeous green. For those people who are accustomed to finding ferns in tropical or coastal locales, seeing them for the first time in the Sierra can prompt a double take.

Foxtail Pine (*pinus austrina*). Endemic to California, these gray-barked trees are not nearly as tall as other pines found in the parks, but they can live for more than 2,000 years. Their seeds are an important food source for bears, birds, squirrels, and other creatures.

Giant Sequioa (*sequoiadendron giganteum*). Also referred to as "big trees," these red- and soft-barked evergreen wonders can live for more than 2,500 years. They do not grow as tall as the coastal redwoods but still are capable of shooting more than 300 feet into the air. Considering how large their bases (up to 40 feet in diameter) and trunks (up to 8 feet in diameter) can be, the fact that their cones are no bigger than chicken eggs seems a bit incongruent.

Incense Cedar (*calocedrus decurrens*). These tall trees, often confused with sequoias because of their similarly grooved and colored bark, grow in abundance from Baja California up to central Oregon. They can be found in all mid-altitude parts (elevation 7,000 feet or lower) of the three national parks and can top out above 200 feet.

Lupine (*magnoliophyta*). Purple flowers distinguish these perennials when they are in late spring or summer bloom in the parks' meadows. Some gardeners like to use lupines (often spelled without the "e") as an ornamental, although others (perhaps anti-purple people) consider them to be weeds.

Manzanita (*arctostaphylos patula*). Omnipresent in California's mountains, as well as a popular planting in many of California's low-lying urban areas, these bushes are easily identified by the startling (but pleasing) contrast between their bright-green leaves and purplish-color bark. ■TIP→**If you hike on Yosemite's spectacular Panorama Trail, you will pass through a veritable forest of manzanita on the hillside just beyond Illilouette Falls.**

Mule's Ear (*wyethia mollis*). A perennial with narrow, yellow flowers, this herb grows above elevations of 4,000 feet and is a bright, mid-summer sight in Sequoia's Crescent Meadow and other mountain areas of the three national parks. It is native to California and not found very far beyond its borders.

Ponderosa Pine (*pinus benthamiama*). One identifying feature of these tall, mountain trees is that their bark resembles jigsaw-puzzle pieces, with the lining between them deep and dark. Another species that is capable of being more than 200 feet tall, ponderosas tend to have broad bases and limbs that begin far from the ground. The cones, renowned for their simple beauty, typically are 3 to 6 inches long. ■TIP→**If you see football-size cones on a trail, it's likely they fell from sugar pines, not ponderosas.**

Sierra Tiger Lily (*lilium columbianum*). Native Americans used this native plant as a food source; in dried form, it reportedly has a sweet-and-sour taste. Found in higher altitudes throughout the West, it provides flashes of orange color in the parks' meadows and forested areas.

FAUNA

It is no wonder that bird-watching is a popular activity in all three national parks: Yosemite has almost 250 confirmed species, while Sequoia and Kings Canyon can claim more than 200. Angling is not nearly as big a deal here, which is just as well due to declining fish populations and the principle that national parks are sanctuaries for all creatures. Eighty-five species of mammals live within Yosemite's boundaries, along with more than 175 other vertebrates; inside Sequoia and Kings Canyon are some 260 native vertebrate species. Bears get most of the attention in all three parks, but to remain a vibrant presence, they must maintain an independence from human beings and, more specifically, from humans food.

BIRDS

Bullock's Oriole (*icterus bullockii*). This small blackbird, commonly spotted in Sequoia and Kings Canyon, is orange underneath and has a white wing patch. At one time, it and the Baltimore oriole were considered to be the same species.

California Thrasher (*toxostoma redivivum*). Generally brown and possessing dark eyes, this foot-long (or so) bird lives in lower-mountain, or foothill, regions of California and Baja California. It's a challenge to spot them, as they tend not to fly much in the open, preferring to be camouflaged in dense bush areas.

Clark's Nutcracker (*nucifraga columbianan*). Kind of an ash-gray with black-and-white wings, this bird can be seen throughout the western North American continent. Among its characteristics are an impressively varied voice and the occasional tendency to dine on carcasses.

Golden Eagle (*aquila chrysaetos*). Possessing a dark brown body to go along with wings that indeed can look golden, this famous raptor can be found at most elevations and in many countries. Occasionally spotted in Yosemite Valley, golden eagles tend to be more easily seen at higher elevations, such as off Tioga Road. When soaring, they hold their wings in a shallow V shape.

Great Gray Owl (*strix nebulosa*). Large by owl standards, the great gray has a big gray head, strikingly yellow and small eyes, and a long tail. Logging poses a major threat to these owls, which in California are listed as an endangered species. They seem to be holding their own in the national parks, which are free of logging. In addition to being found in Canada, as well as the western and upper midwestern sections of the U.S., they also have a presence in Scandinavia and parts of Asia. Listen for their distinctive, deep hoots.

Peregrine Falcon (*falco peregrinus*). Capable of flying at more than 175 mi per hour, this is the planet's fastest animal. For meals, it swoops down on smaller birds, mid-flight. Widespread spots are a prominent feature of its appearance, as are the yellow rings that circle its dark eyes. Insecticides such as DDT put this bird in peril in the middle to late 20th century, but it has rebounded in these three national parks and can be seen throughout the world. Peregrine falcons often perch high on big-city buildings and prey on pigeons.

Steller's Jay (*cyanocitta stelleri*). Bright blue with a gray-black crest, this jay emits a screech that other birds recognize as a signal that food is available. It has a longer head and more slender bill than does a blue jay. Steller's jays like to travel in groups of 10 or more and often can be seen flying en masse over lightly forested areas in the three national parks. They are especially fond of picnic areas.

White-Headed Woodpecker (*picoides albolarvatus*). Partial to ponderosa pine forests in the American West, this medium-size bird has a black body and a white head. Males have red spots on the nape of their lightly colored noggins. This species of woodpecker is quieter than many others because rather than hammering on trees, it pries off the bark. It also forages for cones.

FISH

Brook Trout (*salvelinus fontinalis*). A member of the salmon family, this fish is actually native to the eastern United States but at some point was introduced to the west. Its presence in the three parks is mostly at higher elevations, in small streams and creeks. Fly-fishermen like to go after brook trout, which are brownish and can be up to 10 inches long.

Brown Trout (*salmo trutta*). Greenish with black spots, this fish is also a non-native species to the High Sierra—by most accounts, it is native to Europe and Asia, although a broader native presence is possible. Larger than brook trout, brown trout are a popular game fish and receive high marks for taste. Attempts to farm them have been problematic.

Cutthroat Trout (*oncorhynchus clarki*). This species is native to North America but not to the three national parks. Their size can vary great, from 6 to 40 inches long. They tend to be brownish, with small black spots and larger, lighter splotches. Closely related to rainbow trout, they are another frequent target of fly fishermen.

Golden Trout (*oncorhynchus aquabonita*). This little fish (a size approaching 12 inches is unusual) is native to California and tends to inhabit streams and lakes way up in the High Sierra—at 10,000 feet and above. Chuck Yeager, famed 20th-century aviator and a Northern Californian, maintains that golden trout represent the West's best game fish and make for an excellent main course.

Rainbow Trout (*oncorhynchus mykiss*). Native to North America and parts of Asia, rainbow trout have been introduced to dozens of countries, and this has wreaked havoc on other fish populations. This predator can grow up to 36 inches in length. It is the only trout that is native to Yosemite, originally limited to the Merced River as it flowed through the Valley, down through the Central Valley and toward the Pacific Ocean.

Sacramento Sucker (*catostomus occidentalis*). For Native Americans, this was a major source of food. Green or brown on top with bellies of a lighter shade, Sacramento suckers most commonly keep to streams and lakes at moderate elevations. At maturity, they can be up to 36 inches long.

MAMMALS

Black Bear (*ursus americanus*). Most visitors to the parks want to see bears, although the chances of that happening seem greater in Sequoia than in Yosemite or Kings Canyon. More often brown than black, these bears can weigh up to 350 pounds. They beef up on berries, grasses, and acorns, and routinely rip into the bark of fallen trees in search of termites and other insect treats. From December to April, most of them hibernate, although Sequoia rangers say the furry mammals occasionally wake up in the winter and make quick food-seeking forays into the foothills. Cubs tend to be born in pairs, and for the first year follow their mothers very closely. ⚠ **Do not feed these beautiful creatures, nor leave food where they can get at it—which includes inside locked cars.**

Bobcat (*lynx rufus*). This adaptable predator, which also can be found in semi-arid and subtropical regions of North America, is found in the parks' foothills and in the lower montane (elevation 3,000 feet to 7,000 feet). Weighing in the neighborhood of 30 pounds and standing about 16 inches tall, adult bobcats have grayish brown fur that is spotted. They prefer a diet of rabbits but will on occasion go after deer. They are most active in the hours right after sunrise and right after sundown, spending the rest of the time in shallow caves.

Coyote (*canis latrans*). The scientific name for these creatures, who are found in all three parks, translates as

Bringing Your Pet

"Dogs chase wildlife, pollute water sources, and can become defensive and dangerous in unfamiliar surroundings," says the National Park Service Web site.

When deciding whether or not a trip to Yosemite, Sequoia, and Kings Canyon is right for your pet, consider these regulations: Pets must be kept on leashes shorter than 6 feet in length, they are not permitted in wilderness areas, they may not be left unattended or tied to an object, they are not allowed on shuttle buses or inside any lodging accommodations, and their feces must be picked up. They are forbidden on all trails except for the Meadow Loop in Wawona and on the fully paved paths in Yosemite Valley. They are barred from Tamarack Flat and Porcupine Flat campgrounds, and from all walk-in campgrounds.

In Sequoia and Kings Canyon, all trails are off-limits to dogs. In all other respects, the situation is similar to those in Yosemite, including the leash law.

Ideally, you will leave your pets at home, in the care of family, friends, or neighbors. Otherwise, you can kennel your dog in Yosemite Valley provided it is at least 6 months old and weighs at least 10 pounds, you can provide written proof of registration and up-to-date immunizations, it is between Memorial Day and Labor Day, and the kennel has space available. Call ☎ 209/372–8348 for more information. The nearest kennels to Sequoia and Kings Canyon National Parks are in Visalia and Fresno.

Some people will travel with their pet no matter what rules they break and what practicalities they override. If that describes you, at least have the good sense to leave someone in your party with the pet(s) when the rest of you are in a restaurant or on a trail. Make sure that water always is available, and be aware that potentially deadly ticks can infiltrate your pets' fur and skin.

"barking dogs." At night, you might be able to hear them as they bark, howl, and even yodel. Larger than bobcats, they have light-brown fur and look so much like a dog that upon seeing one on the side of the road, you may for a second wonder, "Where's the collar?" They tend to hunt in pairs, and for the most part eat small mammals such as rodents. However, they've also been known to carry off and devour family pets. They tend to live in elevations between 4,000 feet and 9,000 feet and frequently are spotted off Tioga Road in Yosemite.

Mountain Lion (*puma concolor*). Sometimes referred to as pumas or the North American cougar, these graceful cats live in all three parks, though they are seen only rarely by humans. Their fur a light beige on top and white on their chests; they stand more than 2 feet tall and can be 8 feet long, from nose to tail. They are not picky eaters, as long as dinner is some sort of insect or animal. In the three parks, they go after mule deer and raccoons, among other things. ⚠ **If you ever encounter a mountain lion, and in the very unlikely event it attacks rather than walks away from you, fight for your life.**

Mule Deer (*odocoileus hemionus*). Visitors to all three parks see these graceful creatures on hiking trails, in campgrounds, and by the side of roads. By taking one look at their ears, you understand their name. They have brown fur and short tails, stand 3 to 4 feet tall, and males (bucks) can weigh up to 300 pounds. For sustenance, they graze on berries in season, conifers in the winter, and acorns year-round. Do not assume that you can safely approach these animals because they are vegetarians: they attack humans more than any other animal does in the High Sierra. (Mosquitoes have that distinction in the broader scheme of things.)

Northern Water Shrew (*sorex palustris*). Found on the banks of lakes in Sequoia National Park, this little rodent resembles a mole and, believe it or not, walks on water. Somehow, its hairy hind feet allow the holier-than-thou maneuver.

Spotted Bat (*euderma maculatum*). This flying mammal is distinctive from the other 15 bat species that can be found in the parks by the three white spots on its black back. Reportedly it has the largest ears of any other North American bat. (Regarding this claim, for some reason, proof has been elusive.) Sometimes at night, you might be able to hear them squeak, which signifies they are eating.

Western Gray Squirrel (*sciurus griseus*). Of the six squirrel species in Yosemite, this is the one you will see most often. Although their survival is precarious in other parts of the west—in 1993, the state of Washington classified them as threatened—Western gray squirrels seem to be doing well in the Sierra Nevada, and are more than happy to pounce on food you might drop in the most public of places, such as the small shaded area between Yosemite Lodge's main building and food court.

Western Rattlesnake (*crotalus oreganus*). Of Yosemite's 13 snake species, this is the only one that is venomous. Ranging in color from creamy to black with splotches, "rattlers" can exceed 5 feet in length. Although their bite is indeed poisonous, they do not pose a particularly deadly threat to humans, nor are they much interested in confrontations. Even so, a reptile that a half-century ago was common in Yosemite Valley now is not found there, nor in many other parts of the park, because humans have killed them off.

IF YOU LIKE

ARCHITECTURE

The Ahwahnee Hotel is one of the more famous buildings in California. Designed by Gilbert Stanley Underwood, an early-20th-century architect whose other national parks projects included the lodges in Bryce Canyon and Zion, is the ultimate mountain resort lodge. Its six-story central area and three-story wings look for all the world as though they are made from massive pieces of timber, but actually the hotel's outer layer is composed entirely of wood-shaped, dark-brown concrete—to protect against fires. The hotel's appearance blends perfectly with its incomparable setting. Inside, the Great Lounge deserves to be admired from one of its comfortable chairs, and the Dining Room provides a gorgeous atmosphere for one of the state's celebrated restaurants.

CAMPING

Combined, the three parks contain more than 2,700 campsites. On some summer weekends, they are not enough to accommodate everyone who wants to pitch a tent or park an RV amid giant sequoias or in the shadow of the immense granite domes. Reservations, therefore, are a good idea, especially for the campgrounds in Yosemite Valley and Sequoia's Giant Forest area. You can find many first-come, first-served sites in all the parks, but you might need to find them before noon in order to secure a spot. Fees are low, never more than $20 for individual sites. All sites come with tables, grills or pits, and bear boxes. Most have parking spots, but none have hookups. Yosemite has four all-year campgrounds (Camp 4, Hogdon Meadow, Upper Pines, and Wawona); Sequoia and Kings Canyon have three (Azalea, Lodgepole, and Potwisha).

1

Tips for RVers

Those of you planning to visit Sequoia whose vehicle length exceeds 22 feet are advised take Route 180 from Fresno to the Kings Canyon entrance near Grant Grove, then turn right on Generals Highway to reach Sequoia's attractions as far south as the Grant Museum. The 12-mi stretch beyond that, on down to the Ash Mountain entrance, has 130 curves (many with suggested speeds of 10 MPH), 12 switchbacks, and a 4,709-foot drop in elevation.

If your RV is 40 feet long (or your trailer get-up measures 35 feet), you can park it in one of 12 sites in Yosemite Valley's Lower Pines and Upper Pines. Otherwise, lengths of up to 35 are possible in most Yosemite campgrounds, but you will need to check the specifics listed at ⊕ www.nps.gov/yose/planyour-visit/rvcamping.htm. In Sequoia and Kings Canyon, 40-foot RVs can fit in a few places; 30-footers are not likely to cause a problem anywhere.

No sites in any of the three parks have RV or trailer hook-ups. In Yosemite, you'll find RV dump stations at the three Pines campgrounds in Yosemite Valley, near Tuolumne Meadows, and in Wawona. In Sequoia, Lodgepole and Potwisha have RV dump stations.

You can reserve spaces online, at ⊕ www.recreation.gov, for these campgrounds: Crane Flat, Hogdon Meadow, Tuolumne Meadows, Wawona, and all three Pines campgrounds in Yosemite Valley (Yosemite); and Dorst Creek and Lodgepole (Sequoia).

Eight campgrounds do not allow RVs of any size: Camp 4, Tamarack Flat, and Yosemite Creek (Yosemite); Atwell Mill, Buckeye Flat, and Cold Springs (Sequoia); and Canyon View (Kings Canyon). Note that both campgrounds along Mineral King Road in southern Sequoia National Park are tent-only.

For information about camp-grounds outside the parks, visit ⊕ www.gorving.com.

GAZING AT SCENERY

If you are not impressed by the General Sherman Tree in Sequoia, the scope of Kings River Canyon, or the granite domes and waterfalls of Yosemite, maybe it's time you pursued sightseeing on an intergalactic level. These three parks contain some of the best scenery on Earth. Although you can enjoy most of it by merely looking out a car window, you can attain better views—and from many more intriguing angles—by strapping on hiking boots or stepping into snowshoes or cross-country skies. Take gobs of photographs and leave with everlasting memories.

HIKING

You cannot find mountain trails that are more scenic than those in Yosemite. As you traverse the Panorama Trail, make your way up to Yosemite Point, or walk through a high-altitude forest to emerge on the top of North Dome, where you will see Half Dome, Yosemite Falls, and Yosemite Valley in all their glory. On much shorter and easier paths in Sequoia and Kings Canyon national parks, you can crane your neck and blow your mind by examining the world's biggest trees, mature sequoias that will be so close that you can touch their spongy bark without stepping off the trail. In all three parks, you can disappear deep into the wilderness on multiday backpacking trips or spend less than an hour on well-thought-out nature trails.

PICNICKING

This book highlights 20 of the best picnic areas, half in Yosemite and the rest in Sequoia and Kings Canyon. You cannot go wrong by having lunch at any of them. For each table, there is a grill or pit and a parking space. Shade is most everywhere, with the exception of tables on the beach of the Merced River in Yosemite Valley. On occasion, you may forgo the formality of established picnic areas and instead eat while perched on a smooth rock—perhaps on one of the many at Glacier Point that overlook Yosemite Valley and across to Half Dome. Or, you may want to pause while hiking in Kings Canyon's Redwood Forest, plop down on a soft cushion of pine needles, and nibble on trail mix. All three parks have stores where you can buy snacks and prepackaged sandwiches and salads.

FAMILY FUN

Bringing your children to any national park is one of the best ways to teach them about the wonders of nature. If El Capitan and the General Sherman Tree look big to you, think about how much bigger they must look through your kids' eyes. In these magnificent parks, children also can see animals in their natural habitats, as opposed to in zoo cages or on the Discovery Channel. What person, of any age, is going to forget the first time she saw a mama bear and cub romping across a meadow?

The joys of outdoor adventures extend beyond staring at humongous trees and wild animals. Nature trails, such as the one at Happy Isles in Yosemite Valley, can educate children and perhaps enlighten you, too. The same can be said for the parks' visitor-center exhibits and museums, such as the one in Sequoia's Giant Forest. All three parks offer ranger-led campfire programs during summer evenings, where kids can roast marshmallows or sing songs or, away from the fire, look up at more stars than they could count in a hundred lifetimes.

For detailed information about children's activities at the national parks, look on the National Park Service Web site. Be sure to check out all the fun things that the park system's Junior Ranger program offers, including some activities that children can work on at home before your trip.

IN YOSEMITE

Some of the Yosemite Valley's trails, including Lower Yosemite Falls and Mirror Lake, are level enough to keep kids from getting too tired. If your children are ages 10 and older, they probably will get a kick out of mounting the moderately challenging Mist Trail—because they (and you) are likely to get wet. (And what kid doesn't enjoy the sight of a soaked parent?) In the summer, families can swim in the pools at Yosemite Lodge or Curry Village. In the winter, Curry has an ice-skating rink, and snowshoe outings can be a novel and fun experience for all. You'll also find children's activity books at many of the park's stores. By completing exercises in the "Little Cubs" booklet, smaller kids (ages 3 through 6) earn a "Little Cubs" button.

IN SEQUOIA & KINGS CANYON

In Sequoia, taking the kids to see the world's largest tree, named after General Sherman, is a must. Follow up with a 45-minute stroll around sublime Round Meadow near the Giant Forest Museum—another good stop for children, who will love spinning the sequoia-seed "Win BIG!" wheel. The nearby Beetle Rock Family Nature Center has nature programs throughout the summer. Here, little children are catered to with coloring books and other playthings. Crystal Cave is a good option for teens, especially those who have never been in a cave before and may not be bothered by this one's extensive human-caused damage. Climbing about Moro Rock's etched-in-granite staircase is another fun activity for older kids.

In Kings Canyon, summer camping in the bustling Cedar Grove area is likely to amuse children for a day or two, although this portion of the park is more suited for the serious backpacking crowd. Grant Grove, with its short trail to the General Grant Tree and lively shops and restaurants, is more likely to keep the kids occupied.

Exploring
Yosemite

WORD OF MOUTH

"Yosemite is my place. I love, love, love it! I usually go once or twice a year for 2–3 nights, by myself, and spend my days hiking. To me, it is paradise. Although I've been several times, it never gets old, and, since I'm alone, I do appreciate the familiarity."

—Iregeo

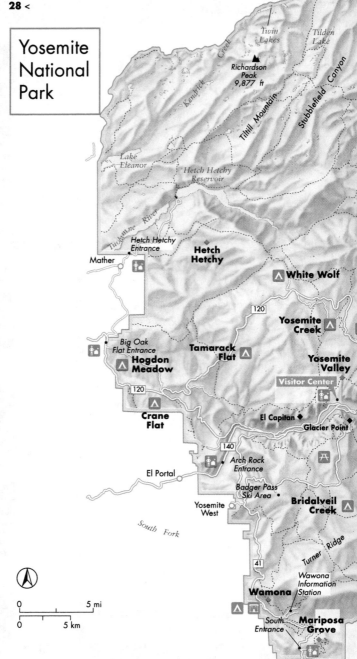

Yosemite National Park

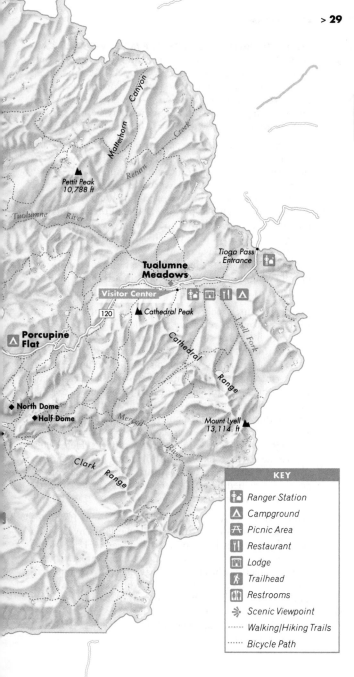

KEY

👫	*Ranger Station*
⛺	*Campground*
🔴	*Picnic Area*
🍴	*Restaurant*
🖼	*Lodge*
🥾	*Trailhead*
🚻	*Restrooms*
⚜	*Scenic Viewpoint*
······	*Walking/Hiking Trails*
······	*Bicycle Path*

By Reed
Parsell

YOSEMITE VALLEY IS ONE OF THE MOST VISUALLY CAP-TIVATING places on the planet. Millions of people come every year, from practically everywhere, to see and do all sorts of memorable things. So for those of you planning a trip here—especially a first visit—the great anticipation you have about sights and activities may be mixed with anxiety about the crowds you are likely to encounter.

Aside from visiting off-season, say in October or February, there really is nothing you can do to avoid the swarms of sightseers who congregate around Yosemite Village, Curry Village, and (to a slightly lesser extent) Yosemite Lodge. But you can lighten your own impact on the bustling scene by doing things such as parking in one of the day lots and relying on the free shuttle to get you places within the Valley. You also can plan your meals at off-peak times to avoid long lines and waits for tables, or you can start your day early enough that by the time eateries and shops are in full swing, you will be traipsing up a trail, away from the growing commotion.

Venturing out farther from the Valley is another good strategy, provided you have the time. It's fair to say that Yosemite has three subregions that will be of interest to most visitors. (Hard-core backpackers consider the park's 747,956 acres to all be at their disposal.) Tuolumne Meadows, to the east, is a high-altitude oasis of lush vegetation on a 2-mi-long flat plain, surrounded by granite peaks and full of hiking possibilities. Wawona, to the south, has a lovely 19th-century whitewashed hotel and a Sequoia grove that's almost—but not quite—as spectacular as what you will see in Kings Canyon and Sequoia National Parks. Hetch Hetchy, to the north, is like a beautiful young person who has sustained a disfiguring accident: Its valley, whose appearance once rivaled that of Yosemite Valley, has been partly submerged under a reservoir for more than 80 years.

From Yosemite Valley, you can take a day trip to Tuolumne on a hikers' bus, or you can visit Glacier Point by hopping aboard a tour bus that departs from Yosemite Lodge three times a day. (Both routes are seasonally operated.) There's a free summertime bus between Wawona and Yosemite Valley, but it's aimed toward visitors who park at Wawona: The once-a-day bus departs from outside the Wawona Store at 8:35 AM, with the return leg boarding at 3:30 PM outside Yosemite Lodge. The only way you can get to Hetch Hetchy is to drive.

Of the park's four entrances, Arch Rock is the closest to Yosemite Valley. The road that goes through it, Route 140 from Merced and Mariposa, represents the most scenic approach from the west as it snakes alongside the boulder-packed Merced River. Route 41, through Wawona, is the way to come from Los Angeles; if you have flown into dreary Fresno and are renting a car, this is also the entry route you will use. Route 120, through Crane Flat, is the most direct route from San Francisco. The only way in from the east is on Tioga Road, which may be the best of all in terms of scenery, but due to snow accumulations it's open for a frustratingly short amount of time: typically, from early June through mid-October.

PLANNING YOUR TIME

YOSEMITE IN ONE DAY

If you have a single day to devote to Yosemite, get here early because you are going to have a very busy day. Begin at the **Valley Visitor Center,** where you can quickly peruse the recently updated exhibits and watch the inspiring documentary "Spirit of Yosemite." A minute's stroll from there is the **Indian Village of Ahwahnee,** which looks at what Native American life was like here around 1870. Take another 20 minutes to see the **Yosemite Museum.** Step onto the free shuttle, as you will do many times today, and get off minutes later at the Yosemite Falls stop (Stop 6). Take an hour to explore the **Lower Yosemite Falls Trail** that leads to the base of the falls before proceeding on—via shuttle or a 20-minute walk—to **Yosemite Lodge** (Stop 8), where you can grab a snack at the food pavilion. Now it's time to choose from among three diverse activities, each taking about two hours and all accessed by the shuttle. The more sedentary visitor may enjoy a leisurely exploring the stores and setting of **Curry Village** (Stops 13, 14, and 20), perhaps going for a swim (summer) or ice skating (winter), renting a bike for an hour, or having a beer on the deck. If you have kids in tow, take them to the **Happy Isles Nature Center** (Stop 16) and its adjacent nature trail, then buy them an ice cream treat on the walk back to Curry Village. The more adventurous may want to hike up the **Mist Falls Trail** (also Stop 16) nearly 1 mi to the Vernal Fall Footbridge, catch your breath and admire the view, then walk back to Curry Village.

Keep shuttling, this time disembarking at the **Ahwahnee Hotel** (Stop 3). Step into the Great Lounge, with its magnificent fireplace and Indian artworks, and sneak a peek into the

TOP REASONS TO GO

■ **Yosemite Valley:** In some respects, the Valley is like the Disneyland of the Sierra Nevada. You'll see people everywhere. However, nature's creations here are so striking—Half Dome, Yosemite Falls, etc.—you must come here, and you will not regret it.

■ **Half Dome:** Remember how the World Trade Center towers continually would draw your attention in New York? Half Dome has a similar magnetism. It's perhaps the most awesome singular thing you can stare at in California (certain movie stars excepted).

■ **Waterfalls:** When they're at their fullest in late spring and early summer, Yosemite Falls, Bridalveil Falls, and Sentinel Falls are something to behold.

■ **Hiking:** To whatever extent you can, sample Yosemite's 800 mi of trails, some easy (Lower Yosemite Falls), others supremely challenging (Half Dome), some pleasantly in between (Wapama Falls). All are scenic.

■ **Tioga Road:** In summertime, this high-altitude route that begins on the Sierra Nevada's steep eastern side, near mystical Mono Lake, unveils incomparable mountain views.

Dining Room—make dinner reservations, if you're up for a splurge. Get back on the shuttle, having absorbed the Ahwahnee's luscious setting and its architectural grandeur. In **Yosemite Village** (Stops 4, 5, 9, and 10), visit the **Ansel Adams Gallery,** if you make it there before closing time. Then, assuming you didn't make reservations at the Ahwahnee, consider having dinner at the popular **Curry Village** buffet or buying sandwiches, chips, and the like from the massive **Village Store.** It's a good place to grab souvenirs, too. If you bought sandwiches, then get back in your car and drive to the **El Capitan Picnic Area** and enjoy an outdoor evening meal as you squint at the famously tall and vertical rock face, trying to spot specs of color that incredibly are rock climbers. At this time of day, "El Cap" should be sun-splashed. (You will have gotten several good looks at world-famous **Half Dome** throughout the day.) Any sunlight left? If so, continue driving on around to see **Bridalveil Falls** before saying good-bye to Yosemite—or better yet, see you next time.

YOSEMITE IN THREE DAYS

Up to one year, plus one day, in advance, make reservations online to spend your two nights at the **Ahwahnee** (big bucks), **Yosemite Lodge** (standard motel experience), or in one of **Curry Village**'s tents (somewhat rustic, and least-expensive, if not cheap). Follow the one-day plan outlined above, perhaps setting aside a few of the activities to plug gaps later during your stay. On the second morning, either drive or take one of the tour buses (three depart daily from Yosemite Lodge, starting at 10 AM) to **Glacier Point** and gaze down upon the Valley from its overlook, which is a short, paved walk from the parking lot. For another bird's-eye view of the Valley, take the 2.2-mi round-trip trail from Glacier Point to **Sentinel Dome.** To see **Half Dome** from many intriguing angles, opt instead for the 8-mi **Panorama Trail** back down to the Valley, via the complete **Mist Falls Trail.** However you return to the Valley, have lunch at a place you haven't tried yet in **Yosemite Village** (the grill there is filling and affordable), and spend the afternoon walking about the Valley floor, or take the flat 1-mi trail out to **Mirror Lake** (Shuttle Stop 17). After dinner, see what's playing at the Yosemite Theatre: the live presentation of "John Muir Is Back—And Boy, Is He Ticked Off!" is one popular possibility.

For the final day, choose from among these three diverse options: drive down Route 41 to the Wawona area, devoting the morning to **Mariposa Grove** and having a late lunch at the **Wawona Hotel;** drive up Route 120 and take the side road to **Hetch Hetchy** to walk the **Wapama Falls Trail** and get a feel for what the "restore Hetch Hetchy" movement is all about; or take the hikers' bus (departing at 8:20 AM from Yosemite Lodge) to spend four hours at **Tuolumne Meadows,** or get off at Porcupine Flat to take the underrated, 8-mi **North Dome Trail,** after you and the bus driver have worked out pickup details. If you have any time left, treat yourself to dinner at the Ahwahnee.

YOSEMITE VALLEY

The Yosemite Valley Visitor Center is 11 mi from the Arch Rock entrance on Rte. 140, 25 mi from the Big Oak Flat entrance on Rte. 120, 35 mi from the south entrance on Rte. 41, and 62 mi from east entrance on Tioga Rd.

So many attractions are packed into this 7-mi-long, 1-mi-wide valley that you might have difficulty deciding what

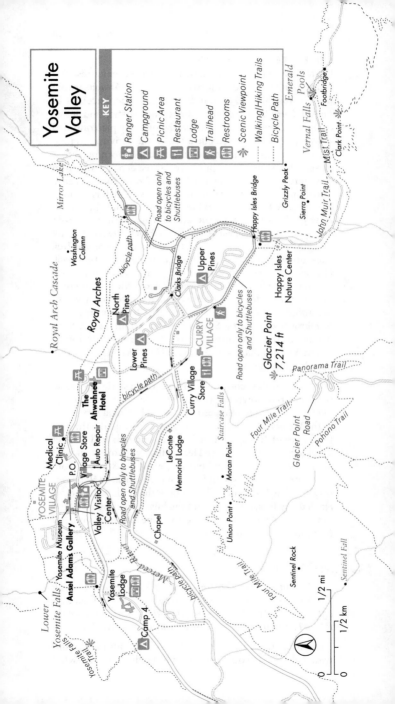

Yosemite Valley

KEY

🏠	Ranger Station
🏕	Campground
🌲	Picnic Area
🍴	Restaurant
🛏	Lodge
🥾	Trailhead
🚻	Restrooms
🌲	Scenic Viewpoint
····	Walking/Hiking Trails
····	Bicycle Path

Mirror Lake

Royal Arch Cascade

Washington Column

Royal Arches

Road open only to bicycles and Shuttlebuses

bicycle path

North Pines

Clarks Bridge

Upper Pines

Happy Isles Bridge

Happy Isles

Grizzly Peak

Sierra Point

Emerald Pools

Vernal Falls

Footbridge

Mist Trail

Clark Point

John Muir Trail

Lower Pines

CURRY VILLAGE

Happy Isles Nature Center

Road open only to bicycles and Shuttlebuses

Glacier Point
7,214 ft

Panorama Trail

Staircase Falls

Curry Village Store

LeConte Memorial Lodge

bicycle path

The Ahwahnee Hotel

Medical Clinic

Village Store

Auto Repair

P.O.

YOSEMITE VILLAGE

Yosemite Museum

Ansel Adams Gallery

Valley Visitor Center

Road open only to bicycles and Shuttlebuses

Chapel

Union Point

Moran Point

Four Mile Trail

Glacier Point Road

Pohono Trail

Merced River

Yosemite Falls

Lower Yosemite Falls

Yosemite Falls Trail

Yosemite Lodge

Camp 4

bicycle path

Four Mile Trail

Sentinel Rock

Sentinel Fall

1/2 mi

1/2 km

0

to do. Start by parking at either the Curry Village or, better yet, Yosemite Village daily lot. From the latter, stroll over to the Yosemite Visitor Center and get your bearings. After that, the free shuttle buses (which operate on low emissions, have 21 stops, running every 10 minutes or so from 9 AM to 6 PM) can take you to, or very near, most of the Valley's most popular sights. In late spring and early summer, Valley scenery arguably is at its best because the magnificent waterfalls are all in full flow. Late summers can be a bit of a drag, what with Yosemite Falls usually running dry, temperatures stubbornly sticking in the 90s, and fellow humans encountered at every turn. If you do insist on driving about the Valley, be aware that roadside parking is limited, and the Southside Drive/Northside Drive loop is one-way. Lots of people tour the Valley via bicycle; Curry Village and Yosemite Lodge have rentals.

DID YOU KNOW? Native Americans' name for the Valley was *Ahwahnee,* which originally might have referred only to the large meadow on the Valley's eastern side. Language experts generally translate *Ahwahnee* as "site of the gaping mouth." Alternatively, the name *Yosemite* may stem from an Indian word that could be written as *u-zu-ma-ti,* or "place of the grizzly bears." That phrase is thought to describe the Miwoks who lived north of the Merced River. *Yosemite* also has been translated as "some of them are killers."

VISITOR CENTERS

Le Conte Memorial Lodge. This small but striking National Historic Landmark, with its granite walls and steeply pitched shingle roof, is named after 19th-century geologist and charter Sierra Club member Joseph Le Conte. A good friend of John Muir's, Le Conte served as Sierra Club president for six years after its founding in 1892. He died in Yosemite Valley in 1901, and a couple of years later the lodge was opened in his honor. Yosemite's first permanent public information center, the lodge has always been operated by the Sierra Club, and its curators include world-famous photographer Ansel Adams (from 1920 to 1923). Step inside to see the cathedral-like interior, which contains a library and environmental exhibits. To find out about evening programs, check the kiosk out front, or look in the park's newspaper. Le Conte Memorial Lodge (relocated from Camp Curry in 1919) is across from

Housekeeping Camp. ✉ *9002 Southside Dr., about ½ mi west of Curry Village, Curry Village* 🎫 *Free* ⊘ *May–Oct., Wed.–Sun. 10–4.*

Nature Center at Happy Isles. Designed for children, this small museum could use some updating. One of its dioramas has several stuffed animals, including a baby bear. Taxidermy hardly promotes a spirit of conservation and respect for living creatures; carvings and synthetics are better alternatives these days, examples of which are in the Valley Visitor Center. Another exhibit recounts how on July 10, 1996, two massive chunks of granite snapped off a cliff southeast of Glacier Point and slammed, intact, onto a slope near the center. The force of the rock fall created a high-velocity wind burst that toppled or snapped about 1,000 trees and damaged the nature center. See evidence of that terrifying event (one person was killed) on a short path outside, and take a few minutes to explore the nature trail. The center also has a small gift shop, with coloring books, T-shirts, and water bottles; this is one of the better kid-oriented gift shops. ✉ *Center of Curry Village Loop, about ¾ mi east of Curry Village, Curry Village* 🎫 *Free* ⊘ *Mid-May–Oct., daily 10–noon and 12:30–4.*

Valley Visitor Center. Exhibits at this visitor center focus on how Yosemite Valley was formed and about its vegetation, animals, and human inhabitants over the past thousands of years; it was thoroughly overhauled in 2007. Read about the Valley's most noteworthy conservationists and artisans, past and present, in a well-conceived exhibit. For fun, have your picture taken next to a life-size bronze statue of an older John Muir, who is sitting on a large rock. In the lobby, rangers and volunteers can answer most any question you have about Yosemite and provide pamphlets and maps; a pool-table–size relief map of the Valley will help with your bearings. Don't leave the area without watching the superb "Spirit of Yosemite," a 23-minute introductory film that runs every half-hour in the theater behind the visitor center. ✉ *Center of Curry Village Loop, Yosemite Village* ☎ *209/372–0299* ⊕ *www.yosemitepark.com* 🎫 *Free* ⊘ *Memorial Day–Labor Day, daily 8–6; Labor Day– Memorial Day, daily 9–5.*

Yosemite Valley Wilderness Center. Backpackers come here for free wilderness permits, which are mandatory for overnight trips into the mountains. They also can purchase maps, check on current weather conditions and campsite availability, rent bear canisters to store their food, and tap into the expertise of the staff members. When the center is closed for the season, the nearby Valley Visitor Center dispenses wilderness permits. ✉ *9039 Village Dr., between the Ansel Adams Gallery and the post office, Yosemite Village* ☉ *Memorial Day–Labor Day, daily 7:30–6.*

2

HISTORIC SITES

★ **Ahwahnee Hotel.** Gilbert Stanley Underwood, the architect for Grand Canyon Lodge on the North Rim in Arizona, also designed the Ahwahnee. Opened in 1927, it is generally considered to be his best work. One of its distinctive construction features is that the exterior walls, though shaped and colored to look like wood, actually are granite and concrete—in order to reduce the danger of fire. Wood balconies and green shutters and awnings add to the grace of a building whose designs are a triumphant mixture of art deco, Arts and Crafts, Middle Eastern, and Native American. The Great Lounge, 77 feet long with magnificent 24-foot ceilings and all manner of Indian artwork on display, is the most special interior space in Yosemite by a long shot. Sit quietly for five minutes in one of the room's comfortable chairs, and you will agree. You can stay here, for $450 a night, or simply explore the first-floor shops and perhaps have breakfast or lunch in the lovely Dining Room. Its windows soar from the floor 34 feet on up to the ceiling, which has interlaced sugar-pine beams. Dinner here is a more formal, and much more expensive, proposition than anywhere else in the park, but if you have the money it's worth a splurge. As you sip your coffee or dive into dessert, take a moment to reflect that actor and environmental activist Robert Redford once bussed tables here. ✉ *1 Ahwahnee Rd., about ¾ mi east of Yosemite Valley Visitor Center, Yosemite Village* ☎ *209/372–1489.*

Indian Village of Ahwahnee. The Southern Sierra Miwok tribe inhabited what's now known as Yosemite Valley for thousands of years. The Gold Rush of the mid-19th century brought enormous changes and dangers, including decimation of the population through violence, disease, and forced resettlement. The Valley's last few Indian homes were razed in 1969. This solemn smattering of re-created structures, accessed by a short loop trail, is an imagination of what Indian life might have resembled here in the 1870s. The roundhouse, reconstructed in 1992, is the site of several ceremonial events throughout the year, none open to the general public. One interpretive sign points out that Miwok referred to the 19th-century newcomers as *Yohemite* or *Yohometuk*, which have been translated as "some of them are killers." ⊠ *Northside Dr., behind the visitor center, Yosemite Village* ⌦ *Free* ⊙ *Daily sunrise–sunset.*

Ansel Adams Gallery. Here you can purchase gorgeous prints by the nature photographer, from posters that cost about $30 apiece to more expensive framed images. Adams' pictures are stunning and many have a timeless, dreamy quality, so the temptation to spend is understandable. Contemporary photographers' works are sold here, too, along with American Indian jewelry and handicrafts. The gallery's elegant camera shop conducts photography workshops and sometimes holds private showings of fine prints on Saturday. ⊠ *9031 Village Dr., between the visitor center and Wilderness Center, Yosemite Village* ☎ *209/372–4413 or 888/361–7622* ⊕ *www.anseladams.com* ⌦ *Free* ⊙ *Apr.–Oct., daily 9–6; Nov.–Mar., daily 9–5.*

☾ **Curry Village.** A couple of school teachers from Indiana, Jenny and David Curry, founded Camp Curry in 1899. Their idea was to make staying overnight in Yosemite Valley affordable for people of modest means, a tradition that continues today. Back then, $2 got you a cot in one of the dozen tents and all your meals. Today, you'll spend considerably more than that, but less than you would at Yosemite Lodge and a fraction of what you'd fork out at the Ahwahnee. Curry's 628 lodging options, most of them tent cabins, are spread over a large chunk of the Valley's southeastern side. The central dining area does boffo business for its breakfast and dinner buffets, and on warm summer days the pool practically overflows with kids. In wintertime, you can ice skate here. This is one of the park's most family-friendly places, but it's one that is more functional than attractive. It's too big and sprawling to have much mountain charm. ⊠ *Southside Dr., about ½ mi east of Yosemite Village, Curry Village.*

Yosemite Museum. In this small museum, which consists of a permanent exhibit room and an adjacent gallery that promotes contemporary Yosemite art, an American Indian sometimes is on hand to demonstrate the ancient techniques of beadwork and basket weaving, as well as answer your questions. You also find examples of arrowheads and other Indian weaponry, limited displays of clothing, and a tribute to Lucy Telles, a member of the Paiute tribe that was

Yosemite in Black & White

What John Muir did for Yosemite with words, Ansel Adams did with photographs. Born in 1902 in San Francisco, Adams first came to the Valley when he was 14, photographing it with a Box Brownie camera. He later said his first visit "was a culmination of experience so intense as to be almost painful. From that day in 1916 my life has been colored and modulated by the great earth gesture of the Sierra." By 1919, he was working in the Valley, as custodian of LeConte Memorial Lodge, the Sierra Club headquarters in Yosemite National Park.

Adams had harbored dreams of a career as a concert pianist, but the park sealed his fate as a photographer in 1928, the day he shot "Monolith: The Face of Half Dome," which remains one of his most famous works. Adams married Virginia Best in 1928, in her father's studio in the Valley (now the Ansel Adams Gallery).

As his photographic career took off, Yosemite began to sear itself into the American consciousness. David Brower, first executive director of the Sierra Club, said, "That Ansel Adams came to be recognized as one of the great photographers of this century is a tribute to the places that informed him."

In 1934, Adams was elected to the Sierra Club's board of directors, where he would serve until 1971. As a representative of the conservation group, he combined his work with the club's mission, showing his photographs of the Sierra to influential officials such as Secretary of the Interior Harold L. Ickes, who showed them to President Franklin Delano Roosevelt. The images were a key factor in the establishment of Kings Canyon National Park.

In 1968, the Department of the Interior granted Adams its highest honor, the Conservation Service Award, and in 1980 he received the Presidential Medal of Freedom in recognition of his conservation work. Until his death in 1984, Adams continued not only to record Yosemite's majesty on film but to urge the federal government and park managers to do right by the park.

In one of his many public pleas on behalf of Yosemite, Adams said, "Yosemite Valley itself is one of the great shrines of the world and—belonging to all our people—must be both protected and appropriately accessible." As an artist and an activist, Adams never gave up on his dream of keeping Yosemite wild yet within reach of every visitor who wants to experience that wildness.

centered in the nearby Mono Lake region. For a quarter-century until her death in 1955, Telles demonstrated to Yosemite visitors her legendary basket-making abilities. ⊠ *9039 Village Dr., Yosemite Village* ☎ *209/372–0299* 🗃 *Free* ⊙ *Daily 9–noon and 1–4:30.*

SCENIC STOPS

★ **El Capitan.** You almost certainly will do a double-take the first time you see "El Cap," the largest exposed-granite monolith in the world, more than twice as tall as the Rock of Gibraltar. Equally mind-blowing is the fact that, since 1958, people have been climbing the thing. On July 2, 2008, Hans Florine of California and Yuji Hirayama of Japan set a record scaling El Capitan's 2,900-foot "nose," a feat that usually takes five days, in 2 hours, 43 minutes. ⚠ **If you are at all tempted to follow in their footsteps, even at a "sane" pace, keep in mind that a couple of dozen climbers have died trying to climb El Cap.** A more sensible idea: Scan the smooth and nearly vertical cliff for specks of color (other than the rock face's various shades of beige and brown), and with your binoculars safely zoom in on the adventurers. The free El Capitan Shuttle, which connects to the Valley's year-round shuttle loop and goes to the El Capitan Picnic Area, operates from mid-June into early September. ⊠ *Off Northside Dr., about 4 mi west of the Valley Visitor Center*

★ FodorśChoice **Glacier Point.** If you lack the time, desire, or stamina to hike more than 3,200 feet up to Glacier Point from the Yosemite Valley floor, you can drive here for a bird's-eye view. Once upon a time there were lodges up here, and for nearly a century, burning embers were pushed off one of its ledges to create the famous "Yosemite Firefall" seen nightly by meadow-tramping crowds below. (Due to environmental considerations, the tradition was swept under the proverbial rug in 1968.) These days, you are likely to encounter a lot of day-trippers on the short, paved trail that leads from the parking lot to the main overlook. Take a moment to veer off a few yards to the Geology Hut, which succinctly explains and illustrates how the Valley appeared 10 million, 3 million, and 20,000 years ago. If you get here via the morning guided-tour bus ($25 one way, $41 round-trip), consider a return trip via the 8-mi Panorama Trail, one of the most visually stunning hikes in the state, if not the world. The shuttle bus runs whenever Glacier Point Road is open, which tends to be from late May through early November. During the winter, the road is plowed only

Celebrating an 'El Cap' milestone

Although today's ascents of El Capitan typically take a few days, the first trek up the 3,000-foot rock face took 16 months.

Bill "Dolt" Feuerer, Warren Harding, and Mark Powell began the climb on July 4, 1957. They and others in the group of adventurers would go up a little each day, set fixed lines, and rappel down until the next time. Everyone had other things to do in life, such as jobs or taking classes, so "El Cap" was a weekend thing and progress was slow.

By the next summer, the group's progress up the cliffside was causing traffic problems below, where park visitors stopped to gawk. Rangers asked the climbers to hold off until after Labor Day, in the interest of easing congestion. Finally, early on November 12, 1958, Harding went all the way to the top with Wayne Merry and George Whitmore.

When rock-climbing pioneers got together in November 2008 to celebrate the 50th anniversary of that first successful scaling, Whitmore was among them. "We realized what we were doing was out of the ordinary and special, but it's safe to say we didn't realize how special it would be," he told the gathering. "To this day, my life is influenced by that climb."

Also in 2008, Kelly Perkins climbed the 2,000-foot rock face of Half Dome. What's notable about that is the 46-year-old underwent heart-transplant surgery in the mid-1990s. Since his operation, he also became the first heart-transplant patient to ascend Mount Whitney in the southern Sierra, the Matterhorn in Switzerland, Mount Fuji in Japan, Mount Kilimanjaro in Tanzania, and the face of El Cap.

to the Badger Ski Area, from which hearty souls can snowshoe or cross-country ski on up to Glacier Point. ■TIP→ **To take the best photographs of Yosemite Valley from Inspiration Point, which is on the route to and from Glacier Point, go in late afternoon, when the sun shines from behind you to most dramatically spotlight Half Dome and other landmarks.** ⊠ *Glacier Point Rd., 16 mi northeast of Rte. 41, Glacier Point.*

★ **Half Dome.** When visiting Yosemite National Park, people's eyes are continually drawn to this remarkable granite formation that tops out more than 4,700 feet above the Valley floor. It is the park's premier attraction. Waterfalls, though spectacular, ebb and flow at Yosemite, while Half Dome has had a steady and commanding presence for some 87 million years. And contrary to its name, the dome is about three-quarters "intact." Judge for yourself as you view it from different parts of the park—from beneath on the Valley floor, from behind on the Panorama Trail, or from across, on North Dome. You can hike to the top of Half Dome, as thousands do every summer, on an 8.5-mi (one-way) trail whose last 400 feet must be ascended by your holding tightly onto a steel cable. To see Half Dome reflected in the Merced River, regard it while standing on Sentinel Bridge just before sundown. ⚠ **Beware that people have died on this hike, whether by falling off the edge or being struck by lightning.** ✉ *Trailhead is off Happy Isles, near Curry Village (the first 3.5 mi of the hike are along the Mist Trail to Nevada Fall).*

Sentinel Dome. The view from here is similar to that from Glacier Point, except you can't see the Valley floor. A 1.1-mi path climbs to the viewpoint from the Glacier Point parking lot. If you come up here via the 10 AM guided-tour bus, you will have plenty of time to climb atop Sentinel and still catch the last bus back to the Valley. The trail is long and steep enough to keep the crowds away, but it's not overly rugged. Topping out at an elevation of 8,122 feet, Sentinel is more than 900 feet higher than Glacier Point. ✉ *Glacier Point Rd., off Rte. 41,Glacier Point.*

WATERFALLS

When the snow starts to melt (usually peaking in May), almost every rocky lip or narrow gorge in the Yosemite Valley becomes a spillway for streaming snowmelt churning down to meet the Merced River. But even in drier months, the waterfalls can be breathtaking. If you choose to hike any of the trails to or up the falls, be sure to wear shoes with good, no-slip soles; the rocks can be extremely slick. Stay on trails at all times.

Bridalveil Fall. A filmy fall of 620 feet, which is often diverted as much as 20 feet one way or the other by the breeze, is the first marvelous view of Yosemite Valley you will see if you come in via Route 41. ✉ *4 mi west of Yosemite Lodge, at the junction of Southside Dr. and Wawona Rd.*

Nevada Fall. Climb Mist Trail from Happy Isles for an up-close view of 594-foot Nevada Fall, the first major fall as the Merced River plunges out of the high country toward the eastern end of Yosemite Valley. Along the way, you will pass Vernal Fall, which is a sensible place to turn around for those hikers who are (justifiably) leery of the strenuous stepping needed to reach Nevada Fall. ■TIP→ **If you don't want to hike, you can see both falls—distantly—from Glacier Point.** ⊠ *South of Curry Village and Upper Pines Campground, just past Happy Isles; Shuttle Stop 16.*

Ribbon Fall. At 1,612 feet, Ribbon Fall is the highest single waterfall in North America (Yosemite Falls is actually the highest, but it's not a single waterfall). It's also the first Valley waterfall to dry up in summer; the rainwater and melted snow that create the slender fall evaporate quickly at this height. Look just west of El Capitan from the Valley floor for the best view of the fall from the base of Bridalveil Fall. ✤ *For the best view of the waterfall, park off Southside Dr., a few hundred yards east of the Rte. 41 junction and Bridalveil Fall lot.*

Vernal Fall. Fern-covered black rocks frame 317-foot Vernal Fall, and rainbows play in the spray at its base. Take Mist Trail from Happy Isles to see it—or, if you'd rather not hike, go to Glacier Point for a distant view. ⊠ *3-mi from the trailhed just off Happy Isles to the top of the waterfall*

★ Fodor's Choice **Yosemite Falls.** The park's namesake waterfall is actually is composed of three falls, and together they constitute the highest waterfall in North America and the fifth-highest in the world. The water from the top descends a total of 2,425 feet, and when the falls run hard, you can hear them thunder all across the Valley. When they dry up, as often happens in late summer, the Valley seems naked without the wavering tower of spray. ■TIP→ **To view the falls up close, head to their base on the trail from Camp 4.** ⊠ *About halfway between Valley Visitor Center and Yosemite Village off Northside Drive; Shuttle Stop 6.*

DID YOU KNOW? **The world's tallest cascade is in Venezuela, where Angel Falls tumbles some 3,212 feet. In second place comes South Africa's Tugela Falls, at 2,800 feet; third is Norway's Utigordsfossen, 2,626 feet; fourth is Norway's Mongelfossen, 2,540 feet; and fifth is Yosemite Falls at 2,425 feet. Yosemite National Park's Sentinel Fall, at 2,000 feet, ranks eighth, just after Norway's Espelandsfoss (2,307 feet), which is tied for sixth with Venezuela's Cuquenan Falls. Rounding out the planet's Top 10 are New Zealand's Sutherland Falls (1,904 feet) and Norway's Kjellfossen (1,841 feet).**

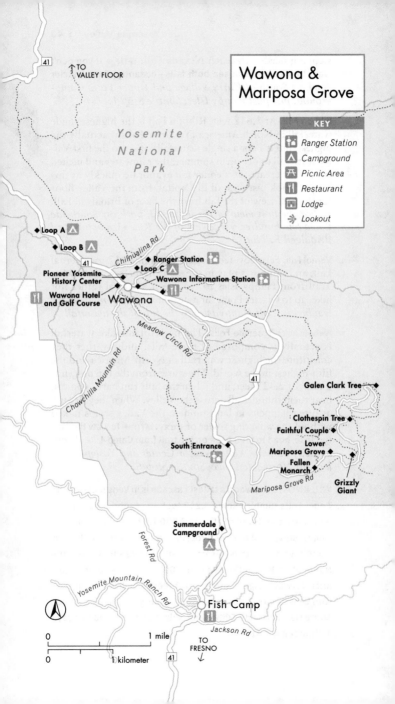

Wawona & Mariposa Grove

KEY

- 🏕️ Ranger Station
- ⛺ Campground
- 🏕️ Picnic Area
- 🍴 Restaurant
- 🖼️ Lodge
- 🔭 Lookout

Yosemite National Park

41 ↑ TO VALLEY FLOOR

◆ Loop A ⛺
◆ Loop B ⛺

Chilnualina Rd

◆ Ranger Station 🏕️
◆ Loop C ⛺

41

Pioneer Yosemite History Center ◆
◆ **Wawona Information Station** 🏕️

Wawona Hotel and Golf Course 🍴
◆ 🍴
○ **Wawona**

Meadow Circle Rd

Chowchilla Mountain Rd

41

Galen Clark Tree ◆

Clothespin Tree ◆
Faithful Couple ◆

Lower Mariposa Grove ◆
Fallen Monarch ◆

Grizzly Giant ◆

South Entrance ◆ 🏕️

Mariposa Grove Rd

Summerdale Campground ◆ ⛺

Forest Rd

Yosemite Mountain Ranch Rd

○ **Fish Camp** 🍴

Jackson Rd

TO FRESNO ↓

41

0 _____ 1 mile
0 _____ 1 kilometer

WAWONA

Wawona Hotel is approximately 7 mi north of park's south entrance, and 27 mi southwest of Yosemite Valley Visitor Center.

Way back in 1864, President Abraham Lincoln acknowledged the special nature of Mariposa Grove when he bundled it with Yosemite Valley as a public trust granted to the young state of California. More than 140 years later, the grove of some 500 Sequoias represents the biggest tourist attraction in the park's southwestern section. If you are unable to visit Giant Forest in Sequoia National Park or Grant Grove in Kings Canyon National, Mariposa Grove is the next best thing. It can feel frenzied there in the summer, however, when innumerable tour buses stop by. By contrast, the whitewashed Wawona Hotel, just 4 mi away, has a perpetually relaxed air. Opened in 1879 and now a National Historic Landmark, the modestly priced (compared with the Ahwahnee Hotel) lodging sprawls leisurely on the gently hilly area across from Wawona Golf Course and Meadow. Adirondack chairs on the green lawns beckon you to bring over a good book and rest your traveling feet for a while.

VISITOR CENTERS

Wawona Information Station. Find out more about this region of the park by talking with rangers here in what's also known as Hill's Studio. Born in England in 1829, Thomas Hill was a teenager when his family immigrated to the United States. He made a lot of money—up to $10,000 per painting—selling his landscapes that depicted Yosemite Valley, and in his later years he operated a gallery and studio here next to the Wawona Hotel. Today, some of Hill's works are exhibited in the information center. You can purchase maps and guide books, as well as secure free wilderness permits and rent bear canisters. ✉ *Forest Dr., off Rte. 41, Wawona* ☎ *209/375–9531* ✉ *Free* ☉ *Apr.–Nov., Sun.–Thurs. 8–5, Fri. and Sat. 8–6.*

SCENIC DRIVES

Route 41. Entering the park via this road, which follows an ultimately curvy course 55 mi from Fresno and through the Yosemite gateway towns of Oakhurst and Fish Camp, presents you with an immediate, important choice: Turn right to visit the Mariposa Grove of giant sequoias 4 mi to the east, or turn left to travel via Wawona to Yosemite Valley, 31 mi away. Try to do both options. (You can get by with an hour in Mariposa Grove, if you're really pressed for time.) As you approach the Valley, you will want to pull into the Tunnel View parking lot (it's on the east side of the mile-long tunnel) and gawk at what lies ahead: from left to right, El Capitan, Half Dome, and Bridalveil Falls. From there, the Valley is another 5 mi. The driving time alone on Wawona Road is about an hour. Make a full day of it by adding Glacier Point to the itinerary; get there via a 16-mi seasonal road that shoots east from Route 41 and passes the Badger Ski Area. ⊠ *Wawona.*

HISTORIC SITES

Pioneer Yosemite History Center. Some of Yosemite's first structures—those not occupied by Native Americans, that is—were relocated from various parts of the park and placed here in the 1950s and 1960s. You can spend a pleasurable and informative half-hour walking about them and reading the signs, perhaps springing for a self-guided tour pamphlet (50¢) to further enhance the history lesson. Among other things, you will see the **Anderson Cabin,** home to the first person credited with climbing Half Dome; the **Blacksmith Shop,** which tended to horses that in the years around 1900 pulled wagons that took eight hours to go between here and Yosemite Valley; and the **Ranger Patrol Cabin,** which harks back to when civilian park rangers took control of the park from the U.S. Army, which had been on patrol here since 1890. Wednesday through Sunday in the summer, costumed docents conduct blacksmithing and "wet-plate" photography demonstrations for free, and for a small fee ($3 at this writing) you can take a 10-minute horse-drawn stagecoach ride. ⊠ *Rte. 41, Wawona* ☎ *209/375–9531 or 209/379–2646* ⊠ *Free* ☉ *Building interiors open mid-June–Labor Day, Wed. 2–5, Thurs.–Sun. 10–1 and 2–5.*

★ **Wawona Hotel.** You might blink when you first come across this 19th-century hotel, because there is something about it that suggests not just another time, but another place. Its architecture, sometimes referred to as "Victorian resort," has a certain elegance. One can imagine an older Mark Twain relaxing in a rocking chair on one of the broad verandas. There is history here, all right, but it appears time has passed without great incident. Across the road is a somewhat odd sight: Yosemite's golf course, which claims to be the first golf course in the Sierra Nevada, and one of the few links in the world that does not employ fertilizers or other chemicals. The Wawona is an excellent place to stay or to stop for lunch when making the drive from the South entrance to the Valley, but be aware that the hotel is closed in January. ⊠ Rte. 41, *Wawona.* ☎ *209/375–1425.*

SCENIC STOPS

★ **Mariposa Grove of Big Trees.** Of Yosemite National Parks' three sequoia groves—the others being Merced and Tuolumne, both near Crane Flat well to the north—Mariposa is by far the largest and easiest to navigate by foot. Actually, you can take quite an extended hike here, if you are so inclined, but many of the so-called "big trees" are near the correspondingly massive parking lot. **Grizzly Giant,** whose base measures 96 feet around, has been estimated to be the world's 25th-largest tree by volume. Perhaps more astoundingly, it's about 2,700 years old. On up the hill, find many more sequoias, a small museum, and fewer people. Summer weekends are especially crowded here. During those or any other occasions, instead of driving here you may be better off taking the free shuttle from Wawona; it operates daily from 9 to 6; the trip takes about 15 minutes each way. The access road to the grove may be closed by snow for extended periods from November to mid-May; you can still usually walk, snowshoe, or ski in. ⊠ *Rte. 41, 2 mi north of the South entrance station, Wawona.*

TUOLUMNE MEADOWS

Approximately 7 mi west of the east entrance on Tioga Rd., 39 mi east of Crane Flat, and 55 mi northeast of the Yosemite Valley Visitor Center.

Most park visitors do not have the time, and in some cases the inclination, to make the 56-mi drive here from Yosemite Valley. The setting is not as dramatic, admittedly, but Tuolumne Meadows is intriguing in its own way. You are confronted, practically out of the blue, with an almost perfectly flat basin, about 2.5 mi long, that in July is resplendent with wildflowers. Backpackers love to launch their journeys into remoteness here, and active day-trippers can work up a sweat on several scenic trails, mostly notably the one that mounts Lembert Dome, which offers breathtaking views of the basin below. Driving here from Lee Vining, on the eastern portion of Tioga Road, is a scenic experience that would not soon be forgotten. Do not count on the high-altitude road being open, however, sooner than June or later than mid-October.

VISITOR CENTERS

Tuolumne Meadows Visitor Center. The standard services are available here at Yosemite's highest and easternmost visitor center: You can get free wilderness permits, rent bear canisters, or shop for various maps, books, and limited souvenirs. Rangers can fill you in on the area's many trails, which vary from an easy stroll about the meadow, to a very long day's trek down the Pacific Coast Trail to Mammoth Lakes, to a multiday backpacking adventure past Waterwheel Falls into the Grand Canyon of the Tuolumne River. Nearby, there's also a mountaineering school and sport shop, as well as a little gem of a grocery store. ⊠ *Rte. 120, approximately 55 mi from the Yosemite Valley Visitor Center, Tuolumne Meadows* ☎ *209/372–0263* 🖾 *Free* ☉ *Early June–late Sept., daily 9–5.*

SCENIC DRIVES

Tioga Road. Few mountain drives anywhere can compare visually with this 59-mi seasonal road, especially its eastern half, between Lee Vining and Olmstead Point. As you climb 3,200 feet up to the 9,945-foot summit of Tioga Pass (Yosemite's sole eastern entrance for automobiles), you are entertained with broad vistas of the granite-splotched High Sierra and its craggy but hearty trees and shrubs. The road, completed by the Great Sierra Consolidated Silver Co. for wagons in 1883, slices across mountain slopes that are visible ahead. Past the bustling scene at Tuolumne Meadows, soon you come upon picturesque Tenaya Lake, named after the Native American who was in charge of Yosemite Valley before Caucasians came upon the scene mid-19th century. At Olmstead Point, you get your first peak at Half Dome, rising dramatically beyond the Tenaya Canyon. From there the road, formally Route 120, goes through thickly forested areas, into which go several enticing trails, most notably the 9-mi round-trip to North Dome. At Crane Flat, where you can gas up, either turn right to head out of the park or south toward Yosemite Valley. Driving Tioga Road one-way takes approximately 1½ hours. Try not to exceed 40 MPH at any point, even where the posted speed limit is 45 MPH, in deference to the many

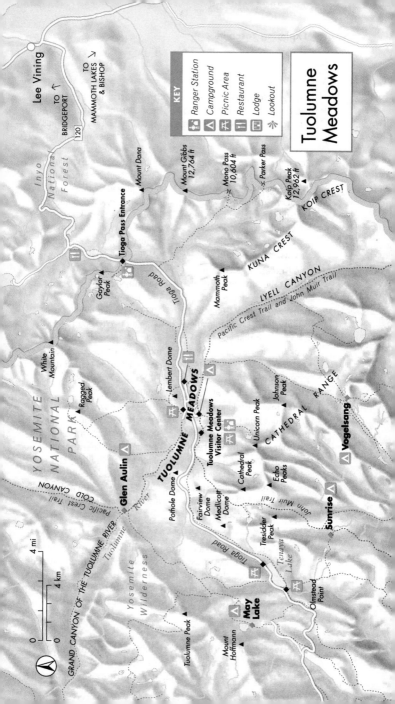

Tuolumne Meadows

KEY

- 🏚 Ranger Station
- ◮ Campground
- 🞂🞁 Picnic Area
- 🍴 Restaurant
- 🏠 Lodge
- 📯 Lookout

Lee Vining

TO ← BRIDGEPORT

TO MAMMOTH LAKES & BISHOP →

120

Inyo National Forest

Mount Dana

Mount Gibbs 12,764 ft

Mono Pass 10,604 ft

Parker Pass

Kolp Peak 12,962 ft

KOIP CREST

KUNA CREST

Tioga Pass Entrance

Gaylor Peak

White Mountain

Tioga Road

Mammoth Peak

LYELL CANYON

Pacific Crest Trail and John Muir Trail

YOSEMITE NATIONAL PARK

Ragged Peak

Lembert Dome

TUOLUMNE MEADOWS

Tuolumne Meadows Visitor Center

Johnson Peak

CATHEDRAL RANGE

Vogelsang

Pothole Dome

Unicorn Peak

GRAND CANYON OF THE TUOLUMNE RIVER

Pacific Crest Trail

COLD CANYON

Glen Aulin

Tuolumne River

Cathedral Peak

Echo Peaks

Fairview Dome

Medlicott Dome

John Muir Trail

Sunrise

Yosemite Wilderness

Tresidder Peak

Tioga Road

Tenaya Lake

Tuolumne Peak

May Lake

Mount Hoffmann

Olmstead Point

4 mi

4 km

0

0

CLOSE UP

Yosemite Events

Vintners' Holidays. Free two- and three-day seminars by California's most prestigious vintners are held midweek in November and December in the Great Room of the Ahwahnee Hotel in Yosemite Village and culminate in an elegant—albeit pricey— banquet dinner. Arrive early for seats in the free seminars; book early for lodging and dining packages. ☎ 559/253–5641 ⊕ www.yosemitepark.com.

The Bracebridge Dinner. Held at the Ahwahnee Hotel in Yosemite Village every Christmas since 1928, this 17th-century–theme madrigal dinner is so popular that you must book by mid-May to secure a seat. ☎ 559/252–4848 ⊕ www.yosemitepark.com.

Chefs' Holidays. Celebrated chefs present cooking demonstrations and five-course meals at the Ahwahnee Hotel in Yosemite Village on weekends from early January through early February. Special lodging packages are available; space is limited. ☎ 559/253–5641 ⊕ www.yosemitepark.com.

Strawberry Music Festival. Held over the Memorial Day and Labor Day holiday weekends at Camp Mather near Hetch Hetchy, the festival features many styles of music (bluegrass, blues, gospel, and rock among them) played by individuals and bands of varying quality. People have been known to attend every day of both annual editions—for decades. ☎ 209/984–8630 ⊕ www.strawberrymusic.com.

Mammoth Lakes Jazz Jubilee. This festival, founded in 1989, is hosted by the local Temple of Folly Jazz Band and takes place in 10 venues, most with dance floors, each July. ☎ 760/934–2478 or 800/367–6572 ⊕ www.mammothjazz.org.

Bluesapalooza. For one long weekend every August, Mammoth Lakes hosts a blues and beer festival—with an emphasis on the beer tasting. ☎ 760/934–0606 or 800/367–6572 ⊕ www.mammothmountain.com.

animals (coyotes are a common sight). Wildflowers bloom here in July and August. By November, the high-altitude road will have closed for the winter, not reopening again until as late as early June. ✉ *Rte. 120, between Lee Vining and Big Oak Flat Rd., Tuolumne Meadows*

SCENIC STOPS

Olmstead Point. About midway between Tuolumne Meadows and the White Wolf turnoff, this overlook provides an introductory—or parting, if you are exiting Yosemite to the east—look at Half Dome, which as the crow flies is about 5 mi to the southwest. In the foreground stands Cloud's Rest, which at 9,926 feet rises nearly 1,100 feet higher than its famous granite-faced counterpart that presides over the Valley. ■TIP→ **Take a quarter-mile trail down a bit from the road to get an even more dramatic look at the two domes and, below, Tenaya Canyon.** ⊠ *Alongside Rte. 120, 2.5 mi west of Tenaya Lake, Tuolumne Meadows.*

★ **Tuolumne Meadows.** Nowhere in the Sierra Nevada mountain range will you find a larger sub-alpine meadow. At an elevation of 8,600 feet, Tuolumne is a place where the air is very crisp and thin, which is something to keep in mind if you are contemplating any form of exercise. Your heart is pounding not because you suddenly are out of shape, but because there is not as much oxygen to breathe. The area's two most popular day hikes are the 1-mi Soda Springs/Parson's Lodge Trail, a flat and easy path that cuts through the meadow north of the road, and the considerably more strenuous, 4-mi round-trip to the top of Lembert Dome. Rangers conduct walks and talks throughout the summer, including three-hour bird-watching hikes. Campfire programs are held nightly at the Tuolumne Meadows Campground. ⊠ *Tioga Rd. (Rte. 120), about 8 mi west of the Tioga Pass entrance station, Tuolumne Meadows.*

HETCH HETCHY

Hetch Hetchy parking lot is 12 mi north of the Big Oak entrance on Rte. 120 and 37 mi northwest of the Yosemite Valley Visitor Center.

If you think that by visiting the Valley, the Wawona area, and Tuolumne Meadows you have seen all the good parts of Yosemite National Park, you are missing out on what John Muir described as "a great landscape garden, one of nature's most precious mountain temples." He was referring to Hetch Hetchy, a 38-mi drive from the Valley that is reached via a 9-mi paved road off Route 120, just outside the Big Oak Flat entrance. Until the early 1920s, Hetch Hetchy was a valley whose scenery rivaled that of Yosemite Valley, what with its flat, meadow floor, long waterfalls, and looming granite formations, most notably Kolana Rock. For the past 86 years, however, Hetch Hetchy has been underwater. The O'Shaughnessy Dam first plugged the Tuolumne River here in 1923, and it was expanded in 1938. Many preservationists and others who long for the Hetch Hatchy Valley of old continue to lobby hard for the

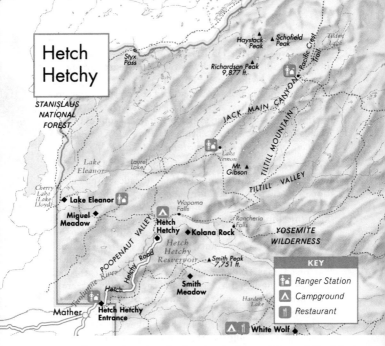

dam's relocation farther downstream. Meanwhile, hikers can get an idea of the area's charms by taking the mildly strenuous, 5-mi round-trip Wapama Falls Trail.

Backpacking is the only way to see the rest of Yosemite National Park—and there is a lot more to see. Of the park's 1,169 square mi, more than 94% are designated as wilderness.

SCENIC STOPS

Hetch Hetchy Reservoir. When Congress gave O'Shaughnessy Dam the green light here in 1913, pragmatism triumphed over aestheticism. Some 2.4 million residents of the San Francisco Bay Area continue to get their water from this 117-billion-gallon reservoir, although spirited efforts are being made to move the dam farther down the Tuolumne River so that the Hetch Hetchy Valley can be restored to its former, pristine glory. Eight miles long, the reservoir is Yosemite's largest body of water, and one that can be seen up-close from several trails that begin at the backpackers camp, a 9-mi paved drive off Route 120. ✉ *Hetch Hetchy Rd., about 12 mi northeast of the Big Oak Flat entrance station, Hetch Hetchy*

Yosemite Hikes & Other Activities

WORD OF MOUTH

"We loved sunset from Sentinel Dome. Drove up to Glacier Point early enough to do the short hike out to Taft Point for that great view then back around to be up on Sentinel in time to get our cameras set up for sunset. The walk back to our car in the Alpine glow was magical, as well. A large buck crossed the trail right in front of us. He stopped and just looked at us for a few moments before he trotted off."

—floridafran

By Reed
Parsell

A COMMON COMPLAINT ABOUT YOSEMITE NATIONAL PARK is that it often is too busy. Crowds are to be expected, perhaps, when so many of the attractions are not only astounding (Half Dome, El Capitan, Yosemite Falls) but easily visible from the road. Indeed, summer days in the Valley can feature long backups of idling automobiles, shoulder-to-shoulder maneuvering in the Valley Visitor Center and surrounding Village, and standing-room-only in the dining halls. What is so back-to-nature about all that?

You can exert some control in this matter. One way is to visit Yosemite off-season. Another is to take a hike, ideally a longer one. It will carry you far enough from the Valley throngs that, although you still might run into a lot of people, at least they won't be carrying ice cream cones and taking pictures of squirrels. You also can examine the park's landmark features from different, interesting perspectives. Checking out Half Dome from atop North Dome, for example, is an even more awesome experience than gazing at it from the Valley floor. Looking down on Tuolumne Meadows and across the horizon from the top of Lembert Dome gives you a better appreciation of the vast and largely unspoiled High Sierra. Venturing even a few hundred feet off any road greatly improves your chances of seeing wildlife, maybe even a bear.

Give yourself time to step off the pavement in Yosemite, even if it's for just an hour or two. You will be rewarded with many lasting memories. Take a look at our recommended hikes, decide which one sounds like a good match for your fitness level and interests, and go for it. Rest assured, the people-packed dinner buffet at Curry Village will be waiting for you whenever you get back.

DAY HIKES

Easy, hard, short, long, paved, rugged—Yosemite has a day hike appropriate for your abilities and interests. You can take a leisurely stroll to Lower Yosemite Falls without breaking a sweat, spend a day alternating between walking the Valley Floor Trail and riding the free shuttle, put your fitness to a test by climbing 3,000 feet up from the Valley to Glacier Point or Yosemite Point, or go crazy by going full-bore up Half Dome. To whatever extent you exert yourself, the scenery will be 100% spectacular.

BEST HIKES & ACTIVITIES

■ **Gawk:** People come from all over the world to see Half Dome, El Capitan, and the waterfalls. It's OK to stand with your fellow travelers and stare.

■ **Take a Short Trail:** After your initial gawking phase (which you can return to later), pick an attraction that looks especially interesting and walk closer to it.

■ **Take a Longer Trail:** Yosemite Valley can feel claustrophobic on a busy summer's day. Escape out into a meadow, up a mountain, or deep into a forest and listen to the birds and the breeze. Breathe deeply that fresh air.

■ **Ride a Bike:** Yosemite Valley's attractions are scattered about, and although the free shuttle buses go to most of them, you might prefer the freedom and exercise that bicycling offers.

■ **Go for a swim:** Yosemite Lodge and Curry Village welcome nonguests swim in their pools—for a fee. For free, people also plop into the Merced River or Tenaya Creek.

It is difficult to identify a "must-do" trail, because you can actually have a good experience at most of Yosemite's signature attractions without straying too far from your car. (One exception is at Mariposa Grove, where you must walk slightly uphill for a half-mile or so to see Fallen Monarch and the Grizzly Giant.) The one-day trail that gets the most buzz, and would give you bragging rights for a lifetime, is Half Dome. Relentlessly you climb, up steep steps carved into granite, slowed by stragglers ahead or pushed by sprinters from behind, getting sprayed by waterfalls along the way—and you still have 3 mi to go, because you have reached only the top of Nevada Fall. You have another 3,000-plus feet to ascend, including the final 400 feet by going hand-over-hand on a steel cable. All that, and the hike's most dangerous aspect is the return journey, when you are dog-tired and the trail's slippery nature comes most into play.

You may encounter some nonhuman mammals that are larger than the omnipresent squirrels (of which there several varieties), but chances are you will not—especially in high tourist season—in the middle of the afternoon, when bears tend to nap and other creatures know to stay out of the way. Bird-watching is a more promising proposition, as 247 species have been spotted in the

Tips for the Trails

Know Your limitations: You must know what they are, to paraphrase Harry Callahan in "Magnum Force." Several of Yosemite's trails are very difficult, most notably the one up Half Dome, so carefully consider what you are capable of before setting off. Remember, there is a lot less oxygen available at 8,000 feet than there is in your hometown—unless you reside in, say, Leadville, Colorado.

Bring Refreshments: A simple rule of thumb regarding water is to take twice what you figure is necessary. That way, you might be able to help hikers in need by giving them your liquid leftovers. Trail mix is good to pack, too.

Watch Your Feet: Most of Yosemite's trails have sandy, or pebbly, portions that can cause you to slip, especially when you are going downhill. In such cases, you should carefully measure each stride. Sightsee only after you have come to a full stop.

Two's company: And three is not really a crowd, when you are hiking into wilderness. In the extremely unlikely event that something goes wrong, you will appreciate the backup personnel.

Beware All Animals: Do not approach, do not heckle, do not feed. Outside the Valley, park rangers enforce a rule that all food and other fragrant items must never be left in an unattended vehicle. Use the public bear boxes.

---

park. Bald and golden eagles inhabit areas above 3,000 feet, so with binoculars you may be able to inspect one of those winged predators. The vegetation you see, of course, depends on the elevation. Possibilities abound in the lower montane (3,000–7,000 feet), upper montane (6,000–9,000 feet), sub-alpine (8,000–11,500 feet), and alpine (11,000 feet and above) regions. Canyon live oak and Pacific dogwood bring vibrant natural colors to the Valley in spring and fall, while distinctive manzanita bushes can be seen most anywhere.

In the Valley, all the major trailheads have restrooms nearby, some of them the pit variety. Snack stands and restaurants are never more than a few shuttle stops away, as are stores ready to assist you with sunscreen and insect repellent.

The staff at the **Wilderness Center** (✉ *Yosemite Village, next to the post office* ⏚ *Yosemite Wilderness Reservations, Box 545, Yosemite Village,* ☎ *209/372–0740* ⊕ *www.nps.*

gov/yose) provides free wilderness permits, which are required for overnight camping (advance camping reservations are available for $5 and are highly recommended for popular trailheads from May through September and on weekends). It also provides maps and advice to hikers heading into the backcountry.

Yosemite Mountaineering School & Guide Service (⊠ *Yosemite Mountain Shop, Curry Village* ☎ *209/372–8344* ⊕ *www. yosemitepark.com*) can take you on guided two-hour to full-day treks from April through November.

3

HIKES TO LOOK OUT FOR

Very short hikes (less than two hours): Bridalveil Fall, "Changing Yosemite" Interpretive Trail, Mariposa Grove (abbreviated option), Meadow Loop, Mirror Lake, Sentinel Loop, Twin Bridges, Lower Yosemite Falls.

Half-day hikes (up to five hours): Lembert Dome, Mariposa Grove (extended option), Four-Mile Trail, Mist Trail, Wapama Falls.

Full-day hikes: Chilnualna Falls, Half Dome, North Dome, Panorama, Upper Yosemite Falls (including Yosemite Point).

YOSEMITE VALLEY

SPOTLIGHT HIKE: PANORAMA TRAIL

Few hikes come with the visual punch that this 8.5-mi trail provides. The star attraction is Half Dome, visible from many intriguing angles, but you also see three waterfalls up close and walk through a manzanita grove. Before you begin, look down on Yosemite Valley from Glacier Point, a special experience in itself. ⊠ *End of Glacier Point Rd., Glacier Point* ☞ *Moderate to difficult.*

0.0 MI: PANORAMA POINT TRAILHEAD

From the Glacier Point parking lot, walk toward the overlook but look right. You should see a trail sign. Go directly past it, up a small hill, and when the right option of a "V" points toward Sentinel Dome, veer left instead.

0.7 MI: INCOMPORABLE VISTAS

As you round a bend you will get your first look at Illilouette Fall. Not long after, you will be able to see Half Dome, Vernal Fall, and Nevada Fall all at once. Pause to soak in the sensational scene. At this point, Half Dome rather resembles a big toe.

2.0 MI: ILLILOUETTE FALL

As you cross Illilouette Creek on a bridge just above the 370-foot waterfall, you may spot brave (foolish?) souls swimming in the pools of water in between. Shortly beyond the bridge is where you encounter the hillside of manzanita bushes, with their distinctive purplish bark and bright-green leaves. If you took the morning tour bus to Glacier Point and want to catch an afternoon bus back to the Valley—or if you want to avoid the mild dangers of descending between Nevada Fall and Vernal Fall—turn around here.

3.5 MI: A LOOK BACK

As you make your way to this plateau, on the Panorama Trail's mile-long stretch of moderate uphill climbing, at several points Half Dome will be directly in front of you. See if you agree that an optional illusion occurs: The Yosemite landmark will appear as though it is merely a large boulder, just a few hundred yards ahead. Upon reaching the clearing, use your binoculars to spot Glacier Point's Geology Hut and, perhaps, hikers who are a few hours behind you.

5.0 MI: A CHOICE

If you spot an abandoned phone kiosk—that's not a joke; there used to be a telephone on this trail—look around the immediate vicinity for a sign for the John Muir Trail. Take it for a slightly longer and safer trek down to the Valley. Otherwise, continue on to Nevada Fall and the only imperfect part of this hike: Steep, rocky steps between Nevada Fall and Vernal Fall can be extremely slippery.

SPOTLIGHT TRAIL: UPPER YOSEMITE FALLS

Fitness gurus constantly tell us to take the stairs rather than the escalator or elevator. Well, here's your chance to obey their orders—big-time. Take this relentlessly uphill, 3.8-mi (one-way) path from the Valley floor to the top of the waterfalls, and you'll swear you have lost five pounds. ⊠ *Trailhead at Camp 4 Campground, ½-mi west of Yosemite Lodge ☞ Difficult.*

0.0 MI: THE TRAILHEAD

Begin a few hundred yards west of the Lower Yosemite Falls Trail, past a large and persistently stinky restroom building. Walk through the Camp 4 Campground's parking lot to find the trail sign, and immediately begin climbing. The first half-mile contains more than 50 switchbacks.

PANORAMA TRAIL TIPS

■ Considering that the trail goes from Glacier Point down to the Valley (or by listening to other hikers on the bus ride up), you might conclude that it's all downhill. Sorry, but beginning at Illilouette Fall you'll have to walk up for a solid mile.

■ Actually, it's a downhill portion that you will have to worry about. The 1.7-mi descent from Nevada Fall to the Valley is dicey, with a frightening number of opportunities to slip-slide on the steep steps and injure yourself. Go slowly on this stretch.

■ Bring your binoculars so that you can zoom in on the top of Half Dome, where you might spot hikers who probably are more winded than you are.

■ For an even bigger sense of accomplishment, leave early in the day and walk *up* the trail, then take the afternoon tour bus from Glacier Point back down to the Valley.

1.0 MI: COLUMBIA ROCK
Getting to this point is a real grind, although things will get easier for a while once you are past the sand-dune-like stretch that is immediately ahead. Meanwhile, take a breather to gaze out over the Valley. Yosemite Lodge's swimming pool may look especially inviting to you from this vantage point, but let that temptation go unheeded and press on.

2.0 MI: MIDDLE OF YOSEMITE FALLS
This small clearing provides you with a breathtaking, mid-falls view. Just before you arrive there, you will have passed a tree that is touchable from the trail, on the right. Its red, stringy bark might make you think it's a sequoia. Rather, it is an incense cedar, common in Yosemite and commonly confused with sequoias.

3.8 MI: TOP OF YOSEMITE FALLS
After another grinding and seemingly never-ending series of seriously steep switchbacks, you get to a free-for-all area of smooth granite on which you might have to search a few moments to find the trail sign that points you onward. Actually, you must *descend* to the small overlook area via a carved-from-the-granite staircase that, if you have been to Sequoia National Park, will remind you of Moro Rock.

UPPER YOSEMITE FALLS TRAIL TIPS

■ Even though Upper Yosemite Falls Trail has less elevation gain than the Four-Mile Trail across the Valley, it covers a shorter distance, is steeper, and is more difficult. Pace yourself carefully.

■ Carry as much water as you can. You might be surprised at how much you will need to drink within the first mile, before you even get to Columbia Rock.

■ Be careful, oh so careful, as you descend. Pebbles atop the rocks you step down upon can cause you to slip. Acting legend William Holden died from a fall in his living room, remember, so it is prudent to exercise extreme caution on this steep and potentially treacherous trail.

■ Do not plan any other physical activity for the day. And there is no need to feel guilty about ordering dessert after dinner. After all, you have just completed the ultimate Stairmaster workout!

4.7 MI: YOSEMITE POINT

If you made it to Upper Yosemite Falls, you might as well add another hour to your round-trip trek by taking this gentler (compared with what you already have been through) uphill path to an overlook that offers broader views of the Valley than does the falls' overlook. Along the way, you will have crossed Yosemite Creek just above the falls, which provides an interesting perspective.

OTHER HIKES IN YOSEMITE VALLEY

🏵 **Bridalveil Fall.** A paved but uphill—too steep for wheelchairs, but OK for strollers—trail leads to a cul-de-sac area from which you can see the 620-foot waterfall. Though much shorter than Yosemite Falls, Bridalveil is dramatic for the "veil" of water it produces at its peak flow in late spring and early summer. About 1 mi round-trip, this hike is one of the park's most consistently crowded, even in September and October, when there might not be much to see, water-wise. ⊠ *4 mi west of Yosemite Lodge, at the junction of Southside Dr. and Wawona Rd.* ⚐ *Easy.*

🏵 **"A Changing Yosemite" Interpretive Trail.** Take this 1-mi, wheelchair-accessible, looped path about Cook's Meadow to see and learn the basics about Yosemite Valley's past, present, and future. You can buy a self-guiding trail guide for 50¢ and read about how Half Dome and other granite formations you see got their start 100 million years ago; learn the differences among oaks, cedars, and pines; be reminded that Native Americans arrived in the Valley as many as 8,000 years ago; that fires are a natural part of keeping the Valley floor healthy; and that human factors such as pollution from the Central Valley and climate change pose significant challenges for the years, and millennia, ahead. ⊠ *Yosemite Valley, across from the Valley Visitor Center Yosemite Village* ☞ *Easy.*

Four-Mile Trail. Not quite as difficult as the Upper Yosemite Falls Trail, this path is the other major hiking route from the Valley to an overlook—in this case Glacier Point. You begin calmly enough, striding mildly uphill from the Sentinel Picnic Area and Sentinel Bridge through the forest. From there, three sections of rather spirited switchbacks lead you under Sentinel Dome to Glacier Point. Along the way, you are treated to fabulous views of the Yosemite Falls (although by August it becomes a trickle, if that) and you actually can take a reverse look through Tunnel View, part of Wawona Road to the west. You'll actually travel 4.7 mi because the original 4-mi path first built in the 1870s has been modified in the interest of ease and safety. Hiking the round-trip certainly is doable in a fairly full day, but you may prefer taking the 10 AM tour bus ($25 one-way) from Yosemite Lodge to Glacier Point and hiking down—or walking up in the morning and catching a return bus (same one-way price). The trail's total elevation gain is 3,240 feet; find restrooms on either end. ⊠ *Approx. 1 mi south of Yosemite Lodge, off Southside Dr., between Sentinel Beach and Swinging Bridge campgrounds* ☞ *Moderate.*

★ FodorsChoice **John Muir Trail to Half Dome.** Ardent and courageous trekkers can continue on from the top of Nevada Fall, off Mist Trail, to the top of Half Dome. Some hikers attempt this entire 10- to 12-hour, 16.75-mi round-trip trek from Happy Isles in one day; if you're planning to do this, remember that the 4,800-foot elevation gain and the 8,842-foot altitude will cause shortness of breath. Another option is to hike to a campground in Little Yosemite Valley near the top of Nevada Fall the first day, then climb to the top of Half Dome and hike out the next day; it's highly recommended that you get your wilderness permit reservations for this trail at least a month in advance. Be sure to wear hiking boots and bring gloves (for the steel cable up Half Dome). The last pitch up the back of Half Dome is very steep—the only way to climb this sheer rock face is to pull yourself up using the steel cable handrails, which are in place only from late spring to early fall. Those who

Half Dome: A Miwok Legend

In the 1980 book *The Natural World of the California Indians*, by Robert F. Heizer and Albert B. Elsasser, the authors describe in detail how the Southern Sierra Miwoks came to be the prevailing tribe of what's now known as Yosemite Valley. They also share the Miwoks' explanation of how the Valley and Half Dome came to be.

"Half Dome (then a person) lived with her husband, Washington Tower, near the edge of the San Joaquin Valley along the Merced River," Heizer and Elsasser write. "After a quarrel with her husband, Half Dome ran away to the east and in the process made the Merced River and gouged out the Valley of the Yosemite. She was carrying her baby in her arms and the baby's cradle on her head.

"Washington Tower, on finding that his wife had left him, cut a white oak club and pursued her. Reaching her, he beat her with the club. Half Dome threw the baby's cradle, with its arched basketry sunshade, against the north wall of the Valley, where it became the Royal Arches. Half Dome herself was transformed into the great rock bearing that name.

"What became of her baby we are not told; perhaps the baby only served as the reason for her carrying the cradle that became the Royal Arches."

brave the ascent will be rewarded with an unbeatable view of Yosemite Valley below and the high country beyond. Before heading out, check conditions with rangers, and don't attempt the final ascent if there are any storm clouds overhead. Lightning strikes have killed people atop the dome. ✉ *South of Curry Village and Upper Pines Campground, just past Happy Isles; Shuttle Stop 16 ☞ Very difficult.*

Mirror Lake Trail. Because this hike is short (2.4-mi round-trip), easy (much of it is paved, with a total elevation change of only 100 feet), and in a busy part of Yosemite Valley (it has its own shuttle stop, No. 17), plenty of people give it a go. Despite the name, there is no lake, and despite what you may have heard or read, geologists no longer believe that this flat area near the foot of Half Dome is transitioning into a meadow. Rather, Tenaya Creek pools here in enough spots to create that misconception. Swimming is popular here, especially on warm days early in the summer, when there is more water. Bathrooms and pay phones are at the trailhead. ✉ *Approx. 1 mi east of Curry Village; Shuttle Stop 17 ☞ Easy.*

★ **Mist Trail.** More visitors take this trail, or portions of it, 🐾 than any other in the park other than Lower Yosemite Falls. Word of mouth, as much as the worth of the trail, keep it bustling from late spring to early fall. From the Happy Isles area you start off innocuously enough, striding steadily up a paved trail that leads to a bridge that serves three purposes: It gives you a first good look at the 317-foot Vernal Fall; it offers a convenient spot where you can fill up your water bottle courtesy of the faucets here (yes, with stainless steel sinks); and if you want to avoid the most strenuous stretch ahead, it gives you a handy opportunity to turn around. Make the final approach to Vernal Fall on a cliffside staircase. In summer, you may want to join many others in swimming behind the waterfall—some adventurers even take a dip below, which is decidedly off-trail. The trek up to and back from Vernal Fall is 3 mi. Add another 4 mi total by continuing up to 594-foot Nevada Fall; the trail becomes quite steep and slippery in its final stages. The elevation gain to Vernal Fall is 1,000 feet, and to Nevada Fall an additional 1,000 feet. Merced River tumbles down both falls on its way to a tranquil flow through the Valley. ⊠ *South of Curry Village and Upper Pines Campground, just past Happy Isles; Shuttle Stop 16, Curry Village* ☞ *Moderate.*

Sentinel Loop Trail. If Glacier Point's vistas have you yearning for more, and you have another hour or two at your disposal, hop on this 2.2-mi (round trip) path to the top of Sentinel Dome. At 8,122 feet, it is 908 feet higher than the overlook at Glacier Point, and its views are more encompassing. If your camera has a "panorama" setting, use it here (if you're ever going to use it at all; "panorama" is pretty worthless unless it comes with an extreme wide-angle feature). The trail is easy until the final, steep push up the dome. If you have taken the tour bus up to Glacier Point ($25 one-way from Yosemite Lodge), you will have time to take this hike. For a really full day of exercise, tack it onto the Four-Mile Trail. ⊠ *End of Glacier Point Rd., Glacier Point* ☞ *Moderate.*

★ **Lower Yosemite Falls Trail.** One of the park's easiest hikes is 🐾 also one of its most spectacular, especially when the three cascades that constitute the 2,425-foot Yosemite Falls are at full volume. The paved trail, the eastern portion of which is wheelchair-accessible, begins to the left of shuttle Stop 6 not far from Yosemite Village. Take a clockwise approach for the quickest way to the observation platform. You can

Q & A with Ranger Scott Gediman

What's your favorite thing to do in the park?

I really enjoy hiking in Yosemite; in my opinion there's no better way to see the park. My favorite is the classic hike up the Mist Trail to Vernal Fall. I've done it literally hundreds of times—I've got family photos of my folks pushing me up the trail in a stroller. If you can only take one hike in Yosemite, do this one, especially in spring and summer.

Which time of year is best for visiting Yosemite?

The spring is wonderful, with the waterfalls going full blast and the meadows so green. The fall colors are beautiful, too. But in winter, the weather is great. The most stunning time in the valley is when a winter storm clears and there are incredible blue skies above the granite rocks, and the snow. There's a feeling you get seeing Half Dome with snow on it, or doing a winter hike on the Four-Mile Trail, Yosemite Falls Trail, or the Glacier Point trails.

What's there to do here in winter?

There's the ice skating rink at Curry Village, and up at Badger Pass there's a wonderful ski school that specializes in teaching kids. There's cross-country skiing on groomed tracks along Glacier Point Road. Snowshoeing is really catching on, and families can do it. You don't need special skills or a bunch of gear to go hiking through the snow; just put some snowshoes on your sneakers or hiking boots, and you're off. Every morning from about mid-December to mid-March, park rangers lead free snowshoe walks from Badger Pass. We talk about winter ecology and adaptations animals make, or we hike up to the old Badger Summit for some fantastic views.

What about summer?

There's a misperception that the crowds are unmanageable, but it's not true. It's very easy to get away from the crowds in the Valley. One easy way is to hike the Valley Loop Trail, which a lot of people don't even know about. It goes all around the valley perimeter. Five minutes from Yosemite Lodge, and you won't see anybody.

How crowded does the Valley really get?

At the busiest time, probably Memorial Day Weekend, there can be as many as 25,000 people in the park at one time, many of them in the Valley. The biggest mistake people make in summer is to drive everywhere. It's frustrating because of the traffic, and it takes longer even than walking. Park your car in the day-use lot or leave it at your hotel, and take the free shuttle around.

get misted here in the late spring and early summer, but by late August you might not even see water, much less feel it. Continuing clockwise, the trail takes a meandering path through trees back to the road, with at least one good small side trail that leads to another falls lookout, perhaps providing yet another photo op. If this little trek has whetted your appetite for more, so to speak, consider taking the strenuous Upper Yosemite Falls Trail. ■TIP→ **If you happen to spend the night in Yosemite Valley when the sky is clear and there is a full moon, come here to see how the falls give off a magical moonglow.** ✉ *Off Northside Dr., about halfway between Valley Visitor Center and Yosemite Village; Shuttle Stop 6* ☞ *Easy.*

WAWONA

Chilnualna Falls Trail. This Wawona-area trail runs 4.2-mi one-way to the top of the falls, then leads into the backcountry, connecting with miles of other trails. This is one of the park's most inspiring and secluded—albeit strenuous—trails. Past the tumbling cascade, and up through forests, you'll emerge before a panoramic vista at the top. ✉ *About 1½ mi off Rte. 41 on Chilnualna Falls Rd, just north of the Wawona Hotel, Wawona* ☞ *Moderate.*

☺ **Mariposa Grove of Giant Sequoias.** For hikers, Yosemite National Park's largest grove of "big trees" is an multiple-choice proposition. You can order a short and easy hike, or a rather long and strenuous one, or something in between; you can see one or two sequoias, or hundreds of them; you can spend time in or skip a museum that's uniquely plotted far up the mountain; you can drive here or take the free shuttle—or any combination of the above. The grove's biggest attraction, literally, is the Grizzly Giant, estimated to be 2,700 years old. By mature sequoia standards, it is not all that tall, at 209 feet, but its volume is measured as 25th-largest in the world. ("In the world" is being hyperbolic, admittedly, because *all* the world's sequoia groves are here in the Sierra Nevada.) About 100 yards farther uphill is the Telescope Tree, the park's only living sequoia that has a man-made passage bored through its base. The Grove Museum, a good 1 mi farther up the path and set amid the grove's thickest patch of sequoias, has a few displays (be sure to look at the sequoia timeline on the floor, which shows that Grizzly Giant was thriving even before the Parthenon was built in Athens) as well as postcards and water bottles for sale. A restroom with flush toilets, believe it or not, is nearby. If you made it this far, you might as well keep going to Wawona Point Vista, which offers outstanding views of the Wawona Meadow (but you cannot quite make out the hotel). In all likelihood, you will have this pretty perch to yourself. ■TIP→ **Yosemite's other two sequoia groves are near Crane Flat: Merced and Tuolumne. The 2-mi trail down to Merced Grove has its charms, but Tuolumne Grove is a big disappointment to the many, many people who nevertheless trudge down to it.** ✉ *.6 mi east of Wawona and 2 mi east of the south entrance, Wawona* ☞ *Easy to moderate.*

Meadow Loop Trail. Nothing about this level, 3.5-mi trail screams "Yosemite," but it makes for a pleasant stroll through the woods anyway. Start across from the Wawona Hotel by stepping right through the golf course on a paved path, then turn left on an abandoned dirt road that circles the meadow. You will see much of the golf course, but not much of the meadow. Traffic noises from Route 41 almost disappear, though never completely. Lots of horses will share this trail with you, so watch out for a bountiful harvest of what humorously are called "road apples." The Meadow Loop is a good hike for those who are staying at the Wawona Hotel and who already have been to Mariposa Grove. Walking it is a good way to build up an appetite for a late dinner in the Wawona Hotel's fine restaurant, or to burn off calories after an early meal. ✉ *Rte. 41, across the street from the Wawona Hotel, Wawona* ☞ *Easy.*

TUOLUMNE MEADOWS

Many backpacking adventures begin at Tuolumne Meadows, the hiking-boot gateway to wilderness areas in Yosemite's northern, eastern, and central regions. This is also a popular day-hike destination for people who have been to Yosemite Valley and perhaps have grown weary of the crowds there. Parked cars can cram the roadside at Tuolumne Meadows, certainly, but the atmosphere here in the High Sierra is laid-back and, perhaps because of the higher altitude, a bit sleepy. Walk for 10 minutes, and you'll be free of the mild Tioga Road commotion. A fantastic general store can supply your picnic at a table beneath Lembert Dome, or down the road a bit at Tenaya Lake. A snack bar and small gas station could come in handy, too.

Lembert Dome and Dog Lake. Park near the Tuolumne Lodge, hike up and over Tioga Road, and you are well on your way to the top of Lembert Dome, an informal spot (there is no platform or formal overlook) where you can take in the meadows some 900 feet below. You might be surprised at how difficult this 2.8-mi one-way hike seems, until you remember you began at an altitude of some 8,500 feet. Head back down and around on the north side to see Dog Lake, a relatively large body of sub-alpine water that offers secluded—if somewhat chilly—swimming possibilities. ⊠ *On the eastern side of Toulomne Meadows, off the small road that leads to Toulomne Meadows Lodge, Toulomne Meadows ⌇ Moderate.*

North Dome from Tioga Road. If the idea of hiking up 3,000-plus feet from the Valley floor to Glacier Point or Yosemite Point sounds too intimidating, you should give this 8.8-mi round-trip path a try. Basically, you begin at an elevation that's about 600 feet higher than 7,525-foot North Dome and meander your way from Tioga Road down a little bit, then mildly up and down a few more times before arriving at a rocky overlook that hovers directly behind the slightly shorter North Dome. Go either around this big mound, via a somewhat steep trail to the left, or up and over it, then down its steep southern side. Either way, you come to the only difficult part of the trail, where for a few minutes you will be tiptoeing down a carved granite staircase before you reach the free-for-all that is the top of North Dome. Once there, you will see Half Dome from as close up as is possible north of the Valley. The view is so good that many people make this an annual trek. The trail, of course, is open only when Tioga Road is, which typically is from early June through mid-October. ⊠ *Tioga Rd., 21 mi east of Crane Flat at the Porcupine Creek parking area, Toulomne Meadows ⌇ Moderate.*

☾ **Tuolumne Meadows.** There is no formal loop or one-way trail here, but by parking next to the road anywhere along the meadows' 2-mi length, you can pick a path to venture out for a low-impact stroll. Come in July for maximum wild-flower viewing, but whenever you are here, do a "360" to admire all the peaks that surround this low-key spot— which usually is peaceful, too, despite the crowds it can attract on weekends. ⊠ *On the north side of Tioga Rd., between the visitor center and Lembert Dome, Toulomne Meadows ⌇ Easy.*

Twin Bridges. Walk for 10 minutes on this mostly level path, and you will come to a lovely clearing where evergreen trees seem to be growing out of the many smooth granite surfaces, and the gurgling stream (the Lyell Fork of the Tuolumne River) teams with birds chirping to provide the audio entertainment. Visually, you also can enjoy the spare mountaintops that rise in every direction. Two wooden bridges here cross the stream, which pools here in several spots that might appeal to swimmers. On the banks, you will find many good places for a picnic. If you ask rangers, bus drivers, or workers at the nearby Tuolumne Lodge what's a good hike to take in the area, this little beauty is likely to be mentioned. Start at the John Muir Trail sign off the lodge's parking lot. You will walk by lodge's residential housing before turning left over a small bridge. ⊠ *Trailhead at Wawona Hotel parking lot, Toulomne Meadows* ☞ *Easy.*

DID YOU KNOW? In the nearly 120 years since Yosemite National Park was created, no human has been killed there by a bear. Unfortunately, humans have been responsible for countless bear deaths, including the shameful eradication of all grizzly bears in California, which once roamed from the coast to the High Sierra. As you drive about the park, you will see signs that depict bears in bright-red silhouette. Those indicate that a vehicle recently struck a bear in the vicinity. It's a sobering thing to contemplate, and a reminder not to speed.

HETCH HETCHY

Hiking here is a bittersweet experience. As you walk beside the reservoir on Wapama Falls Trail, you need summon only a little imagination to picture the valley as it was before it was dammed—many would say damned—in the early 20th century. Hetch Hetchy is an hour's drive from Yosemite Valley and lacks amenities other than a few flush toilets just before you get to the loop parking lot. Its remoteness comes with a big silver lining, however: few visitors. Also, this is Yosemite's lowest elevation, which means pleasant temperatures in the spring and fall. The Evergreen Lodge, outside the park's borders between Route 120 and the reservoir, has a small snack bar and good little restaurant, in addition to being a nice place to overnight.

Wapama Falls Trail. In several respects, this is one of Yosemite's most scenic hikes. You begin by crossing the O'Shaughnessy Dam, a source of long-standing controversy:

from John Muir's opposition just before his death to the impassioned "Restore Hetch Hetchy" (a common bumper sticker in Northern California) movement of today. From the dam you get an idea of what the valley looked like before its flooding in the early 20th century. After passing through a 500-foot tunnel, you emerge on a reservoir-side trail that often is lightly "decorated" with bear droppings. About halfway along the 2½-mi (one-way) trek to the falls, you come to a large rocky ledge from which you can take artistic pictures of the reservoir and Kolana Rock, which may remind those familiar with Rio de Janeiro of that Brazilian city's landmark Sugar Loaf. Upon arriving at the falls, you may get wet, especially in late spring or early summer when runoff is at its maximum. The observation deck is often closed for repairs. To reach the trailhead, exit the park via the Big Oak Flat entrance on Route 120, turn right (east) on Evergreen Road, then take the first right on Hetch Hetchy Road, which dead-ends 9 mi later at the backpackers camp. ⊠ *End of Hetch Hetchy Rd., 9 mi northeast of Evergreen Lodge, Hetch Hetchy* ☞ *Moderate.*

SUMMER SPORTS & ACTIVITIES

BICYCLING

There may be no more enjoyable way to see Yosemite Valley than to ride a bike in the shadow of its lofty granite monoliths. The eastern valley has 12 mi of paved, flat bicycle paths across meadows and through woods, with bike racks at convenient stopping points. For a greater challenge, you can ride on 196 mi of paved park roads—but bicycles are not allowed on hiking trails or in the backcountry. Kids younger than 18 must wear a helmet.

Yosemite Bike Rentals (⊠ *Yosemite Lodge, Yosemite Village* ☎ *209/372–1208* ⊠ *Curry Village,* ⊕ *www.yosemitepark. com*) rents bikes by the hour ($9.50) or by day ($25.50) from either its Yosemite Lodge or Curry Village bike stand, both of which are open from April through October. Bikes with child trailers, baby-jogger strollers, and wheelchairs also are available.

BIRD-WATCHING

Nearly 250 bird species have been spotted in the park, including the sage sparrow, pygmy owl, blue grouse, and mountain bluebird. Park rangers lead free bird-watching walks in Yosemite Valley one day a week in summer; check at a visitor center or information station for times and locations. Binoculars are sometimes available for loan.

Birding Seminars (☎ *209/379–2321* ⊕ *www.yosemite.org*) are sponsored by the Yosemite Association, which offers one- to four-day seminars for beginner and intermediate birders from April through August. Expect to pay between $82 and $254.

FISHING

The waters in Yosemite are not stocked; trout, mostly brown and rainbow, live here but are not plentiful. Yosemite's fishing season begins on the last Saturday in April and ends on November 15. Some waterways are off-limits at certain times; be sure to inquire at the visitor center about regulations. A California fishing license is required to fish in the park; licenses are $12.60 for one day, $19.45 for two days, and $38.85 for 10 days. Full-season licenses cost $38.85 for state residents, and a whopping $104.20 for nonresidents. Within the park, you can buy a license at the Yosemite Village Sport Shop or at the Wawona Store.

You can also obtain a fishing license in advance of a Yosemite trip by writing the **California Department of Fish and Game** (⌂*3211 S St., Sacramento* ☎ *916/227–2245* ⊕ *www.dfg. ca.gov*).

Southern Yosemite Mountain Guides (☎ *800/231–4575* ⊕ *www.symg.com*) offers fly-fishing lessons and day- and weekend trips deep in Yosemite's backcountry.

GOLF

Wawona Golf course is one of the country's few organic golf courses; it's also an Audubon Cooperative sanctuary for birds. You can play a round or take a lesson from the pro here.

Wawona Golf Course (⊠ *Rte. 41, Wawona* ☎ *209/375–6572 Wawona Golf Shop* ⊕ *www.yosemitepark.com*), a 9-hole, par-35 layout, has different tee positions on the "front" and "back" nines, so it actually provides 18 holes at par

70. The pro shop rents out electric golf carts, rents and sells other equipment, and sells golf clothing. Rangers and others who work at and near the Wawona Hotel, which contains the golf course's pro shop, testify that the snack bar is an especially good one. Green fees are $18.50 for 9 holes, $28.50 for 18 holes, and the course is open from mid-April through October.

HORSEBACK RIDING

Reservations for guided trail rides must be made in advance at the hotel tour desks or by phone. Scenic trail rides range from two hours to a full day; six-day High Sierra saddle trips are also available.

For overnight saddle trips, which use mules, you will need to make reservations for remote lodging. To do so, call the **Delaware North Corporation** (☎ *801/559–5000, option 4*) on or after September 15 to request a lottery application for the following year.

Tuolumne Meadows Stables (✉ *Off Tioga Rd., about 2 mi east of Tuolumne Meadows Visitor Center, Toulomne Meadows* ☎ *209/372–8427* ⊕ *www.yosemitepark.com*) runs two-, four-, and eight-hour trips—and High Sierra four- to six-day camping treks on mules, which begin at $625. Reservations are essential.

Wawona Stables (✉ *Rte. 41, Wawona* ☎ *209/375–6502*) offers rides for $59 (two hours), $79 (four hours), and $119 (eight hours) in the Wawona area. Reserve in advance.

Yosemite Valley Stables (✉ *At entrance to North Pines Campground, 100 yards northeast of Curry Village, Curry Village* ☎ *209/372–8348* ⊕ *www.yosemitepark.com*) offers rides in Yosemite Valley for $59 (two-hour), $79 (four-hour), and $119 (eight-hour). Reserve in advance.

RAFTING

For no charge, you can drop your inflatable on the Merced River between Stoneman Bridge (near Curry Village) and Sentinel Beach Picnic Area. Restrictions apply: Rafting is allowed only between 10 AM and 6 PM, the river level must not be measured above 6½ feet at Sentinel Bridge, and the combined total of the air and water temperatures must exceed 100 degrees. You also can go rafting on the South Fork of the Merced River, in Wawona.

The per-person rental fee at **Curry Village Raft Stand** (✉ *South side of Southside Dr., Curry Village* ☎ *209/372–8319* ⊕ *www.yosemitepark.com*) covers the raft (4- to 6-person), two paddles, and life jackets, plus a shuttle to the launch point on Sentinel Beach. You'll pay $20.50 to ride the river back to Curry Village; rafting happens between late May and July, weather and river conditions permitting.

ROCK CLIMBING

★ ~~Fodor's~~Choice The granite canyon walls of Yosemite Valley are world-renowned for rock climbing. El Capitan, with its long and virtually vertical face, is the most famous and difficult, but there are many other options here for all skill levels.

The one-day basic lesson at **Yosemite Mountaineering School & Guide Service** (✉ *Yosemite Mountain Shop, Curry Village* ☎ *209/372–8344* ⊕ *www.yosemitepark.com*) includes some bouldering and rappelling, and three or four 60-foot climbs. Guided hikes and backpacking adventures are available, too. Climbers must be at least 10 (kids under 12 must be accompanied by a parent or guardian) and in reasonably good physical condition. Intermediate and advanced classes include instruction in belays, self-rescue, summer snow climbing, and free climbing. Expect to pay $117 to $317 depending on what kind of adventure you choose; the school is generally open from April through November.

SWIMMING

The pools at Curry Village and Yosemite Lodge are open to nonguests. Several swimming holes with small sandy beaches can be found in midsummer along the Merced River at the eastern end of Yosemite Valley. Find gentle waters to swim; currents are often stronger than they appear, and temperatures are chilling. To conserve riparian habitats, step into the river at sandy beaches and other obvious entry points. Do not attempt to swim above or near waterfalls or rapids; fatalities have occurred.

Nonguests can swim in the pool at **Curry Village Pool** (✉*Curry Village* ☎ *209/372–8324* ⊕ *www.yosemitepark. com*) for $5. The pool, which does not offer designated times for lap swimming, is open from late May through early September.

Yosemite Lodge (✉ *Yosemite Village* ☎ *209/372–1250* ⊕ *www.yosemitepark.com*) has a slightly larger pool than the one at Curry Village and sets aside two hours each day for adult lap swimming. In general, this pool has fewer children, and splashers than its Curry Village counterpart. It's open from late May through mid-September and is available to nonguests for $5.

WINTER SPORTS & ACTIVITIES

ICE-SKATING

Winter visitors have skated at the outdoor **Curry Village Ice-Skating Rink** (✉ *South side of Southside Dr., Curry Village* ☎ *209/372–8319*) for decades, and there's no mystery why: It's a kick to glide across the ice while soaking up views of Half Dome and Glacier Point. The cost is $8 to skate for up to 2½ hours; skates can be rented for $3. The rink is open from mid-November through mid-March, with daily sessions in the afternoon and evening, as well as morning sessions on weekends.

SKIING & SNOWSHOEING

The beauty of Yosemite under a blanket of snow has long inspired poets and artists, as well as ordinary folks. Skiing and snowshoeing activities in the park center on Badger Pass Ski Area, California's oldest snow-sports resort, which is about 40 minutes away from the valley on Glacier Point Road. Here you can rent equipment, take a lesson, have lunch, join a guided excursion, and take the free shuttle back to the valley after a drink in the lounge.

California's first ski resort, **Badger Pass Ski Area** (✉ *Badger Pass Rd., off Glacier Point Rd., 18 mi from Yosemite Valley, Glacier Point* ☎ *209/372–8430* ⊕ *www.yosemitepark. com*) has 10 downhill runs, 90 mi of groomed cross-country trails, and two excellent ski schools. Free shuttle buses from Yosemite Valley operate during ski season (December–early April, weather permitting). Lift tickets are $38, downhill equipment rents for $24, and snowboard rental with boots is $35. The mix is about 35% beginners, 50% intermediate skiers, and 15% advanced skiers; the longest run is 0.3 mi. The base is at 7,200 feet, and the summit at 8,000 feet.

The gentle slopes of Badger Pass make **Yosemite Ski School** (☎ *209/372–8430*) an ideal spot for children and beginners

Q & A WITH A VOLUNTEER

Every year, Gordon Callander of Elk Grove, CA, and his wife, Gladys, spend a month volunteering in Yosemite Valley.

Please describe your volunteer job at Yosemite.

Our primary job is directing and helping to plan and optimize the visitor's stay, based on time, personal choices, and abilities. Other duties include visitor relations in the museum, assisting with art classes, picture-taking for visitors, assisting in the Valley Visitors Center, selling memberships, and giving directions.

What made you get involved?

We are nature junkies. We wanted to give back to our country and our park system, which has given us so much. To be of service. A great way to spend a month.

Where do you stay?

A designated area in Lower Pines Campground. Some volunteers stay in RVs and others stay in tents. We use Curry Village showers and facilities, which are short walk across the meadow.

Have you had any especially memorable experiences while on duty?

I don't recall any earth-shattering experiences. It makes us feel good when a visitor seeks us out to thank us for our advice. Every day we serve is very gratifying knowing that you have enhanced peoples' Yosemite experience.

What do you like to do in Yosemite when you're off duty?

Gladys hikes almost every off-duty day. I split time between golf, hiking, and art classes. The Yosemite Association provides free watercolor classes by renowned teachers Monday through Saturday all summer. We are on duty six hours a day, four days a week.

Have you seen much wildlife during your volunteer stints?

Deer, numerous varieties of birds, squirrels every day. Occasionally black bears, mountain lions, lynx, wolves, coyotes, foxes, skunks, and raccoons.

If someone has just one day to explore Yosemite, and had never been there before, what would you suggest?

Everyone should see the documentary "Spirit of Yosemite," the museum, Yosemite Falls, Mariposa Grove, and Glacier Point. Families with children should visit the Happy Isles Nature Center. Adults with limited mobility should take the Valley Floor Tour. Physically fit people with kids older than 6 should hike to top of Vernal Fall—a genuine Kodak moment when you get to the footbridge.

to learn downhill skiing or snowboarding for as little as $28 for a group lesson.

The highlight of Yosemite's cross-country skiing center is a 21-mi loop from Badger Pass to Glacier Point. You can rent cross-country skis for $21.50 per day at the **Cross-Country Ski School** (☎ 209/372–8444), which also rents snowshoes ($19.50 per day), telemarking equipment ($29), and skate-skis ($24).

Yosemite Mountaineering School (✉ *Badger Pass Rd., off Glacier Point Rd., 18 mi from Yosemite Valley, Glacier Point* ☎ *209/372–8344* ⊕ *www.yosemitepark.com*) conducts snowshoeing, cross-country skiing, telemarking, and skate-skiing classes starting at $30.

EXPLORING THE BACKCOUNTRY

For people who can spend more than a few days here, backpacking is the only way to explore Yosemite National Park's immense undeveloped wilderness—1,101 square mi of it, to be precise. More than 800 mi of paths crisscross the park, most notably the Pacific Crest Trail, which extends some 2,600 mi through all three North American countries.

If you're up for an overnight trek into the High Sierra, you must obtain a wilderness permit. They are free and available at Big Oak Flat, the Hetch Hetchy Entrance Station, Tuolumne Meadows, Wawona, and Yosemite Valley. For general preservation purposes, access to the backcountry trails is limited to a set number of hikers per day, and 40% of those slots are available on the day of—or the day before—on a first-come, first-served basis. Up to 60% of the backcountry trail slots can be reserved.

Backpacking etiquette includes burying your "human waste," so pack a shovel with all the other equipment you will or might need. To prevent bears from eating your food and to help ensure their survival—bears who become accustomed to human fare can be deemed out of control and executed by rangers—keep your grub in 2.7-pound bear canisters, which can hold a five-day supply of food and can be rented from the wilderness centers listed above. Also, do not hike alone, and share your exact itinerary with someone who is not going along.

One more thing: As a Yosemite backpacker who possesses a wilderness permit and trail reservation, you are entitled to free camping on the night before and the night after your adventure in any of the backpacker's campgrounds—for example, the one that is at the end of the 9-mi Hetch Hetchy Road off Route 120.

You can make reservations for backcountry permits up to 24 weeks in advance (from January through September) through the **Yosemite Association** (✆ *Box 545, Yosemite National Park, CA* ☎ *209/372–0740*). Check the National Park Service Web site (⊕ *www.nps.gov/yose/planyour visit/wildpermits.htm*) for instructions. A table on the site shows a schedule of dates when you can reserve a permit throughout the year, then for a $5 nonrefundable fee, you can make reservations by phone or by mail (make checks payable to YOSEMITE ASSOCIATION). You might be able to make reservations online, although that Web site is not always working.

EDUCATIONAL PROGRAMS

CLASSES & SEMINARS

Free **Art Workshops** (✉ *Art Activity Center, Yosemite Village* ☎ *209/372–1442* ⊕ *www.yosemite.org*) are conducted by professional artists in watercolor, drawing, and other media from early April through late November; most are on Monday through Saturday from 10 to 2. Bring your own materials, or purchase the basics at the Art Activity Center, which is next to the Village Store in Yosemite Village. Call to verify scheduling. On the Yosemite Web site, look for Activities, then Fun Park Activities.

Yosemite Outdoor Adventures (☎ *209/379–2321* ⊕ *www. yosemite.org*) offers educational outings on topics ranging from woodpeckers to fire management to pastel painting. Naturalists, scientists, and park rangers lead the outings, which can last from several hours to several days and cost from $82 to $465. Most sessions take place spring through fall, but a few focus on winter phenomena.

RANGER PROGRAMS

Junior Ranger Programs (✉ *Valley Visitor Center or the Nature Center at Happy Isles, Yosemite Village* ☎ *209/372–0299*) are offered for children ages 3 through 13. Kids can participate in the informal, self-guided Little Cub and Junior Ranger programs. A park activity handbook

($6) is available at the Valley Visitor Center or the Nature Center at Happy Isles; once your child has completed the book, a ranger will present him or her with a certificate and a badge.

Ranger-Led Programs include walks and hikes as well as informative and entertaining talks on a range of topics at different locations in the park several times a day from spring through fall. The schedule is reduced in winter, but most days you can usually find a ranger program somewhere in Yosemite. In the evenings at Yosemite Lodge and Curry Village, lectures by rangers, slide shows, and documentary films present unique perspectives on Yosemite. On summer weekends, Camp Curry and Tuolumne Meadows Campground host sing-along campfire programs. There's usually at least one ranger-led activity every night in the Valley; schedules and locations are posted on bulletin boards throughout the park and published in *Yosemite Today.*

TOURS

★ **Ansel Adams Camera Walks** (☎ *209/372–4413 for Ansel Adams Gallery* ⊕ *www.yosemitepark.com*) are a must for photography enthusiasts. These free two-hour guided camera walks are usually offered several mornings a week by professional photographers. Some walks are hosted by the Ansel Adams Gallery, others by Delaware North Corporation; meeting points vary. All are free, but participation is limited to 25 people. Call two days in advance or visit the gallery to make a reservation. An up-to-date scheduled is printed in *Yosemite Today,* which can be viewed at the National Park Service Web site.

DNC Parks & Resorts (☎ *209/372–1240*), the main concessionaire at Yosemite National Park, operates several guided tours and programs throughout the park.

The open-air **Big Trees Tram Tour** of the Mariposa Grove of Big Trees departs from the Mariposa Grove parking lot every half-hour from June through October (depending on snowfall), covers 7 mi, and takes 1 hour 15 minutes. The tour costs $25.50. As an alternative to driving here, consider parking at the Wawona Hotel and taking the free shuttle, a ride that takes about 15 minutes.

The four-hour **Glacier Point Tour** takes you from Yosemite Valley (you're picked up from your hotel) to the Glacier Point vista, 3,214 feet above the Valley floor. Tours are operated from June through October, and advance reservations are required. The cost is $41 round-trip or $25 one-way. Hikers sometimes take the bus one-way and stroll down to (or trudge up from, for a real aerobics workout) Curry Village.

The **Grand Tour** is a full-day outing ($82) that includes both Mariposa Grove and Glacier Point. The tour stops for lunch at the historic Wawona Hotel, but the meal is not included in the tour price (allow about $10 for lunch). Weather permitting, the tour runs from June through Thanksgiving; reservations are required, and departure is from Yosemite Lodge.

The late-evening **Moonlight Tour** of the Valley floor takes place on moonlit nights, depending on weather conditions from April through September. It costs $25 ($66 for a family of four) and takes about two hours. It departs from Yosemite Lodge.

For a full day's outing to the high country, opt for the **Tuolumne Meadows Tour,** which travels up Tioga Road to Tuolumne Meadows. You'll stop at several overlooks, and you can connect with another shuttle at Tuolumne Lodge if you want to explore the Toulumne Meadows area of the park. This service is mostly for hikers and backpackers who want to reach high-country trailheads, but anyone can ride. Depending on the driver, you will have from three to five hours to spend at Tuolumne. Buses run from July through Labor Day, and reservations are recommended. The trip costs $23, with pickups at Curry Village, Yosemite Village, and Yosemite Lodge.

The **Valley Floor Tour** (☎ *209/372–1240*) is a 26-mi, 2-hour tour of the Valley's highlights, with narration on area history, geology, and plant and animal life. Tour vehicles are either trams or enclosed motor coaches, depending on weather conditions. Tours are operated year-round and cost $25 ($66 for a family of four); departure is from Yosemite Lodge.

Though not really a tour, the free, 45-minute **Wee Wild Ones** program is designed for kids 6 and under. Included are animal-theme games, songs, stories, and craft activities. The event is held outdoors before the regular Yosemite Lodge or Curry Village evening programs in summer and fall; children gather before the Ahwahnee Hotel's big fireplace in winter and spring. All children must be accompanied by an adult.

ARTS & ENTERTAINMENT

From spring through fall, a pianist/singer performs four hours of live old-time folk music at the Wawona Hotel starting at 5:30.

Theatrical and musical presentations are offered at various times throughout the year at the **Yosemite Theatre** (✉ *Valley Visitor Center auditorium, Yosemite Lodge Theater, Yosemite Village* ☎ *209/372–0299*).One of the best-loved is Lee Stetson's portrayal of John Muir in "Conversation With a Tramp," "John Muir Is Back—And Boy, Is He Ticked Off!" and "The Spirit of John Muir." Tickets should be purchased in advance at the Valley Visitor Center. Unsold seats are available at the door at performance time, 8 PM. Tickets are $8 to $10.

SHOPPING

You should be able to find acceptable snack food—at reasonable prices—in any of the parks' many small food stores. What is there to complain about when you can buy a single bottle of beer for $1.50 or less? For the best prepackaged meals, stop by Degnan's Deli in Yosemite Village. The mountaineering shops, and to a lesser extent some of the general stores, sell hiking and camping equipment. Souvenirs and film supplies are sold practically everywhere. Nothing is outrageously expensive, other than ice. There's not much you can do about that, however.

The **Ahwahnee Gift Shop** (✉ *Ahwahnee Hotel, Ahwahnee Rd., about ¾ mi east of Yosemite Valley Visitor Center, Yosemite Village* ☎ *209/372–1409*) sells many comparatively upscale items, such as Native American crafts, photographic prints, nice photo frames, handmade bowls, jewelry, even matching sets of dinnerware. But also look at the book selection, which includes writings by John Muir.

The **Ahwahnee Sweet Shop** (✉ *Ahwahnee Hotel, Ahwahnee Rd., about ¾ mi east of Yosemite Valley Visitor Center, Yosemite Village* ☎ *209/372–1409*) sells "handmade" chocolates created in the Ahwahnee kitchen, along with snacks and juices, plus newspapers and postcards.

Ansel Adams Gallery (✉ *9031 Village Dr., between the visitor center and Wilderness Center, Yosemite Village* ☎*209/372–4413 or 888/361–7622* ⊕ *www.anseladams. com*) has original photographic and fine art prints, Native

American crafts, literature, photography supplies, and camera rentals. Be prepared to pay for your Adams infatuation, however; unframed posters cost $30, and prints mostly go for $150-plus.

Big Trees Gift Shop (✉ *Mariposa Grove, Wawona* ☎ *209/ 372–6551*) is a good place to stop if you're looking for a Yosemite sweat shirt, a sequoia-blazoned mug, or a candy bar. It's open from May through October.

Curry Village General Store (✉ *Across from the post office, Curry Village* ☎ *209/372–8333*) has wide aisles and an impressive selection of souvenirs and groceries—vegans can find tofu and soymilk, for example—at the Valley's eastern hub, Curry Village. Take your grub out onto the patio for an impromptu picnic lunch or snack.

The lodgelike **Glacier Point Gift Shop** (✉ *End of Glacier Point Rd., Glacier Point* ☎ *No phone*), perched at one of Yosemite's most popular scenic overlooks, has a big souvenir and gift department, plus a snack bar. It's open from May through October.

An animal theme permeates **Habitat Yosemite** (✉ *Yosemite Village* ☎ *209/372–1253*), which peddles everything from black bear-patterned socks to mountain lion-shape chocolate bars. It's open from May through October.

Tuolumne Meadows Store (✉ *Toulomne Meadows* ☎ *209/ 372–8428*) is one of the few places in Yosemite that stocks a large variety of organic and biodegradable products. Although you might assume that national park stores would always aim for environmentally sound products, that is not always the case. Here they do, and "crunchy" folks, such as vegetarians and vegans, are sure to approve. The store is open from late May through October.

Village Sport Shop (✉ *Yosemite Village* ☎ *209/372–1286*) carries an extensive selection of outdoor gear, including fishing and camping supplies.

Village Store (✉ *Yosemite Village* ☎ *209/372–1253*), Yosemite Valley's largest store has a huge gift and souvenir shop and a great (for a national park) grocery. Nearby, there's a decent deli (Degnan's), a grill, and a pizza joint.

Wawona Store & Pioneer Gift Shop (✉ *Rte. 41, Wawona* ☎ *209/ 375–6574*), which is attached to the Wawona area's only market, stocks upscale souvenirs, craft items, and books.

In the grocery, you'll find a modest selection of snacks, soft drinks, and prepackaged sandwiches.

At the **Yosemite Art & Education Center** (✉ *Next to the Yosemite Village Store, Yosemite Village* ☎ *209/372–1442* ⊕ *www.yosemite.org*) you can have your artistic needs met at the only art supply store in the Valley. Original artworks are sold here, too, many of them watercolors. The center is closed from November through March.

Yosemite Bookstore (✉ *Valley Visitor Center, Yosemite Village* ☎ *209/372–0299*), which is in the Valley Visitor Center, offers an extensive selection of detailed trail maps and esoteric guide books on the park. Here and at many other stores, you can buy a DVD of the nearby theater's impressive documentary, "Spirit of Yosemite."

In addition to the standard assortment of snacks and beverages, **Yosemite Lodge Gift Shop** (✉ *Yosemite Village* ☎ *209/372–1438*) has an extensive collection of T-shirts (you might find some on sale for $10), sweat shirts, and backpacks. It's open until 10 PM, which can come in handy if you are staying at the lodge and want some late-night refreshments.

Yosemite Lodge Nature Shop (✉ *Yosemite Lodge, Northside Dr., about ¾-mi west of the Visitor Center, Yosemite Village* ☎ *209/372–1438*) is next to the noisy and somewhat stuffy food court, but this small shop is an oasis of calm. Soothing music plays soft in the background as you peruse the jewelry, small wood carvings, handcrafted note cards, wind chimes, and even organic T-shirts (made in Peru).

Yosemite Museum Shop (✉ *Yosemite Museum, Yosemite Village* ☎ *209/372–0295*) seems like a hole in the wall, but it has a decent selection of books on California's Native Americans as well as traditional arts and crafts, necklaces, earrings, and other jewelry.

Lodging & Dining in Yosemite

WORD OF MOUTH

"We have been camping in Yosemite for over 30 years. I'd say we didn't start seeing bears in Yosemite till the last eight years or so. In the last several years we've seen bears in the Yosemite campgrounds, and once I saw a bear just strolling down the path as we rode the Yosemite Valley shuttle."

—utahtea

By Reed
Parsell

THE MOMENT YOU DECIDE TO VISIT YOSEMITE and spend at least one night in the Valley, you should start pursuing reservations for lodging or camping. Actually, you might want to make reservations even as you contemplate coming here and cancel them later if you change your mind. Here in Yosemite National Park, only the fittest planners thrive. Darwinian tactics can be of great help in a place that is this popular.

Dining is not a similarly cutthroat proposition, although reservations are wise to obtain for the Ahwahnee Hotel's amazing Dining Room, as well as for a few other restaurants during the summer. Generally, finding something to eat in Yosemite is not a problem. Picnic possibilities represent an embarrassment of riches, what with all the breathtaking views you can take in as you munch mouthfuls of sandwiches, chips, and carrot sticks.

Speaking of food, take special care not to share yours with bears. Long gone, but not forgotten by some park visitors from the 1970s and earlier, are the days when grown bears and their cubs would lope through campgrounds, gathering scraps and garbage that sometimes were left out intentionally by mischief-makers, cameras at the ready. Even recently, rangers say, bears have broken into cars and carted off things such as a box of doughnuts and even a wedding cake. Tales like that might initially strike you as humorous, but after a little reflection—and education courtesy of park workers, interpretive signs, and other sources—you should acknowledge that the animals' survival depends partly on our maintaining certain boundaries. As the saying goes, food that is rarely great for us is even worse for the bears.

WHERE TO EAT

Yosemite National Park has a couple of moderately priced restaurants in lovely (which almost goes without saying) settings: the Mountain Room at Yosemite Lodge and Wawona Hotel's dining room. The Ahwahnee Hotel is top-of-the-line, but not just as national park restaurants go; it has a longtime reputation as one of the finest dining experiences in the country.

Other than those three restaurants, food service is geared toward satisfying the masses as efficiently as possible. Yosemite Lodge's food court and Curry Village's buffet (breakfast and dinner only) are the Valley's best lower-cost, hot-food options. In Valley Village, the grill whips up burgers and fries, Degnan's Deli makes $5–$7 sandwiches made to order, and Loft Pizzeria has a chaletlike open dining area where you can enjoy pizza, salads, and desserts until 9 PM. (The grill and pizzeria are closed during the winter.) The White Wolf Lodge and Tuolumne Lodge, both off Tioga Road and therefore guaranteed open only from early June through September, have small restaurants where meals are competently prepared. Tuolumne Meadows also has a grill, as does the store at Glacier Point. Sliders Grab-N-Go serves fast food during the ski season at Badger Pass, off Glacier Point Road. All food concessions are run by the Delaware North Corporation.

The one eatery outside the park but nearby that merits a mention is actually a service station: the Tioga Gas Mart & Whoa Nelli Deli, on Route 120, just west of Lee Vining. The food here is foodie-friendly, fun, and funky. Where else can you both fill up your tank and order a pitcher of mango margaritas? Outside, you can take lessons on the trapeze. Really.

WHAT IT COSTS				
¢	$	$$	$$$	$$$$
RESTAURANTS				
Under $8	$8–$12	$13–$20	$21–$30	Over $30

Restaurant prices are for a main course at dinner and do not include any service charges or taxes.

In addition to the dining options listed here, you will find many quick and relatively cheap possibilities throughout the park, including a multitude of vending machines, as well as the seasonal snack shack near the shuttle stop at Happy Isles. The convenience stores all sell picnic supplies, with prepackaged sandwiches and salads widely available. Those options might come in especially handy during the middle of day, when you might not want to spend precious daylight hours, in such a spectacular setting, by sitting in a restaurant for a formal meal. Many dining facilities in the park are open only in the summer.

RESTAURANTS

★ Fodor's Choice ✕ **Ahwahnee Hotel Dining Room.** Raves about the dining room's appearance are fully justified—floor-to-ceiling windows, a 34-foot-high ceiling with interlaced sugar pine beams, massive chandeliers, all in an elegant, refined yet rustic setting. Although many continue to applaud the food, others have reported they sense a recent dip in the quality both in the service and what is being served. Diners must spend a lot of money here, so perhaps that inflates the expectations and amplifies the disappointments. In any event, the Sunday brunch ($40) is consistently praised. The dinner menu includes duck breast, pork shoulder, and the like, as well as a vegetarian dish or two for those who want to honor the environmental spirit of the national parks. The seasonal vegetable tagine, for example, consists of chickpeas, Moroccan spices, and dried fruit. Reservations are always advised, and for dinner, guests are asked to dress "resort casual"—collared shirts and long pants for men, dresses or skirts—or a blouse and slacks—for women. This is, after all, by far the most upscale place to eat in Yosemite, if not the entire Sierra Nevada mountain range. ✉ *Ahwahnee Hotel, 1 Ahwahnee Rd., about ¾ mi east of Yosemite Valley Visitor Center, Yosemite Village* ☎ *209/372–1489* ✍ *Reservations essential* ▭ *AE, D, DC, MC, V.*

$$$–$$$$

$ ✕ **Food Court at Yosemite Lodge.** Despite being framed by floor-to-ceiling windows, this large and light space is oddly claustrophobic. The dated dining area is all about volume. You won't spend much money here, nor are you likely to spend much time. The oval layout of vendors proceeds from a coffee bar next to the entrance, past a pasta bar, pizza counter, and burger grill, to a slightly more costly entrée buffet (expect chicken and fish dishes), then a beverage center (including beer), and on to the row of cash registers, where things can bottleneck. In the middle of all that is a circular unit that stocks prepackaged sandwiches and salads. The dozens of indoor tables are sometimes fully occupied, but turnover is fast. You also can sit outside, where a half-dozen tables or so look inviting until you realize that cigarette smoke wafts there from the nearby bus stop. At breakfast, you can get pancakes and eggs made any way you like. The espresso and smoothie bar near the entrance keeps longer hours. ✉ *Yosemite Lodge, about ¾ mi west of the visitor center, Yosemite Village* ☎ *209/372–1265* ▭ *AE, D, DC, MC, V.*

★ ✕ **Mountain Room.** Though good, the food becomes second-
$$$ ary when you see Yosemite Falls through this dining room's
wall of windows—almost every table has a view. The chef
makes a point of using locally sourced, organic ingredients,
so you can be assured of fresh greens and veggies here.
Grilled trout and salmon, steak, pasta, and several chil-
dren's dishes are also on the menu. The Mountain Room
Lounge, a few strides away in the Yosemite Lodge complex,
has a broad bar with about 10 beers on tap. You also can
order chips and salsa, hot sandwiches, or even something
more substantial, such as vegetarian lasagna. The tall win-
dows and comparatively small, usually uncrowded setting
will make you want to linger. ⊠ *Yosemite Lodge, Northside
Dr., about ¾ mi west of the visitor center, Yosemite Village*
☎ *209/372–1281* ⌚ *Reservations essential* ▭ *AE, D, DC,
MC, V* ⊗ *No lunch.*

$$ ✕ **Pavillion Buffet.** You will not be dining alone here, that's
for sure. Breakfast and dinner are busy, busy times when
the line of buffet items can stretch quite far and when scores
of tables packed into a rather dark dining room are mostly
occupied. (Take your tray outside for what might be a better atmosphere, depending on wind direction and the prox-
imity of smokers.) Also within Curry Village's bustling food
complex, you can pop into the Coffee Corner throughout
the day for caffeinated drinks, pastries, and ice cream. In
the morning, it also sells oatmeal, cereals, fruits, and yogurt.
The Pizza Patio, open noon–10 PM, also serves chili and
salads. If you are so inclined, plop down on one of the hole-
in-the-wall bar's half-dozen or so stools for a mug of beer
or glass of wine. ⊠ *Curry Village* ☎ *209/372–8303* ▭ *AE,
D, DC, MC, V* ⊗ *No lunch. Closed mid-Oct.–mid-Apr.*

$$ ✕ **Tuolumne Lodge Restaurant.** At the back of a small building
that contains the lodge's front desk and small gift shop,
this restaurant serves hearty American fare at breakfast
and dinner. Let the front desk know in advance if you have
any dietary restrictions, and the cooks will not let you
down. ■TIP➜ **Many people treat the tent-cabin lodge as a base
camp for day hikes and backpacking adventures, and take advan-
tage of the box lunches that can be ordered the night before.** ⊠
Tioga Rd. (Rte. 120), Toulumne Meadows ☎ *209/372–8413*
⌚ *Reservations essential* ▭ *AE, D, DC, MC, V* ⊗ *No
lunch. Closed late Sept.–Memorial Day.*

¢ ✕ **Tuolumne Meadows Grill.** Serving continuously throughout
the day until 5 or 6 PM, this fast-food grill cooks up break-

fast, lunch, and snacks. Stop in for a quick meal before exploring the Meadows. ✉ *Tioga Rd. (Rte. 120), 1½ mi east of Tuolumne Meadows Visitor Center, Toulomne Meadows* ☎ *209/372–8426* ▭ *AE, D, DC, MC, V* ⊘ *No dinner. Closed Oct.–Memorial Day.*

¢ ✕ **The Village Grill.** For that burger-joint fix you may be missing from life at lower elevations, this family-friendly eatery in Yosemite Village serves grilled sandwiches from a counter until 6 PM daily. Take your tray out to the deck and enjoy your meal under the trees. ■TIP➔ **The fries are especially good, and the portions are generous.** ✉ *100 yards east of Yosemite Valley Visitor Center, Yosemite Village* ☎ *209/372–1207* ▭ *AE, D, DC, MC, V* ⊘ *No breakfast or dinner. Closed Oct.–May.*

$$-$$$ ✕ **Wawona Hotel Dining Room.** Watch deer graze on the meadow while you dine in the romantic, candlelit dining room of the whitewashed Wawona Hotel, which dates from the late 1800s. The American-style cuisine favors fresh California ingredients and flavors; trout is a menu staple. Steak, pork, chicken, and turkey entrées also are on the dinner menu, while vegetarians are likely to be pleased with the eggplant Parmesan. Salads are made from organic greens, and the wine slection is decently varied. There is a Sunday brunch offered from Easter through Thanksgiving, as well as a barbeque on the lawn every Saturday evening in the summer. Opinions of this restaurant are mixed, as complaints have been lodged lately about food and service. For men, a jacket is required at dinner. ✉ *Wawona Hotel, Rte. 41, Wawona* ☎ *209/375–1425* ⟁ *Reservations essential* ▭ *AE, D, DC, MC, V* ⊘ *Closed Jan. and Feb.*

$$$ ✕ **White Wolf Lodge.** This high-country historic lodge's casual, rustic dining room is small enough that every meal offers four different seating times. Breakfast and dinner (no lunch) are all-you-can-eat affairs, served family-style with some vegetarian options. ✉ *Tioga Rd. (Rte. 120), 45 minutes west of Tuolumne Meadows and 30 minutes east of Crane Flat* ☎ *209/372–8416* ⟁ *Reservations essential* ▭ *AE, D, DC, MC, V* ⊘ *No lunch. Closed late Sept.–June.*

PICNIC AREAS

Considering how large the park is and how many visitors it has—some 3.5 million people come here every year, most of them just for the day—it is somewhat surprising that Yosemite has so few formal picnic areas. Happily, in many places you can find a smooth rock to sit on and enjoy breathtaking views along with your lunch. Wherever you eat, be sure not to litter. Pack out your leftovers if you have picnicked deep into a long day hike or somewhere in the backcountry.

✕ **Cathedral Beach.** The bad news is parking here is limited and not obvious. The good news is very good, however: Far enough off Southside Drive that traffic noise is almost entirely eliminated, the area's shaded tables are comfortably spaced—three are practically on the Merced River's sandy beach. Cathedral Rocks are a challenge to see through the tall trees. There are pit toilets but no water. ⊠ *Off Southside Dr., the westernmost picnic area in Yosemite Valley, between Bridalveil Fall and Yosemite Lodge.*

✕ **Church Bowl.** Tucked behind the Ahwahnee Hotel, this small picnic area nearly abuts the granite walls below the Royal Arches. If you're walking from the Village with your supplies, this is the shortest trek to a picnic area, but there's no drinking water. ⊠ *Behind the Ahwahnee Hotel, Yosemite Village.*

✕ **El Capitan.** In the Valley beside "El Cap" (though on its less-interesting east side), this shaded area has about a dozen tables and grills, plus pit toilets. A trail from here leads to the base of El Capitan's dramatic west side, where you may see climbers, and on to Bridalveil Fall. There are pit toilets but no water. ⊠ *Northside Dr., a few miles west of Yosemite Lodge in western Yosemite Valley.*

✕ **Glacier Point.** Whether you have packed your own lunch or bought something from the indoor snack stand here, you may want to skip the designated picnic area and instead find a place on the rocks near the overlook, where you can enjoy views of the Valley and Half Dome. Take care not to litter. There are toilets; drinking water is nearby. ⊠ *End of Glacier Point Rd., Glacier Point.*

DID YOU KNOW? You can put unwanted paper, plastic, and glass in recycling containers that are sprinkled throughout Yosemite. They, along with all trash cans, are all designed to keep wild animals (especially bears) from digging in. Rangers and other park employees have been known to call the trash cans "little Half Domes" because of their resemblance to Yosemite's famous granite formation.

✕ **Lembert Dome.** Choose from among a half-dozen nicely situated tables next to the meadow and in the shadow (on sunny mornings, anyway) of Lembert Dome. From here, you can burn off a lot of calories by hiking up to the granite formation's top (elevation approximately 9,400 feet), or take a pleasant stroll in the inviting grassy fields to the west. Toilets, water nearby. ✉ *Toulomne Meadows.*

✕ **Sentinel Beach/Yellow Pine.** More accessible than the nearby Cathedral Beach Picnic Area, and equally as far from road noise, this is a great spot to enjoy lunch on a hot summer's day, as the tables are shaded and the Merced River's sandy beach is only a few hundred feet away. In fact, there are a half-dozen tables on the beach. You'll find pit toilets but no water. ✉ *Off Southside Dr., a 10-minute walk from Yosemite Lodge in Yosemite Valley.*

✕ **Swinging Bridge.** A couple of dozen tables make this a comparatively large picnic area, and its wide and soft beach, at an especially wide and calm part of the Merced River, makes this a popular summer destination. The area's only downside is that it is very close to the road. There are pit toilets but no water. ✉ *Off Southside Dr., just west of Yosemite Lodge, Yosemite Village.*

✕ **Tenaya Lake.** You can picnic at either end of this extraordinarily scenic and high-altitude (8,150 feet) lake that is the source for Tenaya Creek, which flows through Tenaya Canyon down toward the Valley. Tenaya was an Indian chief who encountered the invading Mariposa Battalion here in the early 1850s. Told the lake would be named in his honor, Tenaya reportedly pointed out it already had a name: "Pie-we-ak," or lake of the shining rocks. There are pit toilets but no drinking water. ✉ *Tioga Rd., 8 mi west of Tuolumne Meadows and 31 mi east of Crane Flat.*

✕ **Yosemite Creek.** About halfway along Tioga Road—and near the North Dome Trail parking area at Porcupine Creek—you will encounter a smattering of aging tables in a down-slope area where the creek sounds compete with too-near traffic noise. Kids will enjoy climbing over the creek's big rocks, though parents might get a bit nervous watching them. There are pit toilets but no drinking water. ⊠ *Tioga Rd., 5 mi east of the White Wolf turnoff.*

✕ **Wawona.** You'll find a half-dozen or so tables between the store's parking lot and the South Fork of the Merced River. Some people go for a swim here. There are toilets and drinking water nearby. There are two other public picnic areas in the Wawona area: up the road a bit near Wawona Campground, and another small one between the park's South entrance and the Mariposa Grove parking lot. ⊠ *Wawona.*

WHERE TO STAY

4

Indoor lodging options inside the park's boundaries may seem a bit more expensive than initially seems warranted, but that small premium pays off big-time in terms of time saved. Unless you are bunking in one of the gateway towns that are a few miles from a Yosemite entrance, perhaps in one of the options listed later in this chapter, you will face long commutes. (Only the Yosemite View Lodge and Yosemite Cedar Lodge, both on Route 140, are within a reasonable hour's drive of Yosemite Valley.) If you can, book some kind of lodging appropriate to your needs and bank balance in the Valley itself, which offers the most central location and access to most of the trails and services in the park.

Because of Yosemite National Park's immense popularity, not just with tourists from around the world but with northern Californians who make weekend trips here, reservations are essential throughout the year. The Delaware North Corporation takes reservations beginning one year and one day in advance of your proposed stay. You can roll the dice by showing up at the front desk and asking if there have been any cancellations, but don't expect to be lucky in the busy seasons.

If you plan to spend just one full day in Yosemite National Park, the idea of paying less for a motel in one of the towns listed in Chapter 8, "What's Nearby," begins to make more sense. To the south, Oakhurst is about a 90-minute drive from the Valley; to the west, Mariposa also is about 90 minutes away; and to the east, Mammoth Lakes is more than a two-hour drive; from summer to early fall, the trip to Mammoth Lakes is via the extraordinarily scenic Tioga Road. From Mariposa, you can take the public bus (known as YARTS) to and from the park, allowing you to spend up to 12 hours in the Valley between the first bus in and the last bus out.

WHAT IT COSTS				
¢	$	$$	$$$	$$$$
HOTELS				
Under $70	$70–$120	$121–$175	$176–$250	Over $250

Hotel prices are for a double room in high season and do not include taxes, service charges, or resort fees.

IN THE PARK

Almost all reservations for lodging in Yosemite (Redwood Guest Cottages is the exception) are made through the concessionaire, **Delaware North Corporation** (☎ *801/559–4884* ⊕ *www.yosemitepark.com*). Within an hour or two of reservations becoming available—and remember, you can start reserving one year and one day in advance of your proposed stay—the Ahwahnee Hotel, Yosemite Lodge, and Wawona Hotel sometimes are fully booked for weekends, holiday periods, and all days between Memorial Day and Labor Day.

★ Fodor'sChoice 🍴 **Ahwahnee Hotel.** From its shiny wood-plank
$$$$ floor, on which stand many comfortable chairs, up past the big windows with magnificent views and walls that contain marvelous artwork, all the way to its lovely crossed-beam ceiling, decorated with colorful Indian designs, the Ahwahnee's Great Lounge is one of California's best interiors. A National Historic Landmark, the hotel is constructed primarily of concrete and sugar-pine logs. Guest rooms have Native American design motifs; public spaces are decorated with art deco detailing, oriental rugs, and elaborate iron-and woodwork. Some luxury hotel amenities, including turndown service and guest bathrobes, are standard here. The Dining Room is by far the most impressive restaurant in the park and one of the most beautiful rooms in California. If you stay in a cottage room, be aware that each cottage has multiple guest rooms, though all have an en suite bath. If you cannot afford to stay here, take the time to stroll about the main floor. **Pros:** best lodge in Yosemite, if not all of California. **Cons:** expensive; some reports that

CLOSE UP

The 2008 Curry Village Rockslide

Mother Nature gave fair warning to those who oversee lodging in Yosemite Valley when granite broke from a cliffside and sent the equivalent of 200 dump-truck loads of rock onto cabins at Curry Village. Miraculously, no one was injured in the 7 AM incident, which sent panicked visitors running away from the crash through clouds of dust. Reportedly, a large group of schoolchildren had just left the area to go to breakfast.

One cabin was completely destroyed, and a dozen others were significantly damaged. More than 1,000 people were evacuated.

Six weeks later, National Park Service officials announced that more than one-third of Curry Village's permanent lodging units would be closed. Having studied the vulnerable rock face on the side of Glacier Point that hovers over the village, they decided to tear down 233 units.

"The NPS can no longer treat each rock fall as an isolated incident," the agency said in an official statement. "Instead, we must look at the area comprehensively and recognize that geologic processes that have shaped Yosemite Valley since the last glaciers receded will continue to result in rock fall."

In October 1996, a much-larger rockslide killed one young man near Happy Isles Nature Center and destroyed more than 1,000 trees. Another young man was killed by a smaller rockslide at Curry Village in June 1999. Four years later, yet another rockslide prompted the NPS to permanently close 27 cabins in the village.

A representative of the Sierra Club, George Whitmore, told the *Fresno Bee* he believes the lodging units were too close to the cliffs. "I don't know why it has taken so long to close those cabins," he said.

4

service has slipped in recent years. ⊠ *1 Ahwahnee Rd., about ¾ mi east of Yosemite Valley Visitor Center, Yosemite Village* ☎ *209/372–1407 front desk, 801/559–4884 reservations* ⊕ *www.yosemitepark.com* ⌁ *95 lodge rooms, 4 suites, 24 cottage rooms* ⌂ *In-room: no a/c (some), refrigerator, Wi-Fi. In-hotel: restaurant, room service, bar, tennis court, pool* ⏸*EP* ⊟ *AE, D, DC, MC, V.*

$–$$ ▩ **Curry Village.** Low on charm but comparatively good on value, Curry Village is the favored place for families on a budget. In summer, expect to be absorbed in a swarm of happy kids and their sometimes harried parents trying to keep the peace. Opened in 1899 as a place where travelers could enjoy the beauty of Yosemite for a modest price,

Curry Village has plain accommodations: standard motel rooms, cabins, and tent cabins, which have rough wood frames, canvas walls, and roofs. The tent cabins are a step up from camping, with linens and blankets provided (maid service upon request). Some have heat. Most of the cabins share shower and toilet facilities. Dining options abound here, with the breakfast and dinner buffets drawing big crowds. At this writing, renovations to Curry's guest registration, lounge, and ampitheater were expected to be completed by mid-May 2009. Happy Isles and the popular Mist Trail are a few minutes' walk away. Reserve far in advance, especially for summer and holiday stays. **Pros:** comparatively economical; family-friendly atmosphere. **Cons:** can be crowded and, for the great outdoors, a bit noisy. ⊠ *910 Curry Village Dr., Curry Village, 95389* ☎ *209/372–8333 front desk, 801/559–4884 reservations* ⊕ *www.yosemitepark.com* ⇨ *18 rooms, 390 cabins (most are tent cabins, some have baths)* ⚓ *In-room: no a/c, no phone, no TV. In-hotel: 3 restaurants, bar, pool, bicycles, no-smoking rooms* ⊚|*EP* ⊟ *AE, D, DC, MC, V.*

$$$–   ▦ **Redwoods Guest Cottages.** The only lodging in the park
$$$$ not operated by Delaware North Corporation, this collection of more than 125 privately owned cabins and homes in the Wawona area is a great alternative to the overcrowded Valley. Fully furnished cabins range from small, romantic one-bedroom units to bright, resortlike, six-bedroom houses with decks overlooking the river. Most have fireplaces, TVs, and phones. On the Redwoods Web site, you can specify whether you want such amenities as high-speed Internet service and a washer/dryer. The property rarely fills up, even in summer, so it's a good choice for last-minute lodging; there's a two-night minimum in the off-season and a three-night minimum in summer. **Pros:** staying in private homes can be very nice; peaceful setting. **Cons:** remote from the Valley; no guarantees you will like everything about where you stay. ⊠ *8038 Chilnualna Falls Rd., off Rte. 41, Wawona, Box 2085, Wawona Station, Yosemite National Park* ☎ *888/225–6666* ⊕ *www.redwoodsinyosemite.com* ⇨ *130 units* ⚓ *In-room: no a/c (some), no phone (some), kitchen, no TV (some). In-hotel: no-smoking rooms, some pets allowed* ⊚|*EP* ⊟ *AE, D, MC, V.*

$ ▦ **Tuolumne Meadows Lodge.** Day hikers and backpackers are served well here at Yosemite National Park's highest (elevation: 8,775 feet) formal accommodations. The tent cabins, sprinkled not too densely on the gentle hills of this spacious property, come equipped with beds, linens, wood stoves, and candles; there's no electricity. You can have breakfast and dinner in the lodge's inviting dining room, although you need to let the friendly front-desk staff know in advance. Box lunches are available, too. Vegetarians and vegans eat well here. **Pros:** convenient for hikers; comparatively inexpensive; friendly. **Cons:** a bit rustic; reservations must be made far in advance. ⊠ *Tioga Rd., Toulomne Meadows* ☎ *209/372–8413 front desk, 801/559–4884 reservations* ⊕ *www.yosemitepark.com* ⮑ *69 tent cabins* ⭤ *EP* ⊟ *AE, D, DC, MC, V* ⊗ *Closed mid-Sept.–early June.*

$$–$$$ ⌑ **Wawona Hotel.** This 1879 National Historic Landmark sits at Yosemite's southern end, a 15-minute drive (or free shuttle bus ride) from the Mariposa Grove of Giant Sequoias. It's an old-fashioned New England-style estate, with whitewashed buildings, wraparound verandas, and pleasant, no-frills rooms decorated with period furnishings. About half the rooms share bathrooms; those that do come equipped with robes. The romantic, candlelit dining room lies across the lobby from the cozy Victorian parlor, which has a fireplace, board games, and a piano, where a pianist plays ragtime most evenings. **Pros:** lovely, peaceful atmosphere; close to Mariposa Grove. **Cons:** few modern in-room amenities. ⊠ *8308 Wawona Rd.(Hwy. 41), Wawona* ☎ *209/375–6556 front desk, 801/559–4884 reservations* ⊕ *www.yosemitepark.com* ⮑ *104 rooms, 50 with bath* ё *In-room: no a/c, no phone, no TV. In-hotel: restaurant, bar, golf course, tennis court, pool* ⭤ *EP* ⊟ *AE, D, DC, MC, V* ⊗ *Closed Jan. and Feb.*

$–$$ ⌑ **White Wolf Lodge.** Set in a sub-alpine meadow at the end of a slim road that heads north 1 mi from Route 120, White Wolf offers rustic accommodations in tent cabins that share nearby baths or in wooden cabins with baths. This is an excellent base camp for hiking the backcountry. Breakfast and dinner are served home-style in the snug, white main building. Keep in mind that you will be seated in one of four time slots, so you might eat earlier or later than you would prefer if you do not reserve well in advance. **Pros:** quiet; convenient for hikers; good restaurant. **Cons:** far from the Valley; not much to do other than hiking. ⊠ *Off Tioga Rd. (Rte. 120), 45 minutes west of Tuolumne Meadows and 30 minutes east of Crane Flat* ☎ *801/559–4884 (reservations), no phone at hotel* ⮑ *24 tent cabins, 4 cabins* ё *In-room: no a/c, no phone, no TV. In-hotel: restaurant* ⭤ *EP* ⊟ *AE, D, DC, MC, V* ⊗ *Closed mid-Sept.–early June.*

$$-$$$ ⛆ **Yosemite Lodge at the Falls.** This lodge near Yosemite Falls, which dates from 1915, looks like a 1960s motel-resort complex, with numerous brown, two-story buildings tucked beneath the trees around large parking lots. Motel-style rooms have two double beds; the larger rooms also have dressing areas and patios or balconies. A few have views of the falls. Of the lodge's eateries, the Mountain Room Restaurant is the most formal. The cafeteria-style Food Court also serves three meals a day. Many park tours depart from the main building. **Pros:** centrally located; dependably clean rooms; lots of tours leave from out front. **Cons:** can feel impersonal; appearance is little dated. ✉ *Northside Dr. about ¾ mi west of the visitor center, Yosemite Village* ☎ *209/372–1274 front desk, 801/559–4884 reservations* ⊕ *www.yosemitepark.com* ⇨ *245 rooms* ⌂ *In-room: no a/c, no phone, Wi-Fi. In-hotel: restaurant, bar, pool, bicycles, no-smoking rooms* ⏴EP ⊟ *AE, D, DC, MC, V.*

OUTSIDE THE PARK

EL PORTAL

$$-$$$ ⛆ **Yosemite Cedar Lodge.** Families are catered to at this clean and comfortable motel, which is on scenic Route 140, about 6 mi farther from Yosemite National Park than its sister property, the pricier Yosemite View Lodge. That's no big deal, as you can catch a YARTS public bus from either and be in the Valley within an hour. The rooms are modern here, with large, flat-screen TVs and nice furnishings. An unaffiliated restaurant serves meals all day, while the lodge's gift shop and small grocery store are open until 11 PM. There is also a sports bar. **Pros:** good location; clean; modern. **Cons:** appearance from the road is so-so. ✉ *9966 Hwy. 140, El Portal* ⊕ *www.yosemiteresorts.us* ⇨ *210 rooms* ⌂ *In-room: refrigerators, Internet. In-hotel: restaurant, bar, pools, no-smoking rooms* ⏴EP ⊟ *AE, MC, V .*

⛆ **Yosemite View Lodge.** Just 2 mi outside the park's Arch Rock entrance on Route 140, this clean and thoroughly modern property is the most convenient place to spend the night if you are unable to secure lodgings in the Valley. You probably would be more comfortable here than in, say, one of Curry Village's tent cabins, although one must always balance the additional comforts by the higher cost. All the rooms have good views, but ones with balconies that overlook the Merced River are the best. You have your choice of four pools here, one of which is indoors. The restaurant cooks up an impressive breakfast buffet, and there also is a pizza joint on-site. The lodge's gift shop and small grocery store are open until 11 PM. **Pros:** great location; good views; lots of on-site amenities. **Cons:** can be pricey for what you get. ✉ *11136 Hwy. 140, El Portal* ☎ *209/379–2681 or 888/742–4371* ⊕ *www.yosemite-motels.com* ⌦ *335 rooms* ⚥ *In-room: refrigerator, kitchen (some), Internet. In-hotel: restaurant, bar, pools, laundry facilities, no-smoking rooms, Wi-Fi, some pets allowed* ⓘ*EP* ⊟ *MC, V.*

FISH CAMP

$$ 🔲 **Narrow Gauge Inn.** All of the rooms at this well-tended, family-owned property have balconies (some shared) and great views of the surrounding woods and mountains. For maximum atmosphere, book a room overlooking the brook; for quiet, choose a lower-level room on the edge of the forest. All of the rooms are comfortably furnished with old-fashioned accents. Reserve way ahead. The restaurant ($$$, open Wed.–Sun. Apr.–Oct.), which is festooned with moose, bison, and other wildlife trophies, specializes in steaks and American fare, and merits a special trip. **Pros:** close to Yosemite's south entrance; well-appointed; wonderful balconies. **Cons:** rooms can feel a bit dark; dining options are limited (especially for vegetarians). ✉ *48571 Hwy. 41, Fish Camp* ⊕ *www.narrowgaugeinn.com* ⌦ *26 rooms, 1 suite* ⚥ *In-room: no a/c (some), Internet, Wi-Fi (some). In-hotel: restaurant, bar, pool, some pets allowed, no-smoking rooms* ⓘ*EP* ⊟ *D, MC, V.*

$$$$ 🔲 **Tenaya Lodge.** One of the region's largest hotels, Tenaya Lodge is ideal for people who enjoy wilderness treks by day but prefer creature comforts at night. The hulking prefab buildings and giant parking lot look out of place in the woods, but inside the rooms have all the amenities of a modern, full-service hotel. The ample regular rooms are decorated in pleasant earth tones; deluxe rooms have mini-bars and other extras; suites have balconies. Off-season rates can be as low as $100. The Sierra Restaurant ($$$), with its high ceilings and giant fireplace, serves Continental cuisine; the more casual Jackalopes Bar & Grill ($–$$) has burgers, salads, and sandwiches. **Pros:** rustic setting with modern comforts; good off-season deals. **Cons:** so big it can seem impersonal; pricey during summer; few dining options. ✉ *1122 Hwy. 41, Fish Camp* ☎ *559/252–6555 or 888/514–2167* ⊕ *www.tenayalodge.com* ⌦ *244 rooms, 6 suites* ⚥ *In-room: refrigerator, Internet, Wi-Fi. In-hotel: 2 restaurants, room service, bar, pool, gym, bicycles,* *children's programs (ages 5–12), laundry service, no-smok-ing rooms* ⏹EP ⊟ *AE, D, DC, MC, V.*

★ ▦ **Evergreen Lodge.** It feels like summer camp at the Ever-
$$–$$$ green, where you can ditch the valley's hordes for a cozy
☾ cabin in the woods 8 mi from Hetch Hetchy. The perfect
blend of rustic charm and modern comfort, cabins have
sumptuous beds, comfy armchairs, candy-cane-striped pull-
out sofas, and tree-stump end tables. The terrific roadhouse-
style restaurant ($$) serves meaty dishes such as broiled
elk tenderloin and bean burgers, and the long bar has a
friendly feel (perhaps owing to the reggae music that plays
here often). After dinner, shoot pool in the bar, play Ping-
Pong outside, melt s'mores, attend a lecture or film, or play
Scrabble by the fire in the barn-like recreation center. Multi-
night stays are required from April through October, as
well as on holidays. **Pros:** rustic setting is romantic; staff
is very friendly; lots of things to do. **Cons:** far from Yosem-
ite Valley (though close to Hetch Hetchy). ✉ *33160 Ever-
green Rd., 25 mi east of Groveland, 23 mi north of Yosemite
Valley, Groveland* ☎ *209/379–2606 or 800/935–6343* ⊕
www.evergreenlodge.com ⇩ *90 cabins* ☖ *In-room: no a/c,
no phone, refrigerator, no TV. In-hotel: restaurant, bar,
bicycles, children's programs (ages 5–12), Internet terminal,
public Wi-Fi, no-smoking rooms* ⏹EP ⊟ *AE, D, DC, MC,
V* ☯ *Closed Jan.*

WHERE TO CAMP

It should come as no surprise that the 464 campsites within
Yosemite Valley are the park's most tightly spaced and,
along with the 304-site campground at Tuolumne Mead-
ows, the most difficult to secure on anything approaching
short notice—especially less than three months in advance.
If you are spending just one or two nights in the park,
however, and plan to concentrate solely on Valley sites and
activities, you should endeavor to stay in one of the three
"Pines" campgrounds, which are clustered near Curry
Village and within an easy stroll from that busy complex's
many facilities (buffet, shops, pool, bike rentals, etc.). For a
more primitive and quiet experience, and to be near many
backcountry hikes, try one of the Tioga Road campgrounds,
a few of which are several miles off that seasonal road and
therefore quite remote. From the Wawona Campground,
you will have fewer hiking options (although they are

good ones), but you will be close to the Mariposa Grove of Giant Sequoias, Yosemite's most popular attraction outside of the Valley.

All sites come with picnic tables, fire pits or grills, and a food locker to keep bears from ruining your day (and to keep you from helping to put them in mortal danger of being executed by park rangers). At Valley campgrounds, shower and laundry facilities are nearby at Curry Village and Housekeeping Camp; campers at Tuolumne Meadows can use the showers at the Tuolumne Lodge in the summer only. Off the beaten path, at Porcupine Flat, Tamarack Flat, and Yosemite Creek, pit toilets are as good as it gets bathroom-wise; there's no water; and RVs longer than 24 feet are not recommended. No sites, anywhere in the park, have RV hookups.

Aside from group areas, of which there are four, sites are limited to six people and two vehicles apiece. Quiet hours are from 10 PM to 6 AM, although you will not win over new friends or please many old ones by making a lot of noise between 6 and 8 AM. Dogs, which are prohibited at Camp 4, Porcupine Flat, and Tamarack Flat, must be kept on a leash. ■TIP➔ **Better yet, leave Rover at home, or board him with a buddy: National parks are poor places to bring pets.**

The park's backcountry and the surrounding wilderness have some unforgettable campsites that can be reached only via long and often difficult hikes or horseback rides. To camp in a High Sierra campground such as Glen Aulin near Tuolumne Meadows and the centrally placed Merced Lake, you must obtain a wilderness permit. They are free and available at Big Oak Flat, the Hetch Hetchy Entrance Station, Tuolumne Meadows, Wawona, and Yosemite Valley. Access to the backcountry trails is limited to a set number of hikers per day (lotteries are held for some days), and 40% of those slots are available on the day of—or the day before—on a first-come, first-served basis.

Delaware North Corporation (☎ *801/559–4909* ⊕ *www. yosemitepark.com*) operates five High Sierra Camps with comfortable, furnished tent cabins in the remote reaches of Yosemite; rates include breakfast and dinner service. The park concessionaire books the extremely popular backcountry camps by lottery; applications are due by late November for the following summer season. Phone for more information, or check for current availability by navigating through the Web site to the High Sierra Camps pages.

The **Yosemite Association** (✉ *Box 545, Yosemite, CA,* ☎ *209/372–0740* ⊕ *www.yosemite.org/visitor*) manages wilderness permit reservation requests. You can make reservations up to 24 weeks in advance. First, visit the National Park Service Web site (⊕ *www.nps.gov/yose/planyourvisit/ wildpermits.htm*) and check on availability for your trailhead. For a $5 nonrefundable fee, you can make reservations by phone or by mail (make checks payable to YOSEMITE ASSOCIATION). You might be able to make reservations online, although that Web site is not always available.

WHAT IT COSTS				
¢	$	$$	$$$	$$$$
CAMPING				
Under $8	$8–$14	$15–$20	$21–$25	Over $25

Camping prices are for a campsites including a tent area, fire pit, bear-proof food-storage box, picnic table; potable water and pit toilets or restrooms will be nearby.

IN THE PARK

Seven of Yosemite's 13 campgrounds take reservations. If you plan to camp in the Valley, reserve as far in advance as you can. Generally, you can reserve spots four to five months in advance; learn specifics by navigating the National Park Service's official page for Yosemite Between Memorial Day and Labor Day, the first-come, first-served sites can be snapped up before noon. Find group sites at Bridalveil Creek, Hogdon Meadow, Tuolumne Meadows, and Wawona.

All Yosemite National Park campground reservations (except those for Housekeeping Camp) are now are handled through a central system that is not NPS-operated called Recreation One-Stop (☎ *877/444–6777* ⊕ *www.recreation. gov* ▭ *D, MC, V*).

$ ⛺ **Bridalveil Creek.** Sites are first-come, first-served at this seasonal campground that sits among lodgepole pines at 7,200 feet, above the Valley and off Glacier Point Road. From here, you can easily drive to Glacier Point's magnificent views, or lace up your hiking shoes and trek off into the wilderness. ✉ *Glacier Point, 95389* ✛*From Hwy. 41 in Wawona, go north to Glacier Point Rd. and turn right;*

entrance to campground is a few miles past Badger Pass Ski area, and on right side ☎ *877/444–6777 for reservations* ⊕ *www.recreation.gov* ⇨ *110 sites (tent or RV)* ⚒ Flush toilets, drinking water, bear boxes, grills, picnic tables, public telephone ⚓ Reservations taken only for group sites and those with horse corrals ⊟ D, MC, V ⊗ July–late Sept.

¢ ⚠ **Camp 4.** This is the only Valley campground whose sites are available on a first-come, first-served basis. Open year-round, it is near El Capitan, on the Valley's west side far away from the campgrounds near Curry Village, and therefore is a favorite of rock climbers and solo campers. It fills up quickly and can be sold out before noon and on Fridays and Saturdays during the summer. This is a tents-only campground, and all sites are a short walk from the parking lot. ⊹ *The campground is at the base of Yosemite Falls Trail, less than ½-mi west of Yosemite Lodge on Northside Dr.,* ☎ *No phone* ⚓ *Reservations not accepted* ⇨ *35 sites* ⚒ Flush toilets, drinking water, bear boxes, fire grates, picnic tables, public telephone, ranger station ⊗ Open year-round.

$$ ⚠ **Crane Flat.** This camp on Yosemite's western boundary, south of Hodgdon Meadow, at 17 mi from the Valley is far from the bustle. Short hikes to two of the park's three sequoia groves—Merced and Tuolumne—are nearby, although they pale in comparison with what you will see down in Mariposa Grove, near Wawona. ⊹ *From Big Oak Flat entrance on Hwy. 120, drive 10 mi east to campground entrance on right* ☎ *877/444–6777 for reservations* ⊕ *www.recreation.gov* ⇨ *166 sites (tent or RV)* ⚒ Flush toilets, drinking water, bear boxes, fire pits, picnic tables, general store, ranger station ⚓ Reservations essential ⊟ AE, D, MC, V ⊗ Mid-June–mid-Oct.

$$$$ ⚠ **Housekeeping Camp.** This camp is different than your typical Yosemite campground and not counted as one of the park's 13 campgrounds. The units, although technically not tents, will remind you of them. Composed of three walls (usually concrete) and covered with two layers of canvas, each unit has an open-ended fourth side that can be closed off with a heavy, white canvas curtain. Inside, typically, are a bunk bed and full-size bed, dirty mattresses included; outside is a covered patio, fire ring, picnic table, and bear box. You rent "bedpacks," consisting of blankets, sheets, and other comforts, in the main building, which

also has a small grocery. One nice touch is that each unit has a fence-enclosed patio, providing another layer of privacy. They also have electricity (and lights) but no running water. Lots of guests take advantage of the adjacent Merced River and sun on its rocks or drop inflatable rafts onto its gentle surface. Showers ($5 a pop) and a laundry area also are on premises. ✉ *Southside Dr., ½-mi west of Curry Village, Curry Villages, Delaware North Reservations, 6771 N. Palm Ave., Fresno* ☎ *801/559–4884 for reservations* ⊕ *www.yosemitepark.com* ⇴ *266 units* ⚹ *Flush toilets, laundry facilities, showers, bear boxes, fire pits, picnic tables, restaurant, snack bar, electricity, public telephone, general store, swimming* ▤ *AE, D, DC, MC, V* ⊙ *Late Apr.–early Oct.*

$$ ⚠ **Hodgdon Meadow.** On the park's western boundary, at an elevation of about 4,900 feet, this year-round campground is set among vegetation that is similar to that in the Valley—but there's no river and no development. Reservations are recommended May through September. ⊹ *From Big Oak Flat entrance on Hwy. 120, immediately turn left to campground* ☎ *877/444–6777 for reservations* ⊕ *www.recreation.gov* ⇴ *105 sites (tent or RV)* ⚹ *Flush toilets, drinking water, bear boxes, grills, picnic tables, ranger station* ▤ *AE, D, MC, V.* ⊙ *Open year-round.*

$$ ⚠ **Lower Pines.** This moderate-size campground sits directly along the Merced River; it's a short walk to the trailheads for the Mirror Lake and Mist trails. Expect small sites and lots of people. All three Pines campgrounds have accessible sites. Vehicles up to 40 feet long also can be accommodated. ✉ *Near Curry Village, on the eastern end of the Valley, clustered with the North Pines and Upper Pines campgrounds* ☎ *877/444–6777 for reservations* ⊕ *www.recreation.gov* ⇴ *60 sites (tent or RV)* ⚹ *Flush toilets, drinking water, bear boxes, fire grates, picnic tables, public telephone, ranger station, swimming (river)* ⚹ *Reservations essential* ▤ *AE, D, MC, V* ⊙ *Mar.–Oct.*

$$ ⚠ **North Pines.** Adjacent to Tenaya Creek and the Merced River at an elevation of 4,000 feet, this campground also is near many trailheads. Sites are close together, and there is little privacy. All three Pines campgrounds have accessible sites. Vehicles up to 40 feet long also can be accommodated. ✉ *Near Curry Village on the eastern end of the Valley, clustered with the Lower Pines and Upper Pines campgrounds near Curry Village* ☎ *877/444–6777 for* *reservations* ⊕ *www.recreation.gov* ↩ *81 sites (tent or RV)* ⚹ *Flush toilets, drinking water, bear boxes, fire grates, picnic tables, ranger station, swimming (river)* ⚹ *Reservations essential* ▭ *AE, D, MC, V* ☉ *Mid-Mar.– mid-Nov.*

$ ⚿ **Porcupine Flat.** Sixteen miles west of Tuolumne Meadows, this first-come, first-served campground sits at 8,100 feet. Sites are close together, but if you want to be in the high country and Tuolumne Meadows is full, this is a good bet. The North Dome Trail, one of the park's best day hikes and most underrated, begins off the nearby Porcupine Creek parking area. There is no water available. ✉ *Rte. 120, 16 mi west of Tuolumne Meadows* ☎ *No phone* ↩ *52 sites (tent or RV up to 35 feet)* ⚹ *Pit toilets, bear boxes, fire pits, picnic tables, no water* ⚹ *Reservations not accepted* ▭ *AE, D, MC, V* ☉ *July–mid.-Oct.*

$ ⚿ **Tamarack Flat.** This rather primitive campground sits in a forested area at an elevation of 6,300 feet, with lodgepole pines, red firs, and some cedars. Sites are nicely spaced and the atmosphere is fresh-mountain-air peaceful. There's no water, and only small RVs (up to 24 feet) are allowed. To say the 3-mi road to get here from Tioga Road is paved is like saying President Eisenhower had hair—pure flattery. ✛ *From Big Oak Flat entrance station, turn left on Tioga Rd. (Hwy. 120); after 3 mi turn right to enter campground, 2½ mi from Tioga Rd., 95389* ☎ *No phone* ↩ *52 sites (tent only)* ⚹ *Pit toilets, bear boxes, fire grates, picnic tables, no water* ⚹ *Reservations not accepted* ▭ *No credit cards* ☉ *Late June–mid-Sept.*

★ Fodor'sChoice ⚿ **Tuolumne Meadows.** In a wooded area at 8,600
$$ feet, south of Tioga Road and between Tuolumne River and Elizabeth Creek, this is one of the most spectacular and sought-after campgrounds in Yosemite. Backpackers often begin and end their adventures in this large, fairly flat maze of loop drives and one-ways; there's even a horse corral. Hot showers can be had at the Tuolumne Lodge—though only at certain, strictly regulated times. Half the sites are first-come, first-served, so arrive early or make reservations. ✉ *Hwy. 120, 46 mi east of Big Oak Flat entrance station, Touloumne Meadows* ☎ *877/444–6777 for reservations* ⊕ *www.recreation.gov* ↩ *304 sites (tent or RV)* ⚹ *Flush toilets, dump station, drinking water, bear boxes, fire grates, picnic tables, public telephone, general store, ranger station* ▭ *AE, D, MC, V* ☉ *Late June–late Sept.*

$$ ⛺ **Upper Pines.** This is the Valley's largest campground, and the only one that is open year-round. Expect large crowds in the summer—and little privacy. All three Pines campgrounds have accessible sites. ✉ *Near Curry Village on the eastern end of the Valley, clustered with the Lower Pines and North Pines campgrounds* ☎ *877/444–6777 for reservations* ⊕ *www.recreation.gov* ⌁ *238 sites (tent or RV)* ♿ *Flush toilets, dump station, drinking water, bear boxes, fire grates, picnic tables, public telephone, ranger station, swimming (river)* ⚠ *Reservations essential* ⊟ *AE, D, MC, V* ⊙ *Open year-round.*

$$ ⛺ **Wawona.** Near the Mariposa Grove, just downstream from a popular fishing spot, this year-round campground (reservations essential May–September) has larger, less densely packed sites than campgrounds in the Valley, and is located right by the river. The downside is that it's an hour's drive to the Valley's major attractions. At 8 AM daily, take a mug and have "Coffee With a Ranger" at the amphitheater. ✉ *Hwy. 41, 1 mi north of Wawona, Wawona* ☎ *877/444–6777 for reservations* ⊕ *www.recreation.gov* ⌁ *93 sites (tent or RV)* ♿ *Flush toilets, dump station, drinking water, bear boxes, fire grates, picnic tables, ranger station, swimming (river)* ⊟ *AE, D, MC, V* ⊙ *Open year-round.*

★ ⛺ **White Wolf.** In the beautiful high country at 8,000 feet,
$ this is a prime spot for hikers. RVs up to 27 feet long are permitted. From here, the Valley is about an hour's drive away, via Crane Flat. ✛ *From Big Oak Flat entrance, go 15 mi east on Tioga Road (Hwy. 120); campground is on right* ⌁ *74 sites (tent or RV)* ♿ *Flush toilets, drinking water, bear boxes, fire grates, picnic tables, public telephone, ranger station* ⚠ *Reservations not accepted* ⊟ *No credit cards* ⊙ *July–mid-Sept.*

$ ⛺ **Yosemite Creek.** This secluded campground, at 7,600 feet on a dirt road, is not suitable for large RVs. It's a good jumping-off point for spectacular hikes to the rim of the Valley and to the top of North Dome and Yosemite Falls. Drive extra slowly and carefully on the 6-mi side road here; it's brutal. There is no water available. ✛ *From Big Oak Flat entrance station, turn left onto Tioga Rd. (Hwy. 120) and continue 30 mi to the posted turnoff on right; drive 5 mi to campground, 95389* ⌁ *40 sites (tent only)* ♿ *Pit toilets, bear boxes, fire grates, picnic tables, public telephone, no water* ⚠ *Reservations not accepted* ⊟ *No credit cards* ⊙ *July–mid-Sept.*

OUTSIDE THE PARK

$ ⚠ **Dimond-O Campground.** At 4,400 feet elevation, this campground is just 2 mi from Yosemite's western border on the road to Hetch Hetchy Reservoir. It has nicely spaced, well-maintained sites. When the park's campgrounds are sold out and you want to be within an hour's drive of the Valley, this is a good bet. From Route 120, take Evergreen Road (2 mi west of the Big Oak Flat entrance station) north and continue 6 mi to reach the campground. ✉ *34660 Evergreen Rd., Groveland* ☎ *209/379–2258 information, 877/444–6777 reservations* ⊕ *www.recreation.gov* ⇌ *38 sites for tents or RVs* ⚹ *Pit toilets, drinking water, bear boxes, grills, picnic tables* ⚹ *Reservations essential* ▭ *No credit cards* ☼ *Late Apr.–mid-Oct.*

4

CAMPING IN YOSEMITE

Campground Name	Total # of Sites	# of RV sites	# of hook-ups	Drive-to sites	Hike-to sites	Flush toilets	Pit toilets	Drinking water	Showers	Fire grates/pits	Swimming	Boat access	Playground	Dump station	Ranger station	Public tele-phone	Reservations Possible	Daily fee per site	Dates open
Bridalveil Creek	110	110		Y		Y		Y		Y						Y		$14	Jul-Sept
Camp 4	35				Y	Y		Y		Y					Y	Y		$5	Y/R
Crane Flat	166	166		Y		Y		Y		Y					Y		Y	$20	Jun-Sept
Hodgon Meadow	105	105		Y		Y		Y		Y					Y		Y	$20	Y/R
Housekeeping Camp	266	266		Y		Y		Y	Y	Y	Y					Y	Y	$74	Apr-Oct
Lower Pines	60	60		Y		Y		Y		Y	Y				Y	Y	Y	$20	Mar-Oct
North Pines	81	81		Y		Y		Y		Y	Y				Y	Y	Y	$20	Mar-Nov
Porcupine Flat	52	52		Y			Y			Y								$10	Jul-Oct
Tamarack Flat	52			Y			Y			Y								$10	Jun-Sept
Tuolumne Meadows	304	304		Y		Y		Y	Y	Y	Y			Y	Y	Y	Y	$20	Jun-Sept.
Upper Pines	238	238		Y		Y		Y		Y				Y	Y	Y	Y	$20	Y/R
Wawona	93	93		Y		Y		Y		Y				Y	Y	Y	Y	$20	Y/R
White Wolf	74	74		Y		Y				Y						Y		$14	Jul-Sept
Yosemite Creek	40			Y			Y			Y						Y		$10	Jul-Sept

Y/R = year-round ** = Summer Only

Exploring Sequoia & Kings Canyon

WORD OF MOUTH

"I think it would be criminal to visit Sequoia and not visit Kings Canyon. They are practically the same park as far as distance and the route you have to take to get there, and I'm not kidding! There are great hikes in both parks, which are less crowded but smaller than Yosemite, which means less time is needed there."

—npurpleh2

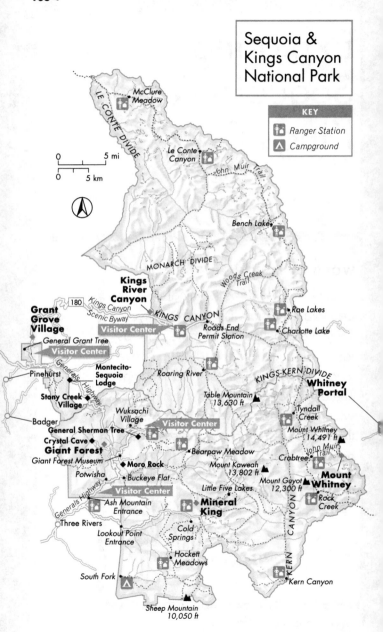

Sequoia & Kings Canyon National Park

KEY
 Ranger Station
△ Campground

By Reed
Parsell

GETTING TO SEQUOIA AND KINGS CANYON NATIONAL PARKS takes time and determination: Their western entrances are 200 mi from Los Angeles, 250 mi from San Francisco, and 375 mi from Las Vegas, mostly via roads that offer little compelling scenery. Nevertheless, the payoff upon arrival is huge—literally, in the form of trees you will never forget.

Although *Sequoiadendron giganteum* is the formal name for the redwood that grows here, everyone outside a classroom calls them sequoias, big trees, or Sierra redwoods. Their monstrously thick trunks and branches, spongy rust-color bark, remarkably shallow root systems, and neck-craning heights are dizzying to comprehend, as is the fact they can live for more than 2,500 years. You will see many of these towering marvels in the Giant Forest stretch of Generals Highway, which connects the two parks. Beside or a few miles off this 43-mi road are most of Sequoia National Park's main attractions and Grant Grove Village, the orientation hub for Kings Canyon National Park.

The two parks share a boundary that runs west–east, from the foothills of the Central Valley to the Sierra Nevada's dramatic eastern ridges. Kings Canyon has two portions, the smaller shaped like a bent finger and encompassing Grant Grove Village and Redwood Mountain Grove (the two parks' largest concentration of sequoias), the larger whose heart is the stunning Kings River Canyon and whose vast, unspoiled peaks and valleys are a backpacker's dream. Sequoia is in one piece and includes Mount Whitney, the highest point in the Lower 48 states, although it is impossible to see from the western part of the park and a chore to ascend from either side.

Generals Highway remains open year-round, but the parks' two largest side roads are closed in winter and during much of the fall and spring as well. Mineral King Road veers off from Route 198 between Sequoia's southern entrance and the small town of Three Rivers, and delves 25 mi into a glacial valley that's comparatively little visited—which pleases those who embrace the concept of quiet and consider the Mineral King area to be a hiker's heaven. Kings Canyon Scenic Byway, a 40-mi road that's a smoother ride than Mineral King Road, passes mostly through Sequoia National Forest and Giant Sequoia National Monument, dead-ending in Kings Canyon National Park just past Cedar Grove Village and peaceful Zumwalt Meadow.

TOP REASONS TO GO

■ **Sequoias:** Join people who flock from around the planet to gape at these giants. Some sequoias are so weirdly thick and tall that even standing among them, you might think you are in a Hollywood film and the trees have been added via special effects.

■ **Kings River Canyon:** It lacks the dramatic, dry appearance of Arizona's Grand Canyon, but Kings River Canyon is deeper in parts, and the granite domes that loom over it are a striking spectacle in their own right.

■ **Hiking:** More than 800 mi of trails offer many satisfying possibilities. Take a quick stroll through a sequoia grove, a sturdy day hike around meadows to mountain lakes, or a multiday adventure into the High Sierra wilderness.

■ **Meadows:** Big trees cannot grow in them because they are too moist, but tall, lush grasses do, with wildflowers abundant in late spring and early summer. Bears frequent the meadows, often with cubs in tow.

■ **Wildlife:** Of the parks' 330 known species of animals, you are practically guaranteed to see California mule deer. Stick around long enough, and you might spot a black bear—who probably will have brown fur.

PLANNING YOUR TIME

SEQUOIA IN ONE DAY

After spending the night in Visalia or Three Rivers—and provided your vehicle's length does not exceed 22 feet— shove off early on Route 198 to the park's **Ash Mountain entrance.** Pull over at the **Hospital Rock** picnic area to gaze up at the imposing granite formation of Moro Rock, which you later will climb. Heed signs that advice 10 MPH around tight turns as you climb 3,500 feet on **Generals Highway** to the **Giant Forest Museum.** Spend a half-hour there, then examine some first-hand by circling the lovely **Round Meadow** on the **Big Trees Trail,** which you must walk to from the museum or from its parking lot across the road. Quite possibly you will see a bear or two on this short hike.

Get back in your car and continue a few miles north on Generals Highway to see the **General Sherman Tree.** Once you have returned your jaw to its upright position and have taken a few pictures, set off on the **Congress Trail** so that you can be further awed by the **Senate** and **House** big-tree clusters. Buy your lunch at the **Lodgepole** complex, 2 mi to the

north, and take it—or what you packed the night before—
to the nearby **Pinewood** picnic area. Now you're ready for
the day's big exercise, the mounting of **Moro Rock.**

You can either drive there or, if it is summer, park at the
museum lot and take the free shuttle. Count on spending
at least an hour for the 350-step ascent and descent, with a
pause on top to appreciate the 360-degree view. Get back in
the car, or on the shuttle, and proceed past the **Auto Log** to
Crescent Meadow. Spend a relaxing hour or two strolling on
the trails that pass by, among other things, **Tharp's Log.** By
now you've probably renewed your appetite, which you can
attend to at the **Wolverton Barbecue** (summer evenings only)
or the highly regarded restaurant at **Wuksachi Lodge.**

KINGS CANYON IN ONE DAY

Enter the park via Route 180, having spent the night in
Fresno. Better yet, wake up already in **Grant Grove Village,**
perhaps in the **John Muir Lodge.** Pop into the **Kings Canyon
Visitor Center** to watch the introductory film and peruse the
exhibits. If need be, stock up for a picnic with takeout food
from the **Grant Grove Restaurant** or prepackaged food from
the nearby store. Drive less than a mile to see the **General
Grant Tree,** as well as the other Sequoias in compact **General
Grant Grove.** Provided it is no later than mid-morning, motor
on up to the short trail at **Panoramic Point,** for a great view
of Hume Lake and the High Sierra beyond.

Return to Route 180 and head east on what is also known
as the **Kings Canyon Scenic Byway.** Be sure to pull off at an
overlook or two as you approach the canyon, which begins
near **Boyden Cave.** Check out the caverns if you don't mind
postponing lunch, but otherwise continue to **Cedar Grove
Village** (having taken 10 minutes for a gander at **Grizzly Falls**
along the way). Eat on a table by the **South Fork of the Kings
River,** or on the deck off the Cedar Grove Snack Bar. Now
you are ready for the day's highlight, a stroll about **Zumwalt
Meadow,** which is a few miles past the village.

After you have enjoyed that short trail and the views it
offers of **Grand Sentinel** and **North Dome,** you might as well
go the extra mile to **Road's End,** where you can wonder at
all the hearty souls who have parked there and backpacked
into the vast wilderness of the High Sierra. Make the return
trip—with a quick stop at **Roaring River Falls**—past Grant
Grove and briefly onto southbound **Generals Highway.** Pull
over at the **Redwood Mountain Overlook** and use binoculars

to look down upon the world's largest sequoia grove, then drive another couple of miles to the **Kings Canyon Overlook,** where you can survey some of what you have done today. If you've made reservations and have time, have a late dinner at the **Wuksachi Lodge.**

SEQUOIA & KINGS CANYON IN THREE DAYS

Follow both one-day suggestions above, spending the night between in either Grant Grove or the Wuksachi/Lodgepole area. Spend the morning on a longer hike, with prime candidates being—from north to south—the 6-mi **Redwood Canyon Trail,** the **Big Baldy Trail,** the **John Muir Trail** (accessed from within Dorst Creek Campground), or the **Tokopah Falls Trail** (from the Lodgepole Campground). In the **Lodgepole Visitor Center,** buy tickets for a tour of **Crystal Cave** that afternoon and for the **Wolverton Barbecue** (summers only; otherwise, dine at **Wuksachi Lodge** again) that evening.

If a fourth day is at your disposal, consider taking one of the longer hikes off the **Kings Canyon Scenic Byway** to the north, or shake, rattle, and roll your way over **Mineral King Road** to one of the hikes in that less-visited part of Sequoia National Park, with dinner at the **Silver City Resort.**

GIANT FOREST

16 mi north of Ash Mountain entrance and 25 mi southeast of the Big Stump entrance on Generals Hwy.

Only Redwood Mountain Grove has a few more sequoias, but Giant Forest is where you will find the world's biggest tree and many of Sequoia National Park's other must-see sights. Step into the Giant Forest Museum, open year-round weather permitting, to learn all you care to the Sierra redwoods. The nearby Big Trees and Congress Trails are two of the most spectacular showcases of mature sequoias, and both are short and paved. Hop on the shuttle to Moro Rock, where you can climb its amazing stone staircase for sweeping views of the Middle Fork Canyon, and then on to Crescent Meadow, reportedly John Muir's favorite place in the Sierra Nevada outside Yosemite. Retreat to the Lodgepole complex and Wuksachi Village for diverse food and lodging options.

Giant Forest merits at least a half-day visit, but spend a full day here if you can. ■TIP→ **And remember that if you intend to tour Crystal Cave, you must purchase tickets at either the Lodgepole or Foothills Visitor Center.**

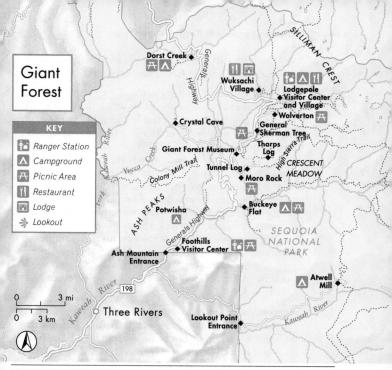

Giant Forest

KEY

Ranger Station
Campground
Picnic Area
Restaurant
Lodge
Lookout

Dorst Creek

Wuksachi
Village

Lodgepole
Visitor Center
and Village

Crystal Cave

Wolverton

General
Sherman Tree

Tharps
Log

Giant Forest Museum

Tunnel Log

Moro Rock

CRESCENT
MEADOW

ASH PEAKS

Potwisha

Buckeye
Flat

SEQUOIA
NATIONAL
PARK

Ash Mountain
Entrance

Foothills
Visitor Center

Atwell
Mill

198

Three Rivers

Lookout Point
Entrance

0   3 mi
0   3 km

VISITOR CENTERS

Beetle Rock Family Nature Center. Across the road from Giant
Forest Museum and a few strides south of the multi-tiered
parking lot, the Sequoia Natural History Association operates a nature center with interactive exhibits and a children's
bookstore with science-oriented books, games, and toys.
"Beetle Rock Rollick," a ranger-led family program, is
conducted at 2 PM daily. On the massive rock, children have
lots of room to run around and climb on smooth and gentle
slopes that should ease parents' anxieties. ⊠ *Generals Hwy.
(Rte. 198), 4 mi south of Lodgepole Visitor Center, Giant
Forest* ☎ *559/565–4251* ☜ *Free* ☾ *Early July–late Aug.,
conditions permitting; daily 10–4.*

Foothills Visitor Center. Learn about foothills resource issues
such as drought and fire in this small center at the southern
end of Generals Highway. You also can pick up books,
maps, and a list of ranger-led walks, and get wilderness permits. Buy tickets here if you plan to see Crystal Cave before
you get to Lodgepole Visitor Center, the only other place
they are sold. (Tickets are not available via telephone or the
Internet.) ⊠ *Generals Hwy. (Rte. 198), 1 mi north of the*

Ash Mountain entrance,Giant Forest ☎ 559/565–3135 ☉ Oct.–mid-May, daily 8–4:30; mid-May–Sept., daily 8–6.

★ **Giant Forest Museum.** Well-imagined and interactive displays
☾ give you the basics about sequoias, of which there are 2,161 with diameters exceeding 10 feet in the 2,115-acre Giant Forest. Be sure to play "Win BIG!", a large spinning contraption in the spirit of TV's "Wheel of Fortune" that illustrates the daunting odds a tiny sequoia seed faces to grow into a "big tree." Also, step into the replicated hollow of a burned-out sequoia and, out front, walk a white line that's the same length as the Sentinel Tree that towers over the museum. Between world wars, motels and other businesses lurked across the highway here, but conservation efforts in the 1970s led to their removal. The museum is entirely wheelchair-accessible. ⊠ *Generals Hwy., 4 mi south of Lodgepole Visitor Center, 18 mi north of Ash Mountain entrance Giant Forest* ☎ *559/565–4480* ⊑ *Free* ☉ *Daily 8–5.*

Lodgepole Visitor Center. Along with exhibits on the area's geologic history, wildlife, and longtime American Indian inhabitants, the center screens an outstanding, 22-minute film about bears. After watching it, you will better understand why the loping mammals need humans' help in continuing their existence—grizzlies, which roamed not just the Sierra Nevada but California's valleys and coastal areas, were wiped out in this state by 1922. Books, maps, and souvenirs are sold here, as are tickets to Crystal Cave. (The only other place to obtain them is at the Foothills Visitor Center.) ⊠ *Generals Hwy. (Rte. 198), 4 mi north of Giant Forest Museum, 22 mi north of Ash Mountain entrance, Giant Forest* ☎ *559/565–4436* ☉ *June–Oct., daily 7–6; Nov.–May, weekends 7–6.*

☾ **Walter Fry Nature Center.** The hands-on nature exhibits here are designed primarily for children, but the center is open only afternoons for a few short weeks in the summer. ⊠ *Lodgepole Campground, ½ mi east of Lodgepole Visitor Center, Giant Forest* ☎ *559/565–4436* ⊑ *Free* ☉ *July–mid-Aug., weekends noon–5.*

SCENIC DRIVES

★ **Generals Highway.** One of the most scenic drives in a state replete with them, this 43-mi road is the main asphalt artery between Sequoia and Kings Canyon national parks. Named after the landmark Grant and Sherman trees that awe so

A Tall Tale About Old Trees

Three species of redwood trees exist on the Earth now, although 175 million years ago there may have been other types and many more groves. Blame the Ice Age for the trees' contemporary rareness. The three species are:

Sequoiadendron giganteum: These are the "big trees," also called "sequoias" or less frequently "Sierra redwoods," that represent the signature attraction of Sequoia National Park. The highest mature sequoia has been measured at 311 feet tall, and the oldest is estimated to have been around for 3,200 years. Among the world's other tree species, only bristlecone pine (found in the American West) and Fitzroya (in the Andes) can live longer lives. Sequoias' seeds are the size of oat flakes and their cones are shaped like chicken eggs.

Sequoia sempervirens: Limited to a narrow band along the Pacific Coast of North American, they are the world's tallest trees, topping out at nearly 370 feet. Their bases tend to be much less thick than those of Sequoias, and their life spans do not exceed 2,000 years. Known popularly as "coastal redwoods," their seeds are roughly the same size as those of tomatoes, and their cones are shaped like large olives.

Metasequoia glyptostroboides: Known as "dawn redwoods," they were believed to be extinct until a small grove of them was found in the Sichuan-Hubei region of China. They are small compared with their two distant cousins, topping out at 150 feet. It is not yet known how long they tend to live. Their cones are egg-shape, with a diameter no greater than 1 inch. Although the species is being grown easily in many other parts of China, the one wild forest, with about 5,000 trees, faces an uncertain future.

5

many visitors (presumably even jaded New Yorkers), it runs from the Foothills Visitor Center north to Grant Grove Village. Along the way, it passes the turnoff to Crystal Cave, the Giant Forest Museum, Lodgepole Village, and Sequoia National Park's other most popular attractions. The lower portion, from Hospital Rock to the Giant Forest, is especially steep and windy. If your vehicle is 22 feet or longer, avoid that stretch by entering the parks via Route 180 (from Fresno) rather than Route 198 (from Visalia). And take your time on this road—there's a lot to stop and see, and wildlife can scamper across at any time. ⊠ *Generals Hwy., Giant Forest.*

SCENIC STOPS

Auto Log. Vehicles used to be driven over this downed sequoia, the kind of forced interaction between natural wonders and man-made contraptions happily has fallen out of favor. Today, be content to stroll along the tree's carved "driveway." ⊠ *Moro Rock–Crescent Meadow Rd., 1 mi south of Giant Forest, Giant Forest.*

Crescent Meadow. John Muir called this the "gem of the Sierra." Take an hour or two to walk around it, and see if you agree. Wildflowers bloom throughout the summer. ⊠ *End of Moro Rock–Crescent Meadow Rd., 2.6 mi east off Generals Hwy., Giant Forest.*

Crystal Cave. A curvy and deteriorating 6½-mi paved road, along with a steep, downhill, half-mile hike from the parking lot, make visiting this cavern a minor challenge. One of more than 200 caves in the two parks, Crystal is unusual in that it's composed largely of marble, the result of limestone being hardened under heat and pressure. It contains several impressive formations that will be more clearly seen once an environmentally sensitive relighting project is completed in the next few years. Unfortunately, some of the cave's formations have been damaged or destroyed by early 20th-century dynamiting. Dust kicked up by the once-unpaved main passageway further lowers the pristine factor. The standard tour allows 45 minutes inside the cave. ■TIP→ **Spend more time, with fewer people, on the Discovery Tour ($19). All tickets must be bought at least 90 minutes in advance at either the Foothills or Lodgepole Visitor Centers.** ⊠ *Crystal Cave Rd., 6 mi west off Generals Hwy., Giant Forest* ☎ *559/565–3759* ⊕ *www.sequoiahistory.org* ✉ *$11* ☉ *Early May–late Oct., daily 11–3; 11–4:30 mid-June–Labor Day.*

★ **General Sherman Tree.** Neither the world's tallest nor oldest
☾ sequoia, General Sherman is nevertheless tops in volume—and it is still putting on weight, adding the equivalent of a 60-foot-tall tree every year to its 2.7 million–pound bulk. On the gently sloping trail coming down from the parking lot, be sure to pause where General Sherman's "footprint," a circumference at ground level of 102-plus feet, is marked on a platform from which the 2,100-year-old tree's 275-foot height also can be appreciated. A small lot immediately off Generals Highway allows wheelchair access. ⊠ *Generals Hwy. (Rte. 198), 2 mi south of Lodgepole Visitor Center, Giant Forest.*

★ **Moro Rock.** Sequoia National Park's best non-tree attraction, Moro Rock offers panoramic views to those fit and determined enough to mount its 350-ish steps. In a case where the journey rivals the destination, Moro's stone stairway (built by the National Park Service in 1931 to replace a 14-year-old wooden structure) is so impressive in its twisty inventiveness that in 1978 it was entered on the National Register of Historic Places. The rock's 6,725-foot summit overlooks the Middle Fork Canyon, sculpted by the Kaweah River and approaching the depth of Arizona's Grand Canyon. ✉ *Moro Rock–Crescent Meadow Rd., 1½ mi east off Generals Hwy. (Rte. 198) to parking area, Giant Forest.*

Tunnel Log. It's been 40 years since you could drive through a standing sequoia—and that was in Yosemite National Park's Mariposa Grove, not here. This 275-foot tree fell in 1937, and soon a 17-foot-wide, 8-foot-high hole was cut through it for vehicular passage that continues today. Large vehicles take the nearby bypass. ✉ *Moro Rock–Crescent Meadow Rd., 2 mi east of Generals Hwy. (Rte. 198), Giant Forest.*

5

GRANT GROVE

3 mi northeast of the Big Stump entrance and 45 mi north of the Ash Mountain entrance on Rte. 180.

What in 1890 was created as the 4-square-mi Grant Grove National Park is now the hub of Kings Canyon National Park's western, smaller portion. Grant Grove Village, 55 mi due east of Fresno via Route 180, has year-round services that include a general store, John Muir Lodge, and even a campground. If you devote two or three days to see both national parks, this is a good place to spend the night: You'll be roughly the same driving distance from the main attractions of Sequoia (General Sherman Tree, Giant Forest, Moro Rock) as you are from those of eastern Kings Canyon (Kings River Canyon, Cedar Grove, Zumwalt Meadow).

However long you stay and whichever direction you head from Grant Grove, take 15 minutes to watch the film about Kings Canyon that airs continually in the visitor center— also open year-round. Then scoot over to the nearby General Grant Tree, part of a lovely grove that includes the fascinating Fallen Monarch.

Mount Whitney

At 14,494 feet, Mount Whitney is the highest point in the contiguous United States and stands on Sequoia National Park's wild eastern side. The peak and several slightly shorter companions loom high above the tiny, high-mountain desert community of Lone Pine, where parts of several TV shows (*Maverick, Rawhide*) and movies (*Charge of the Light Brigade, Gunga Din, High Sierra*) have been filmed. The high mountain ranges, arid landscape, and scrubby brush of the Eastern Sierra are beautiful in their vastness and austerity.

From the west side of the park, Mount Whitney is hidden behind the Great Western Divide. To see it, you must either undertake an extended backpacking trip or drive hundreds of miles around the Sierra Nevada range, via Yosemite National Park's Tioga Pass to the north or around Isabella Lake (and the small resort town of Kernville) to the south. The best vantage point is at the end of 13-mi Whitney Portal Road (closed in the winter) off memorably scenic Highway 395.

The most popular route to the summit, the **Mount Whitney Trail,** can be conquered by fit and moderately experienced hikers, unless there is snow on the mountain, in which case it is a challenge for expert mountaineers only. Day hikers must have a permit to hike the trail beyond Lone Pine Lake, about 2½ mi from the trailhead at Whitney Portal campground (elevation 8,361 feet). All overnighters must have a permit. Reservations for climbing Mount Whitney are difficult to obtain because of a daily limit on the number of hikers allowed that is enforced from May through October. You can apply for overnight and day permits by lottery each winter by mail only; postmarks must be in February. In May, if other hikers have canceled, a few permits become available; permits are arranged through the Wilderness Permit Office of Inyo National Forest. ☎ *760/873–2485 wilderness information line, 760/873–2483 reservation line* ⊕ *www.fs.fed. us/r5/inyo.*

VISITOR CENTERS

Kings Canyon Visitor Center. Acquaint yourself with the varied charms of this two-section national park by watching a 15-minute film and perusing the center's exhibits on the canyon, sequoias, and human history. If you don't have time to drive the 30-mi scenic byway through Kings River Canyon to Cedar Grove, spending a half-hour here serves

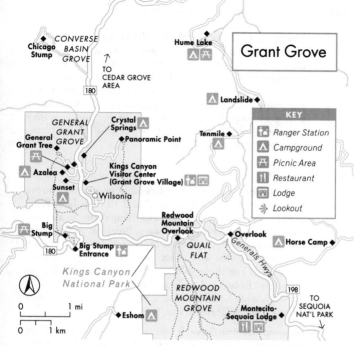

Grant Grove

KEY

🏚 Ranger Station
🔺 Campground
🎪 Picnic Area
🍴 Restaurant
🏨 Lodge
⇴ Lookout

Kings Canyon National Park

as an handy, if inadequate, substitute. Books, maps, and free wilderness permits are available, as are updates on the parks' weather and air-quality conditions. ⊠ *Generals Hwy. (Rte. 198), 3 mi northeast of Rte. 180, Big Stump entrance, Grant Grove* ☎ *559/565–4307* ☉ *Summer, daily 8–6; spring and fall, daily 9–4:30; winter, daily 9:30–4:30.*

HISTORIC SITES

★ **Fallen Monarch.** This sequoia's hollow base was used in the ☾ second half of the 19th century as a home for settlers, a saloon, and even to stable U.S. Cavalry horses. As you walk through it (assuming entry is permitted, which has not always been the case in recent years), check out how little the wood has decayed, and imagine yourself tucked safely inside, sheltered from a storm or protected from searing heat. ■TIP→ **Also look for a chimney that was punched through a sequoia that otherwise is remarkably intact for one that toppled; perhaps it fell on a cushion of thick snow.** ⊠ *Trailhead 1 mi north of Grant Grove Visitor Center, Grant Grove.*

Gamlin Cabin. What you see is only borderline historical, despite its being on the National Register of Historic Places.

The modest lodging that the Gamlin brothers built in 1872 has been moved and rebuilt several times, and a few brain-cramped visitors have carved their initials into its sides. Consider this one-room cabin instead a well-intentioned replica, illustrating what once served as U.S. Cavalry storage space and, during the first decade of the 20th century, a ranger station. The roof and lower timber are made from sequoia wood. ☒ *Trailhead 1 mi north of Grant Grove Visitor Center, Grant Grove.*

SCENIC STOPS

General Grant Tree. President Coolidge proclaimed this to be "the nation's Christmas tree," and 30 years later President Eisenhower designated it as a living shrine to all those Americans who have died in wars. Bigger at its base than the General Sherman Tree, it tapers rather quickly and is estimated to be the world's second- or third-largest sequoia by volume. For those still caught up in the Civil War, an impressive Robert E. Lee Tree is nearby. (It weighs in at No. 11 worldwide.) ☒ *Trailhead 1 mi north of Grant Grove Visitor Center, Grant Grove.*

★ **Redwood Mountain Grove.** If you are serious about sequoias, you should consider visiting this, the world's largest big-tree grove. Within its 2,078 acres are 2,172 sequoias whose diameters exceed 10 feet. Your options range from the distant (pulling off the Generals Highway onto an overlook) to the intimate (taking a 6- to 10-mi hike down into its richest regions, which include two of the world's 25 heaviest trees). To reach the trailhead, you must take a poorly maintained, summer-only dirt road that tumbles down from Generals Highway on the southern edge of Kings Canyon National Park's western portion. ✛ *Drive 5 mi south of Grant Grove on Generals Hwy. (Rte. 198), then turn right at Quail Flat; follow it 1½ mi to the Redwood Canyon trailhead, Grant Grove.*

CEDAR GROVE

30 mi east of Grant Grove Village and 33 mi east of the Big Stump Entrance on Kings Canyon Scenic Byway (Rte. 180).

The gateway to Kings Canyon National Park's large eastern portion and to the pristine wilderness that beckons beyond, Cedar Grove is a popular launching pad for many back-

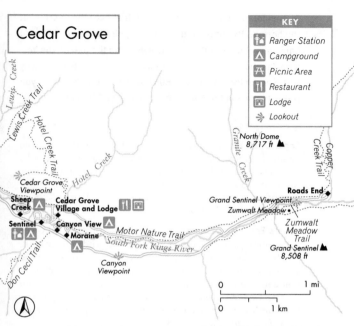

packing trips. In summertime, the Road's End parking lot is crowded with cars whose occupants have disappeared into the High Sierra, sometimes for weeks.

Day-trip opportunities abound here, too, for those who either have seen all the big trees they want or are just ready for a different type of outing. The seasonal, 30-mi road to Cedar Grove Village and to the trailheads beyond has been designated as Kings Canyon Scenic Byway. As you drive through Sequoia National Forest on your way to the park, you will pass through the canyon's deepest point. Be sure to pause at an overlook or two along the way, and once you're in the Cedar Grove area, walk around Zumwalt Meadow and take the short trail to Roaring River Falls. Admire the natural, gray beauty of North Dome and Grand Sentinel that loom above the canyon. Grab a meal from the Cedar Grove snack bar and take it out onto a deck that overlooks the South Fork of the Kings River, which is a mighty force when mountain snowmelt is at its peak.

DID YOU KNOW? The record-keepers at Guinness have said that Kings River Canyon is the deepest canyon in the United States.

At one point, a cliff top hovers 8,200 feet over the riverbed at the bottom. By contrast, the deepest point in Arizona's Grand Canyon is almost 6,000 feet. Elsewhere on the planet, the Yarlung Zangbo Grand Canyon in China is thought to lead the way with a depth that exceeds 17,600 feet. Peru's Cotahuasi Canyon is the deepest in the Americas, at nearly 11,600 feet.

VISITOR CENTERS

Cedar Grove Visitor Center. Off the main road and behind the Sentinel campground, this small ranger station has books and maps, plus information about hikes and other things to do in the area. ⊠ *Kings Canyon Scenic Byway, 30 mi east of park entrance, Cedar Grove* ☎ *559/565–3793* ☉ *April–October, daily 9–5.*

Road's End Permit Station. If you're planning to hike the backcountry, you can pick up a permit and information on the backcountry here. You can also rent or buy bear canisters, a must for campers. When the station is closed, you can still complete a self-service permit form. ⊠ *6 mi east of Cedar Grove Visitor Center, at the end of Kings Canyon Scenic Byway, Cedar Grove* ☎ *No phone* ☉ *Late May–late Sept., daily 7–3:30.*

SCENIC DRIVES

★ **Kings Canyon Scenic Byway.** About 10 mi east of Grant Grove Village is Jackson View, where you'll first see the canyon. Near Yucca Point, Kings River Canyon is thousands of feet deeper than the much more famous Grand Canyon. (A strenuous 1-mi hike gets you to the spot where cliff-tops tower more than 8,000 feet above the confluence of the Middle and South forks of the Kings River.) Continuing through Sequoia National Forest past Boyden Cave, you enter the larger portion of Kings Canyon National Park and, soon, Cedar Grove Village. Past there, the U-shape canyon becomes broader. Be sure to allow an hour to walk through Zumwalt Meadow, which allows you to gawk at North Dome and Grand Sentinel, both granite-faced gems. Also, either coming or going, take a few minutes to park and take less-than-5-minute walks to the base of Grizzly Falls (outside the park, near Boyden Cave) and Roaring River Falls (just east of Knapp's Cabin). The drive dead-ends at a big parking lot, the launch point for many back-

Sequoia & Kings Canyon Events

Annual Trek to the Tree. At 2:30 PM on the second Sunday in December, thousands of Christmas carolers, many of whom arrive en masse from Sanger, gather at the base of General Grant Tree, the nation's official Christmas tree. This event's been going on for more than 80 years. ☎ 559/565–4307 ⊕ www.sanger.org.

Blossom Days Festival. On the first Saturday of March, communities along Fresno County's Blossom Trail celebrate the flowering the area's many orchards, citrus groves, and vineyards. You can drive the 62-mi trail any time of year, but peak blossom season is late February–mid-March. ☎ 559/262–4271 ⊕ www.gofresnocounty.com/BlossomTrail/BlossomIndex.asp.

Jazzaffair. Held just south of the parks in the town of Three Rivers, a festival of mostly swing jazz takes place at several locations, with shuttle buses between sites. The festival is the second or third weekend of April. ☎ 559/561–4549 ⊕ www.jazzaffair.info.

Redbud Festival. This two-day arts-and-crafts festival in Three Rivers highlights work by local artists every May. ☎ 559/561–3300.

Woodlake Rodeo. A weekend-long event thrown by the Woodlake Lions, this rodeo draws large crowds to Woodlake (near Three Rivers) on Mother's Day weekend. ☎ 559/564–8555 ⊕ www.woodlakelionsrodeo.com.

North American Pole Vault Championship. Every August in Old Town Clovis, this competition by top pole-vaulters is accompanied by a farmers market, petting zoo, and other family activities. ☎ 559/278–4097.

Celebrate Sequoias Festival. On the second Saturday of September, rangers guide field trips to the lesser known groves of Sequoia National Park. ☎ 559/565–4307 Grant Grove Visitor Center.

Big Fresno Fair. The Fresno Fairgrounds come alive each October with an old-fashioned county fair that includes a midway, agriculture and livestock shows, horse races, and big-name entertainment. ☎ 559/650–3247 ⊕ www.fresnofair.com.

packers. Stops not included, driving the byway takes about one hour each way. ⊠ *Rte. 180, between the Big Stump entrance and Road's End Permit Station* ☎ *No phone* ☉ *Late May–late Sept., daily 7–3:30.*

HISTORIC SITES

Knapp's Cabin. Stop here not so much for the cabin itself, but as an excuse to get out of the car to stretch and ogle the scenery. George Knapp, a Santa Barbara businessman, stored gear in this small wooden structure when he commissioned fishing trips into the canyon in the 1920s. ⊠ *Kings Canyon Scenic Byway, 2 mi east of Cedar Grove Village turnoff, Cedar Grove.*

SCENIC STOPS

Canyon View. There are many places along the scenic byway to pull over for sightseeing, but this spot is special in that it showcases evidence of the canyon's glacial history. Here, maybe more than anywhere else, you can understand why John Muir compared Kings Canyon vistas with those in Yosemite. ⊠ *Kings Canyon Scenic Byway (Rte. 180), 1 mi east of the Cedar Grove turnoff, Cedar Grove.*

MINERAL KING

25 mi east of Three Rivers and 26 mi from Sequoia National Park's Ash Mountain entrance via Mineral King Rd.

People who come to this remote section at the southern end of Sequoia National Park sometimes make it an annual habit. They love the remoteness and the crisp, light air of 7,800 feet. They enjoy gazing up at Sawtooth Peak, 12,343 high and with a series of sharp granite bumps that do indeed resemble a saw. They venture onto the 11 trails, up mountainsides, past abandoned mine shafts, to gorgeous lakes. They like to watch deer scamper by their cabin at Silver City Resort, or pitch their tents right next to sequoias in the Atwell Mill campground. And secretly, they pray that 25-mi Mineral King Road—which branches here off Route 198 at Three Rivers—remains in crummy condition. Otherwise, more people would come spoil the quiet fun.

Mineral King is the highest spot you can drive to in Sequoia National Park, and the road is open only from late May through October. If you plan to make a day-trip here from Three Rivers, get going very early, pack a picnic lunch, and be prepared to be shaken in your car seat during the drive in and out.

CLOSE UP | Little Facts About Big Trees

■ The National Park Service offers these tidbits about Sequoia National Park's namesake trees:

■ Rather than dying of old age, sequoias fall down. Root systems compromised by eroding ground are often to blame.

■ Mature sequoias produce up to 2,000 cones, containing 400,000 seeds, each year.

■ The egg-size cones can remain hanging from branches for 20 years.

■ Seeds typically are the size of oat flakes.

■ Of the 75 giant sequoia groves in the Sierra Nevada mountain range, only eight lie north of the Kings River—including the three groves in Yosemite National Park.

VISITOR CENTERS

Mineral King Ranger Station. On your way to hiking at the end of Mineral King Road, consider stopping here to ask rangers for suggestions and insights. You also can buy maps, books, and wilderness permits. Take a moment to look out the large side windows at the "exotic sequoia"; in this case, that one that was human-planted. Although less than 80 years old, it has an unusually thick trunk. That's because, a ranger explains, it was planted in the open, and without the need to grow tall quickly to capture sunlight, it starting spreading out instead. ✉ *Near the end of Mineral King Rd., 24 mi east of East Fork entrance, Mineral King* ☎ *559/565–3768* ☉ *Late May–late Sept., daily 8–4.*

SCENIC DRIVES

Mineral King Road. Vehicles longer than 22 feet are prohibited on this side road into southern Sequoia National Park, and for good reason: It contains 589 twists and turns, according to one reputable source. Anticipating an average speed of 20 MPH is optimistic, considering all the potholes, blind curves, and narrow stretches. The scenery is splendid as you climb nearly 6,000 feet from Three Rivers to the Mineral King area, but it's for passengers to admire, not the fully occupied drivers. If you can, trade off with your spouse or companion on the return trip. Allow 90 minutes each way. Make sure you start off with a full tank, too, because gas is no longer sold at Silver City Resort. You can pick up a few snack items there, though, and the restaurant is pretty good. The road is usually closed from late October through late May. *Mineral King.*

SCENIC STOPS

Mineral King. Silver was discovered here at 7,800 feet in the early 1870s. Subsequent attempts to extract the mineral were commercial flops. A road had been probed into the remoteness, however, and the lovely sub-alpine valley lured loggers, hydro-electric power developers, tourists, and people who built mountain cabins as summer retreats from the Central Valley or Los Angeles. ⚠ **If you're hiking very far into the backcountry, be aware that there are abandoned, open mines capable of ruining your day.** ✉ *End of Mineral King Rd., 25 mi east of Generals Hwy. (Rte. 198), east of Three Rivers, Mineral King.*

Sequoia &
Kings Canyon
Hikes & Activities

WORD OF MOUTH

"Both Sequoia and Kings Canyon are fabulous national parks. Depending on your interest, there are many, many hikes into isolated groves that are worthwhile. Kings Canyon has the drive with killer scenery and plenty of great trails for hikers. Sequoia has the mountain scenery, too, but you have to get on the trails to see it. When you drive through on the roads, it's mainly the trees that you see."

—Otis B. Driftwood

By Reed
Parsell

TRAMPING THROUGH A FOREST IS PLEASANT, but strolling through a sequoia grove is unforgettable. Nowhere else but in the Sierra Nevada can you come upon tree trunks that are wider than two-lane highways. Looking up in search of their tops makes your neck ache. Touching the bark makes you wonder at its sponginess. Seeing how the big trees have been blackened by fires, yet live on for hundreds if not thousands of years, can confound your mind.

Sure, you can get a general sense of sequoias by driving through the parks, getting out of the car only to peruse the Giant Forest Museum or to stare at the General Sherman Tree. But to fully appreciate the wonders of Kings Canyon and Sequoia National Parks, you should do more than just stretch your legs. Grab a water bottle and head toward a grove that's a bit off-road. Stand beside the big trees, or amid a cluster of them. See what it's like for sunlight to be filtered through a 250-foot canopy. Some of the best hikes—Congress Trail, Big Trees Trail, Zumwalt Meadow—are short and easy. The most unusual—Moro Rock—might test your fitness level, but it's not to be missed.

Options for longer day hikes abound. Backpacking will take you into vast expanses of pristine wilderness. Experience the thrills of rock-climbing and kayaking in Kings River Canyon. In the winter, explore Sequoia's Giant Forest and Kings Canyon's Grant Grove on snowshoes or cross-country skis. Keep in mind, however, that bicycling options are limited, and boating, rafting, and snowmobiling are prohibited.

DAY HIKES

Rangers report that many people spend less than an hour in the parks, zipping in via Route 198 and taking time only to see the General Grant Tree before turning around and skedaddling up to Yosemite National Park, or back home. How efficient! They will have seen a giant sequoia—something else to check off on the proverbial bucket list.

General Grant and the other so-called "big trees" have been around for hundreds—in many cases for thousands—of years and deserve more respect than merely to be the object of a frantic photo op. At least one full day in the parks is a worthwhile goal. Obligingly, both Kings Canyon and Sequoia National Parks contain several easy hikes

BEST HIKES

■ **Walking the Congress Trail:** If you only have time for one hike, this is the one to take. It conveniently starts beside Sequoia National Park's most famous attraction, the General Sherman Tree.

■ **Taking on Moro Rock:** You cannot help but be impressed with ingenuity it took to fashion a rock staircase up this huge slab of granite. The view on top isn't bad, either.

■ **Meandering about the meadows:** Crescent Meadow on the road past Moro Rock, Round Meadow near the Giant Forest Museum, and Zumwalt Meadow out past Cedar Grove are three varia-

tions on a naturally enchanting expanse.

■ **Listening to the experts:** By attending any of the innumerable and diverse ranger programs offered in both parks, you will come away the wiser—and perhaps thinking about a return visit to these special parks.

■ **Get away from it all:** Backpack in the High Sierra and you may just forget there are such things as 24-hour cable news channels, cell phones that take pictures, and drive-through coffeehouses. And you will approve of the concept.

6

that will allow you to closely examine the rust-barked skyscrapers without taking too much of your time. The best short trails (Big Trees, Congress, Grant Grove, General Sherman Tree) are paved, and parts of them are even wheelchair-accessible.

If you're an ambitious hiker, choose from among many intriguing options, including more than a dozen half- and full-day trails that you might have to yourself. With a wilderness permit, you can venture deep into the High Sierra, trekking for days on trails that pass by lakes and meadows and are shared by other mammals.

Indeed, while walking along whatever path you have taken, keep your eyes open for black bears (many of which are brown), spotted skunks, lizards, squirrels, even foxes and bobcats—more than 260 species of vertebrates are native to the parks. As for vegetation, that depends on the elevation. From the Foothills Visitor Center, at 1,700 feet, to the High Sierra peaks that are topped by Mount Whitney, at 14,494 feet, more than 1,200 species of plants grow. Sequoias are the star attraction, but they have a lot of leafy (and grassy, and shrubby) company.

Free general park maps are available at the entrance stations and visitor centers that probably will serve your purposes unless you are going on a backpacking adventure. Montecito-Sequoia Lodge, in Sequoia National Forest, in its lobby has a bank of free information sheets about several hikes. You can purchase detailed maps at the visitor centers or in most park stores.

HIKES TO LOOK OUT FOR

Very short hikes (less than two hours): Big Stump, Big Trees, Congress, Crescent Meadow (main trail only), General Grant, Panoramic Point, Roaring River Falls, Zumwalt Meadow.

Half-day hikes (up to five hours): Big Baldy, Buena Vista, Crescent Meadow (expanded), Little Baldy, Mist Falls, Muir Grove, Timber Gap, Redwood Canyon (6-mi version), Tokopah Falls.

Full-day hikes: Don Cecil, Eagle Lake, Hotel Creek, Marble Falls, Redwood Canyon (10-mi version).

For books about hikes in Sequoia National Park, contact the **Sequoia Natural History Association** (⊠*47050 Generals Hwy., Three Rivers* ☎ *559/565–3759* ⊕ *www.sequoia history.org*).

SPOTLIGHT HIKE: CONGRESS TRAIL

Although there are many places in Kings Canyon and Sequoia National Parks where you can see giant trees up close, this 2-mi loop goes through the heart of the Giant Forest Grove and contains intense clusters of sequoias into which you can venture, creating memories that will linger for years to come. The clearly marked trailhead is a few strides from the General Sherman Tree. Another positive: You can look up while you are strolling along and not fear tumbling, because the trail is paved, fairly wide, and never too steep. ⊠ *Off Generals Hwy., 2 mi north of Giant Forest Museum and 2 mi south of Lodgepole Visitor Center, Giant Forest* ☞ *Easy.*

0.0 MI: CONGRESS TRAILHEAD

Within minutes of heading away from the commotion that typically surrounds the General Sherman Tree, you notice that the sound of talking tourists gives way to that of chirping birds, a babbling creek, and whispering breezes. A couple of fallen 150-foot-plus cedars help put into per-

CLOSE UP

Tips for the Trails

Water. Figure out what you think you will need, then double that amount, especially on hot summer days—of which there are many in these two California parks next to the smoldering Central Valley.

Binoculars. Avoid disappointment by being able to zoom in on a grazing animal, a distant grove of sequoias, or to the top of a big tree you are standing under; lots can be happening up there.

Footwear. Regular sneakers are good enough for most of the day trails, although during late spring and early summer you might have to cross a small stream or two.

Sunscreen. It is never a bad idea to lather on some SPF 30-plus, although 250-foot-tall sequoias do provide an inordinate amount of shade.

Animals. Do not approach, do not heckle, do not feed. And remember, both parks' rangers enforce a policy that all food and other fragrant items must never be left in an unattended vehicle. Most trailheads have bear boxes.

6

spective that although sequoias are by far the biggest trees in the Sierra, their "neighbors" are hardly short.

1.0 MI: PRESIDENT TREE

A few minutes prior to reaching here, you will pass a sequoia that, although severely scarred by fire (practically gutted at its base), continues to sprout needles and cones in its upper reaches. It's a testament to the sequoias' survival skills, practically without peer on our planet. The President Tree is impressive, standing tall rather on its own in the manner of a strong executive, but its most important function is to alert you that you are approaching the trail's highlight: the legislative branch.

1.1 MI: THE SENATE

If you can stand in the midst of these dozen or so skyscrapers and not mutter "Wow!" then you are either a city slicker through and through, or stoic to the point of soullessness. Here and at the even larger cluster of Sequoias in the House, another 0.2 mi down the trail, you will crane your neck to see the treetops so distant that you might consider employing binoculars—and maybe even lie on your back to spare your upper spine. Check out how close some of these giants grow to each other; several seem, in fact, to be sharing the same base and root system.

Congress Trail Tips

■ To reach the trailhead, you first must walk 0.4-mi down a paved, but fairly steep, path from the main General Sherman Tree parking lot. The return trip should get your heart pumping more than the trail ever does.

■ Thanks to all the big trees, you need not worry about excessive exposure to the sun.

■ Bring binoculars so that you can see what creatures inhabit the sequoias' upper reaches, and perhaps you can spot the egg-shape cones hanging from the massive branches. Mature trees can have up to 11,000 cones at a time.

■ Do not rush. Take the time to step into the Senate, and the House—maybe even lie down and stare up at the sequoias' sublime skyline.

1.8 MI: NEARING THE TRAIL'S END

Throughout this path, you will have passed the pleasant sites of wild grasses, ferns, and large granite boulders. The final few hundred yards can be a bit confusing to negotiate, however, as signage suddenly is not there when you most need it, and you could end up mistakenly in the General Sherman Tree's handicapped-only parking area off Generals Highway. By veering right at one or two forks in the path, however, you should end up back where you started.

OTHER TRAILS

Giant Forest and the Cold Springs campground in Mineral King each has a short, self-guided nature trail.

Big Baldy. After a few short and fairly steep sections, this 4.5-mi, out-and-back trail settles down to a low-key trek through pine woodlands to the 8,209-feet summit of Big Baldy, the park's highest granite peak. All told, you will ascend about 650 feet, and your reward will be a view of Redwood Canyon. You also can see the Great Western Divide to the west; the eastern views can be sweeping provided the air is clear, which rarely is the case. ⊠*Trailhead 8 mi south of Grant Grove on Generals Hwy. (Rte. 198), Grant Grove* ☞ *Moderate.*

Big Stump Trail. Along this relatively short and easy path you will see that old-growth sequoias were once not so much objects of wonder as they were of commerce. From 1883 until 1890, the year Congress set aside Kings Canyon and Sequoia national parks for protection, logging was done here, complete with a mill. The 1-mi loop trail, whose unmarked beginning is a few yards west of the Big Stump entrance, passes by many enormous stumps, as well as by a sequoia that was spared (Resurrection Tree) and another that was sawed one-fourth through, but survived and continues to grow (Sawed Tree). The largest stump is what's left of the Mark Twain Tree, which when cut down for "educational" purposes (a cross-section of it remains on display at the American Museum of Natural History in New York) was nearly 300 feet tall and measured 91 feet around its base. Climbing atop this stump—which has the square-footage of a large bedroom—via a nine-step stairway is one of the reasons to take this trail: You'll see how enormous these trees are, and appreciate how conservation efforts that begun more than a century ago provide hope that sequoias will survive thousands of years into the future. The small parking lot can get busy here; you might have to park on the road's shoulder. ⊠*Trailhead near Rte. 180, directly off the Big Stump entrance's parking lot, Grant Grove ⚲ Easy.*

⟳ **Big Trees Trail.** This one's a must, as it does not take long to stroll and the setting is spectacular: beautiful Round Meadow surrounded by many mature sequoias, with well-thought-out interpretive signs along the path that explain the ecology on display. For example, you will read that big trees do not grow inside meadows because there is too much moisture, but on the adjacent slopes their sprawling root systems soak up water that flows toward the open, level grassland. Be sure to step on the "footprint"—the shape at a tree's base, outlined on a concrete pathway—of the nearby, 251-foot-tall sequoia colorfully called Near Ed by Ned. From the handicapped parking lot off Generals Highway, the 0.7-mi Big Trees Trail is wheelchair-accessible. If you walk there from the Giant Forest Museum, the total loop is 1.5 mi. ∎TIP➜**In June and July, the meadow is likely to be ablaze with wildflowers.** ⊠*Off Generals Hwy. (Rte. 198), near the Giant Forest Museum, Giant Forest ⚲ Easy.*

Buena Vista Peak. For a 360-degree view of Redwood Canyon and the High Sierra, make the 2-mi ascent to Buena Vista. ⊠*Trailhead off Generals Hwy. (Rte. 198), south of Kings Canyon Overlook, 7 mi southeast of Grant Grove, Grant Grove ⚲ Difficult.*

★ **Crescent Meadow Trails.** John Muir reportedly called Crescent Meadow the "gem of the Sierra." It is a pleasant place,

6

Survive an Animal Encounter

CLOSE UP

One of the reasons people come to national parks and go hiking is that they might see wildlife. Sometimes, they do. But very rarely, they wish they had not.

Almost universally, wild animals have zero interest in confronting human beings. Under extraordinary circumstances, however, trouble can brew. Here's what experts say you should do if you are confronted by several animals that are common in these parts.

Bear: Try to be seen by a bear before you see her. Accomplish that by occasionally talking or whistling as you stroll through a forest; some hikers even wear bells. If a bear approaches you, make a lot of noise to try to scare it off. If you are with other people, everybody should shout, but surrounding the bear is a definite no-no. Try not to act afraid and do not run away. If she approaches in what might

be attack mode, try climbing a tree or dropping into a fetal position. She doesn't want to eat you. She just wants to make sure you do not pose a threat to her or, if nearby, her cubs.

Deer: No, they don't eat meat. But these are not domesticated animals that want to be petted. Give them their space. Otherwise, they can attack with hooves and antlers. More people are injured by deer than by any other animal in the Sierra Nevada range.

Mountain lion: Do not run. Either stay put or back away slowly. Make sure your body is turned fully toward the lion, and you are standing upright. Make your appearance as large as possible. Raise your arms, or spread your jacket open. Shout, and throw things at the lion if possible. If he attacks, fight for your life—which means protecting your neck as you do all you can to get it away from you.

---

without question, and you have a couple of good options here if you are looking for a short hike. A 1.8-mi path, much of it paved, traces the meadow's outline. Allow extra time if you can, however, to veer off on an additional 0.8-mi path (one-way) that leads past Log Meadow to Tharp's Log. The fallen, hollowed-out sequoia was converted into a two-room cabin by Hale Tharp, who is dubiously saluted on the National Park Service Web site as being "Giant Forest's first Caucasian resident." Continue the detour to Chimney Tree, a hollowed and blackened—but still very tall—remnant of a sequoia. All told, you could spend two to three agreeable hours in this area. ⊠*End of Moro Rock–*

Crescent Meadow Rd., 2.6 mi east off Generals Hwy. (Rte. 198), Giant Forest ☞ Easy.

Don Cecil Trail. You have to really be into hiking to take this Kings Canyon National Park trail, which at 13 mi and with an elevation gain of 4,000 feet represents a full day's hard work. Consider that its culminating point, the top of 8,513-foot Lookout Peak, is accessible via a much shorter and easier trail off Big Meadows Road in Giant Sequoia National Monument. You do gain, however, outstanding panoramic views of the backcountry. ✉*Trailhead off Kings Canyon Scenic Byway, across from parking lot, 0.2 mi west of Cedar Grove Village, Cedar Grove ☞ Difficult.*

Eagle Lake Trail. Although this is by all accounts the most popular day hike in Mineral King, rangers say that many people give up before completing the 6.8-mi round trip, which includes an elevation gain of 2,170 feet. Those statistics might not seem like deal-breakers to many experienced hikers, but keep in mind that the trailhead starts at 7,800 feet. A couple of miles into the trail, you will encounter one of the area's many abandoned mine shafts—water tumbles down it, you should not. The sight of the alpine lake, once you catch your breath, should please. ✉*At the end of Mineral King Rd., Mineral King ☞ Difficult.*

☺ **General Grant Tree Trail.** Though General Grant Grove is rather small, at 128 acres, it's a big deal. More than 120 sequoias here have a base diameter that exceeds 10 feet, and the grove's signature tree is the world's second- or third-largest by volume. Standing 268 feet tall and containing enough wood to conceivably build 40 five-room houses, the General Grant Tree was declared by President Coolidge in 1926 to be "The Nation's Christmas Tree." Three decades later, President Eisenhower designated it as a living shrine in memory of all Americans who have died in wars. On the second Sunday afternoon of December, the Sanger Chamber of Commerce sponsors a "Trek to the Tree" here for holiday celebrations. Nearby, the vanquished Confederacy is ably represented by the Robert E. Lee Tree, recognized as the world's 11th-largest sequoia. ■TIP→**Before you begin this gentle, paved .3-mi trail, consider purchasing an entertaining trail guide at the trailhead or from the nearby visitor center.** ✉*Trailhead off Generals Hwy. (Rte. 198), 1 mi northwest of Grant Grove Visitor Center, Grant Grove ☞ Easy.*

Hotel Creek Trail. For gorgeous canyon views, take this trail from the canyon floor at Cedar Grove up a series of switchbacks until it splits. Follow the route left through chaparral to the forested ridge and rocky outcrop known as Cedar Grove Overlook, where you can see the Kings River Canyon stretching below. This strenuous 6.4-mi round-trip hike gains 1,200 feet and takes three to four hours to complete. Be prepared for uninterrupted exposure to the sun. For a longer hike, return via Lewis Creek Trail for an 8-mi loop. ⊠*Trailhead at Cedar Grove pack station, 1 mi east of Cedar Grove Village, Cedar Grove* ↻ *Difficult.*

Little Baldy Trail. Climbing 700 vertical feet in 1.75 mi of switchbacking, this trail ends at a granite dome with a great view of the peaks of the Mineral King area and the Great Western Divide. The walk to the summit and back takes about four hours. ⊠*Little Baldy Saddle, Generals Hwy. (Rte. 198), 11 mi north of Giant Forest, Grant Grove* ↻ *Moderate.*

Marble Falls Trail. The 3.7-mi, moderately strenuous hike to Marble Falls crosses through the rugged foothills before reaching the cascading water. Plan on three to four hours one way. ⊠*Off the dirt road across from the concrete ditch near site 17 at Potwisha Campground, off Generals Hwy. (Rte. 198), Foothills* ↻ *Difficult.*

Mist Falls Trail. This sandy trail follows the glaciated South Fork Canyon through forest and chaparral, past several rapids and cascades, to one of the largest waterfalls in the two parks. A 9-mi round-trip, the hike is relatively flat, but it climbs 600 feet in the last mile. It takes four to five hours to complete. ⊠*Trailhead at end of Kings Canyon Scenic Byway, 5.5 mi east of Cedar Grove Village, Cedar Grove* ↻ *Moderate.*

☾ **Moro Rock Trail.** If you enter Sequoia National Park via the Foothills entrance, you can hardly help but notice this magnificent granite dome looming on the cliffside ahead as you head up Generals Highway. Although climbing to its top (elevation 6,725 feet) results in sweeping views of the Middle Fork Canyon and the Kaweah River (as well as General Highway's twisted path), the most distinctive aspect of Moro Rock is the staircase that has been carved and constructed on its backside. Count on needing 15 minutes to mount all 350-plus steps, which have a spot on the National Register of Historic Places. You can drive to Moro Rock's base or, better yet, take the shuttle from the

Giant Forest Museum. From the base, you can take the 4.6-mi Soldiers Trail Loop that, among other things, passes by the Triple Tree (three sequoias that seem to share the same base). ⊠*Moro Rock–Crescent Meadow Rd., 1.5 mi east off Generals Hwy. (Rte. 198), Giant Forest* ☞ *Moderate.*

Muir Grove. You will attain solitude—and possibly see a bear or two—on this unheralded gem of a hike, a fairly easy 4-mi round trip from the Dorst Creek Campground. The remote grove is small but indescribably lovely, its soundtrack provided solely by nature. Halfway there, step out onto a large rock outcropping and get a sneak peak at the grove on a facing slope. Give yourself a couple of hours for this hike, and remember not to disturb the bears. The trailhead is very subtly marked; it is past the group campsite area, on the right. Use the amphitheater parking lot. ⊠*Dorst Creek Campground, Generals Hwy. (Rte. 198), 8 mi north of Lodgepole Visitor Center, Giant Forest* ☞ *Easy.*

Panoramic Point. Obtain a nice view of whale-shape Hume Lake from the top of this Grant Grove path, which though paved and only 300 feet long is fairly steep—strollers might work here but not wheelchairs. Two interpretive signs identify a dozen High Sierra peaks, all above 12,000 feet, that stretch from Mt. Goddard in northern Kings Canyon National Park to Eagle Scout Peak in Sequoia. Trailers and RVs are not permitted on the steep and narrow road that leads to the trailhead parking lot, where you also will find a few picnic tables. ⊠*End of Panoramic Point Rd., 2.3 mi north of Grant Grove Village, Grant Grove* ☞ *Easy.*

6

DID YOU KNOW? Lush mountain greenery can have a whiff of illegitimacy, or more specifically illegality, in and around Sequoia National Park. This region is thought to have the nation's highest concentration of marijuana cultivation. In 2008, federal agents seized more than 525,000 marijuana plants. Agents noted that pesticides and other chemicals that often are used to grow the outlawed "weed" can have a detrimental impact on animals and native plants.

★ **Redwood Canyon.** Avoid the hubbub of Giant Forest and its General Sherman Tree by hiking down to Redwood Canyon, the world's largest grove of sequoias. First, however, you must reach the parking lot via a seasonal, 2-mi road off Generals Highway that is unpaved and crater-plagued

(10 MPH is a reasonably safe speed, both going down and returning up). Opt for the trail toward Hart Tree, and soon you will lose track of how many humongous trees you pass along the 6-mi loop. Beware that at the 4-mi mark, just past the Fallen Goliath, you must cross a small creek (a signpost really is needed here). Taking the 4-mi Sugar Bowl side trail lets you see thousands of baby sequoias that recently have sprouted thanks to the park's prescribed burn program. Count on spending four to six peaceful hours here, although some backpackers linger overnight (wilderness permit required). ⊠ *5 mi south of Grant Grove on Generals Hwy. (Rte. 198), then turn right at Quail Flat; follow it 1.5 mi to the Redwood Canyon trailhead, Grant Grove* ⚲ *Moderate.*

⚙ **Roaring River Falls Walk.** Take a shady three-minute walk to this forceful waterfall that rushes through a narrow granite chute. The trail is paved and mostly accessible. ⊠ *Trailhead 3 mi east of Cedar Grove Village turnoff from Kings Canyon Scenic Byway, Cedar Grove* ⚲ *Easy.*

Timber Gap Trail. In Sequoia National Park's southern section, this is one of two good day hikes in Mineral King (Eagle Lake is the other). If you are fit enough to conquer the first half, a heart-pounding uphill mile that switchbacks relentlessly north from the parking area, you will be rewarded with a more level path and stunning views of the mountaintops to the south—one small and pointy peak after another are at about the same altitude, with Sawtooth Mountain's jagged peak forming a reasonable resemblance to the business edge of a saw. It's within the second of the trail's two forested areas that you will come to the gap, where the trail starts descending in the direction of Moro Rock. That is your signal to turn around, limiting your round-trip to about three hours and making the return portion practically all downhill. ⊠ *Off the Sawtooth parking lot, near the end of Mineral King Rd., Mineral King* ⚲ *Moderate to difficult.*

Tokopah Falls Trail. This trail follows the Marble Fork of the Kaweah River for 1.75 mi one way and dead-ends below the impressive granite cliffs and cascading waterfall of Tokopah Canyon. It takes 2½ to 4 hours to make the 3½-mi round-trip journey. The trail passes through a mixed-conifer forest. ⊠ *Off Generals Hwy. (Rte. 198), ¼ mi north of Lodgepole Campground, Giant Forest* ⚲ *Moderate.*

★ Fodor'sChoice **Zumwalt Meadow Trail.** Rangers agree this is the best, and most popular, day hike in the Cedar Grove area. Just 1.5 mi long, it offers three visual treats: the South Fork of the Kings River, the lush meadow, and the high granite walls above, including those of Grand Sentinel and North Dome. At two points you will need to climb over piles of big rocks, which will require a little effort and concentration, but in general you'll be traipsing over pine needles and, perhaps, pinching yourself to prove that you really are in such a charming place. ⊠*Trailhead 4½ mi east of Cedar Grove Village turnoff from Kings Canyon Scenic Byway, Cedar Grove* ☞ *Easy.*

SUMMER SPORTS & ACTIVITIES

BICYCLING

Cedar Grove has a designated bike trail. Other than that, steep, winding roads and shoulders that are either narrow or nonexistent make bicycling here more of a danger than a pleasure. Outside of campgrounds, you are not allowed to pedal on unpaved roads. Kings Canyon and Sequoia National Parks are best seen by vehicle and on foot.

BIRD-WATCHING

More than 200 species of birds inhabit the two national parks. Not seen in most parts of the United States, the white-headed woodpecker and the pileated woodpecker are common in most mid-elevation areas here. There are also many hawks and owls, including the renowned spotted owl. Species are diverse in both parks due to the changes in elevation, and range from warblers, kingbirds, thrushes, and sparrows in the foothills to goshawk, blue grouse, red-breasted nuthatch, and brown creeper at the highest elevations. Ranger-led bird-watching tours are held on a sporadic basis. Call the park's main information number to find out more about these tours (*see* ⇨ Visitor Information *in* Travel Smart).

Contact the **Sequoia Natural History Association** (☎ *559/565–3759* ⊕ *www.sequoiahistory.org*) for information on bird-watching in the southern Sierra.

FISHING

There's limited trout fishing in the creeks and rivers from late April to mid-November. The Kaweah and Kings rivers are popular spots; check at visitor centers for open and closed waters. Some of the park's secluded backcountry lakes have good fishing. For park regulations, closures, and restrictions, call the parks' general information line (*see* ⇨ Visitor Information *in* Travel Smart) or stop at a park visitor center. Licenses and fishing tackle are usually available in Lodgepole, Grant Grove, and Cedar Grove markets; only Grant Grove is open year-round.

A California fishing license is $12.60 for one day, $19.45 for two days, $38.85 for 10 days (discounts are available for state residents). Licenses are required for those over 16; children ages 15 and younger do not need licenses as long as they are with an adult.

Among many other functions, the **California Department of Fish & Game** (☎ *916/653–7661* ⊕ *www.dfg.ca.gov*) supplies fishing licenses.

HORSEBACK RIDING

Scheduled trips take you through redwood forests, flowering meadows, across the Sierra, or even up to Mount Whitney. One-day destinations by horseback out of Cedar Grove include Mist Falls and Upper Bubb's Creek. In the backcountry, many equestrians head for Volcanic Lakes or Granite Basin, ascending trails that reach elevations of 10,000 feet. Costs per person range from $25 for a one-hour guided ride to around $200 per day for fully guided trips for which the packers do all the cooking and camp chores.

From May through October, you can take a one-day or overnight trip along the Kings River Canyon from **Cedar Grove Pack Station** (⊠*Kings Canyon Scenic Byway, 1 mi east of Cedar Grove Village, Cedar Grove* ☎ *559/565–3464 in summer, 559/337–2314 off-season*). Popular routes include the Rae Lakes Loop and Monarch Divide.

A one- or two-hour trip from **Grant Grove Stables** (⊠*Rte. 180, ½ mi north of Grant Grove Visitor Center, near Grant Grove Village, Grant Grove* ☎ *559/335–9292 mid-June–Sept., 559/337–2314 Oct.–mid-June*) is a good way to get a taste of horseback riding in Kings Canyon. The stables are open daily 8–6 from June through Labor Day.

From May through September, hourly, half-day, full-day, or overnight trips through Sequoia are available from **Horse Corral Pack Station** (⊠ *Off Big Meadows Rd., 10 mi east of Generals Hwy. [Rte. 198] between Sequoia and Kings Canyon national parks, Sequoia National Forest* ☎ *559/565–3404 in summer, 559/564–6429 in winter* ⊕ *www. horsecorralpackers.com*) for beginning and advanced riders, who must be at least 7 years old. Sleigh rides, provided there is enough snow, are offered during the November through January holiday season. Expect to pay $35 to $145 day-trips.

Day and overnight tours in the high-mountain area around Mineral King are available from July through late September at **Mineral King Pack Station** (⊠ *End of Mineral King Rd., 25 mi east of East Fork entrance, Mineral King* ☎ *559/561–3039 in summer, 520/855–5885 in winter* ⊕ *mineralking.tripod.com*). Expect to pay $25 to $75 for a day trip.

SWIMMING

Drowning is the No. 1 cause of death in both Sequoia and Kings Canyon parks. Though it is sometimes safe to swim in the parks' rivers in the late summer and early fall, it is extremely dangerous to do so in the spring and early summer, when the snowmelt from the high country causes swift currents and icy temperatures. Check with rangers if you're unsure about conditions or to learn the safest locations to wade in the water. △ **Stand clear of the water when the rivers are running, and stay off wet rocks to avoid falling in.**

WINTER SPORTS & ACTIVITIES

CROSS-COUNTRY SKIING

For a one-of-a-kind experience, cut through the groves of mammoth sequoias in Giant Forest. Some of the Crescent Meadow hiking trails are suitable for skiing as well. Most of the trails are not groomed. You can park at Giant Forest. Note that roads can be precarious in bad weather. Some advanced trails begin at Wolverton.

Roads to Grant Grove are easily accessible during heavy snowfall, making the trails here a good choice over Sequoia's Giant Forest when harsh weather hits.

Grant Grove Ski Touring Center (⊠*Grant Grove Market, Generals Hwy. [Rte. 198], 3 mi northeast of Rte. 180, Big Stump entrance, Grant Grove* ☎ *559/335–2665*) is set up in the Grant Grove Market in the winter, and you can rent cross-country skis here. The shop is open daily from 9 to 6, and the cost to rent skis runs from $6 to $11 per day. This is a good starting point for a number of marked trails, including the Panoramic Point Trail and the General Grant Tree Trail.

In the backcountry, **Pear Lake Ski Hut** (⊠*Trailhead at end of Wolverton Rd., 1½ mi northeast off Generals Hwy. [Rte. 198], Giant Forest* ☎ *559/565–3759*) offers primitive lodging during the winter ski season. The hut is reached by a steep and extremely difficult 7-mi trail from Wolverton. Only expert skiers should attempt this trek. Space is limited; make reservations well in advance. You'll pay $30 to $38 per night, and the hut is generally available from mid-December through mid-April.

Wuksachi Lodge (⊠*Off Generals Hwy. [Rte. 198], 2 mi north of Lodgepole, Giant Forest* ☎ *559/565–4070*) rents skis ($15 to $20 per day) daily from 9 to 4 in the winter season (usually November through May, unless there is no snow). Depending on snowfall amounts, there may also be instruction available. Reservations are strongly recommended if you want to stay at the lodge. Marked trails cut through Giant Forest, which sits 5 mi south of the lodge.

SLEDDING

The Wolverton area, on Route 198 near Giant Forest, is a popular sledding spot, where sleds, inner tubes, and platters are allowed. You can buy sleds and saucers, starting at $8, at the Wuksachi Lodge, 2 mi north of Lodgepole (*see* ⇨ Cross-country Skiing, *above*).

In winter, Kings Canyon also has a few great places to play in the snow. Sleds, inner tubes, and platters are allowed at both the Azalea Campground area on Grant Tree Road, ¼ mi north of Grant Grove Visitor Center, and at the Big Stump picnic area, 2 mi north of the lower Route 180 entrance to the park.

Grant Grove Market (⊠*Generals Hwy. [Rte. 198], 3 mi northeast of Rte. 180, Big Stump entrance, Grant Grove* ☎ *559/335–2665*) sells sleds, saucers, and other snow-play gear during the winter season; it's open daily from 9 to 6.

SNOWSHOEING

Snowshoeing is good around Grant Grove, which along with Wuksachi has naturalist-guided snowshoe walks Saturdays and holidays from mid-December through mid-March as conditions permit.

Snowshoers may stay at the Pear Lake Ski Hut (*see* ⇨ Cross-country Skiing, *above*). You can rent snowshoes for $15 to $20 at the Giant Forest Museum or Wuksachi Lodge. Make reservations and check schedules at both sites.

Grant Grove Market (⊠ *Generals Hwy. [Rte. 198], 3 mi northeast of Rte. 180, Big Stump entrance, Grant Grove* ☎ *559/335–2665*) rents snow shoes in the winter if you prefer to take a self-guided walk. It's open daily from 9 to 6.

Grant Grove Visitor Center (⊠ *Generals Hwy. [Rte. 198], 3 mi northeast of Rte. 180, Big Stump entrance, Grant Grove* ☎ *559/565–4307*) rents out snowshoes for the ranger-led walks for a $1 donation. Call ahead to check on the schedule; walks are usually on Saturdays and holidays.

EXPLORING THE BACKCOUNTRY

One of the distinguishing characteristics of Kings Canyon and Sequoia National Parks is that you cannot drive directly through them. Rather, you must make enormous detours, hundreds of miles long, to motor from the easily accessible western portions to the rugged eastern side—where you'll still have to get out of your vehicle and hike several miles to reach park boundaries. Beyond are hundreds of thousands of acres unspoiled by humans, which is an extraordinary thing for a state that is as densely populated and heavily visited as California.

The parks' vast wilderness, containing more than 800 mi of trails, represents a veritable buffet of natural wonders for backpackers. They can stroll serenely about the High Sierra, at elevations above 11,000 feet, come upon lakes and spot glaciers, breathe clean air and smell abundant wildflowers, and not encounter another person for days (although surely they will see plenty of wildlife). If you are planning an overnight trip into the parks' mountains, you will need a wilderness permit. They are free (the overnight camping fee is $15, however, and due when you get a permit) and are available on a first-come, first-served basis at the Foothills, Grant Grove, and Lodgepole visitor centers, as well as in advance. A quota system is imposed for backcountry trails, so you might have to settle for a second or third choice.

For more details about backpacking in Sequoia & Kings Canyon National Parks, contact the **Wilderness Permit Office** (☎ 559/565–3766 ⊕ *www.nps.gov/seki/planyourvisit/ wilderness.htm*).

In Sequoia National Park, hikers can reserve spots at the **Bearpaw High Sierra Camp** (☎ 888/252–5757 ⊕ *www.visit sequoia.com*), which is 11.5 mi east of Crescent Meadow via the High Sierra Trail. You will be provided with bedding, towels, linens, and meals—and access to showers and flush toilets. Make reservations, starting January 2 for that year by phone or online.

EDUCATIONAL PROGRAMS

All visitor centers have maps for self-guided tours of Sequoia National Park. Ranger-led walks and programs take place throughout the year in Lodgepole Village and Wuksachi Lodge. Forest Service campgrounds have activities from Memorial Day to Labor Day. Schedules for activities are posted on bulletin boards and at visitor centers.

There are no regularly scheduled guided tours of Kings Canyon. Grant Grove Visitor Center has maps of self-guided park tours. Ranger-led programs take place throughout the year in Grant Grove. Cedar Grove and Forest Service campgrounds have activities from Memorial Day to Labor Day. Check bulletin boards or visitor centers for schedules.

Sequoia Sightseeing Tours (☎ 559/561–4189 ⊕ *www.sequoia tours.com*) is the only licensed tour operator in either park. The company offers daily interpretive sightseeing tours in a 10-passenger van with a friendly, knowledgeable guide. Full-day tours ($88) depart from the town of Three Rivers, and half-day tours ($59) begin at Wuksachi Lodge. Reservations are essential.

CLASSES & SEMINARS

Evening Programs (☎ 559/565–3341) during the summer may include documentary films and slide shows, as well as evening lectures. Locations and times vary; pick up a schedule at any visitor center or check bulletin boards near ranger stations.

★ **Seminars** (☎ 559/565–4251 or 559/565–3759 ⊕ *www.sequoiahistory.org*) led by expert naturalists cover a range of topics, including birds, wildflowers, geology, botany, photography, park history, backpacking, caving, and path-finding. Some courses offer transferable credits. Reserve in advance. For information and prices, pick up a course catalogue at any visitor center or from Sequoia Natural History Association.

RANGER PROGRAMS

Free Nature Programs are offered on almost every summer day. Ranging in length from ½ to 1½ hours, ranger talks and walks explore subjects such as the life of the Sequoia, the geology of the park, and the habits of bears. In Kings Canyon National Park, for example, you can take a "Zumwalt Meadow Meander" in Cedar Grove. In Sequoia National Park, catch free nature events at Giant Forest, Lodgepole Visitor Center, Wuksachi Village, and Dorst Campground. Check bulletin boards throughout the parks for that week's schedule.

Rangers conduct daily **Ranger Walks** to General Grant Tree, the General Sherman Tree, and in various Kings River Canyon locales daily in summer, less often at other times of year. The larger campgrounds typically have some sort of campfire program nightly in summer. Check bulletin boards throughout the park for the week's schedule.

☾ The **Junior Ranger Program** (☎ 559/565–3341 ⊕ *www.nps.gov/webrangers*), a free, self-guided program, is offered year-round for children ages 5 and older. Pick up a Junior Ranger booklet at any of the visitor centers. When your child finishes an activity, a ranger signs the booklet. Kids earn a patch upon completion, which is given at an awards ceremony. (Jay Awards are for ages 5 to 8, Raven Awards for ages 9 to 12, and Arrowhead Awards for ages 13 and older.) It isn't necessary to complete all activities to be awarded a patch.

DID YOU KNOW? Back in 1903, only 450 people visited Sequoia and Grant Grove National Parks. By the middle of this decade, that number had mushroomed to 1.6 million visitors. Not surprisingly, July and August are the most popular months to visit, when all of the parks' attractions are open. As early as Labor Day and as late as mid-June, some of the parks' campgrounds, stores, trails, and roads can be closed.

SHOPPING

Selection can be a bit limited in the parks' general stores, but the prices are reasonable when compared with what you would pay in California's mountain communities or the Central Valley. Beer, for example, in some instances is cheaper—and you can buy single bottles. Ice, however, costs nearly double what it does outside the park.

In the interest of preventing bears from developing bad eating habits, prompting a chain of unfortunate events that can lead to their being killed by rangers, the two parks have a firm policy on keeping foodstuffs out of parked cars and tents. You are required to store grocery bags and coolers in unsecured bear boxes, found at all the campgrounds, picnic areas, and major trailheads. That all suggests that buying packaged, single meals is a practical strategy, as opposed to stocking up and constantly having to shuffle your food between vehicle and bear box. Most of the parks' convenience stores have prepackaged sandwiches and salads, and the eateries offer takeaway.

Cedar Grove Market (⊠*Cedar Grove Village, Cedar Grove* ☎ *559/565–0100*) is small, but stocked with the essentials for RV and auto travelers. The market carries a little of everything, from ice-cream bars to foot powder. The store is open from mid-April through September.

Grant Grove Market is a mini-supermarket that sells basic groceries, camping supplies, and emergency gasoline. This is also the place to rent cross-country skis and snowshoes in winter. ⊠*Grant Grove Village, Grant Grove* ☎ *559/335–2665.*

Lodgepole Market & Gift Shop (⊠*Next to Lodgepole Visitor Center, Giant Forest* ☎ *559/565–3301*) sells gifts, toys, books, souvenirs, and outdoor equipment and is Sequoia National Park's largest store. Its grocery department has a fairly wide selection of items, some of them organic. Across the hall, a deli and snack bar make this centrally located complex a convenient place to obtain nourishment.

Privately owned **Silver City Resort** (✉ *Mineral King Rd., 20 mi east of Hwy. 198, Mineral King* ☎ *559/561–3223*) has a small store next to its cozy and competent restaurant, where grocery options are very limited (there's no alcohol, for instance). You are more likely to be tempted by the T-shirts, postcards, and other souvenirs. It's open only from late May through October.

Stony Creek Market (✉ *Generals Hwy. [Rte. 198], between Sequoia and Kings Canyon parks, 12 mi south of Grant Grove, Sequoia National Forest* ☎ *559/565–3909*) has snacks and basic foodstuffs, plus a wide selection of souvenirs on Generals Highway in the Sequoia National Forest between Grant Grove and Giant Forest. It's open from mid-June through early September.

Wuksachi Lodge Gift Shop (✉ *Wuksachi Lodge, 6 mi north of Giant Forest Museum, Wuksachi Village, Giant Forest* ☎ *559/565–4070*) sells souvenir clothing, Native American crafts, postcards and snacks are for sale at a tasteful shop off the Wuksachi Lodge lobby.

6

Sequoia & Kings Canyon Dining & Lodging

WORD OF MOUTH

"Our little secret (just between you and me) is that Kings Canyon is the place to stay. We now go every summer (I fly out from Alabama) and have a small family reunion in General Grant Grove. We love, love, love Sequoia also so we drive over there at least twice during the week we are camping at Kings Canyon. There are all levels of lodging."
— Hershey

By Reed
Parsell

PITCHING A TENT UNDER BIG TREES AND BILLIONS OF STARS, rather than insulating yourself under a motel's 8-foot painted-white "popcorn" ceiling, is the preferred method of lodging in and around these national parks. Sequoia has the best indoor option, the rustic yet refined Wuksachi Lodge, whose restaurant is the closest thing to fine dining you will find within 50 mi. Other than Wuksachi and the Silver City Resort, however, the accommodations are modest but functional, and the food is little beyond fast.

Campgrounds fill up quickly in the summer, the busiest season by far in two national parks whose most significant secondary roads are snowed shut for half the year. Lodgepole is the largest and is the most centrally located campground in Sequoia. Reservations are all but mandatory there and at Sentinel Campground in Kings Canyon's Cedar Grove; they are highly recommended for Dorst Creek Campground near Sequoia's northern boundary. Camping "off the beaten path" means finding spots farther from Generals Highway and away from the congested Cedar Grove area. If you're not into tenting or RVing, and the parks' lodges are full, the small town of Three Rivers has several nice places to stay, although driving up and down the steep and curvy southern portion of Generals Highway can be tiresome.

Burgers, ice cream, and the like are sold at all the parks' eateries. Picnicking provides a much more personal experience, and a number of tables—especially those in the Pinewood Picnic Area inside the Giant Forest—are in peaceful settings whose trees will continue to astound you with their size, even if they are not Sequoias.

WHERE TO EAT

Treat yourself (or the family) to a high-quality meal in a wonderful setting in the Wuksachi Dining Room, if you would like, but otherwise keep your expectations modest and embrace outdoor eating whenever possible. Grab bread, spreads, drinks, and fresh produce at one of several small grocery stores. Alternatively, you can get take-out food from the Grant Grove Restaurant or Cedar Grove Snack Bar, or from one of the two small Lodgepole eateries. The nightly Wolverton Barbecue is a hybrid experience between dining in and picnicking out; the all-you-can-eat feast is staged on a patio that overlooks a sublime meadow.

Between the parks and just off Generals Highway, the Montecito Sequoia Lodge has a year-round buffet.

WHAT IT COSTS				
¢	$	$$	$$$	$$$$
RESTAURANTS				
Under $8	$8–$12	$13–$20	$21–$30	Over $30

Restaurant prices are for a main course at dinner and do not include any service charges or taxes.

RESTAURANTS

IN THE PARKS

¢–$ ✕ **Cedar Grove Market.** You can pick up sandwiches and, if they're not sold out, salads to go at this market, which in addition to a range of grocery items also stocks firewood and other camping supplies. It's open daily from 7 AM to 9 PM. ⊠ *Cedar Grove Village, Cedar Grove* ☎ *559/565–0100* ▭ *AE, D, MC, V* ⊗ *Closed late Oct.–mid-Apr.*

$ ✕ **Cedar Grove Snack Bar.** For what looks to be a small operation, the menu is surprisingly extensive, with dinner entrées such as pasta, pork chops, and steak. For breakfast, try the biscuits and gravy, French toast, pancakes, or cold cereal. Burgers (including vegetarian patties) and hot dogs dominate the lunch choices. Outside, a patio dining area overlooks the Kings River. ⊠ *Cedar Grove Village, Cedar Grove* ☎ *559/565–0100* ▭ *AE, D, MC, V* ⊗ *Closed Oct.–May.*

$$$ ✕ **Grant Grove Village Restaurant.** In a no-frills, open room, order basic American fare such as pancakes for breakfast or hot sandwiches and chicken for later meals. You can put a $37 dent in your wallet by ordering veal, but why? The kitchen's old-fashioned idea of a healthy plate is a hamburger with cottage cheese; vegetarians and vegans will have to content themselves with a simple salad. Takeout service is available. ⊠ *Grant Grove Village, Grant Grove* ☎ *559/335–5500* ▭ *AE, D, MC, V.*

¢ ✕ **Lodgepole Market, Deli & Snack Bar.** The choices here run the gamut from simple to very simple, with the three counters only a few strides apart in a central eating complex. For hot food, venture into the snack bar, where the usual burgers and fries are amended with chicken-tender and

7

pizza-slice options. The deli sells prepackaged sandwiches along with ice cream scooped from tubs. Find more prepackaged foods, along with picnic supplies, in the market. ⊠ *Next to Lodgepole Visitor Center,Giant Forest* ☎ *559/565–3301* ⊟ *AE, D, DC, MC, V* ☺ *Closed early Sept.– mid-Apr.*

$$ ✕ **Silver City Resort.** Enjoy a rotating, set menu in an informal but friendly setting high in the Mineral King area. Patrons, many of whom return year after year to stay in this family-owned resort, say great things about the food and, especially, the freshly baked pies. On Tuesday and Wednesday, pie and drinks are all that is available. (Although the surrounding land is part of Sequoia National Park, Silver City Resort is privately operated.) ⊠ *Mineral King Rd., 20 mi east of Hwy. 198, Mineral King* ☎ *559/561–3223 or 805/528–2730* ⊕ *www.silvercityresort.com* ⊟ *MC, V* ☺ *No lunch, dinner Tues. and Wed.*

$$ ✕ **Wolverton Barbecue.** The view is bound to be more memo-
☾ rable than the food, no matter how much you enjoy the all-you-can-eat buffet. Weather permitting, diners congregate on a wooden porch that looks directly out onto a small but strikingly verdant meadow. In addition to the predictable meats such as ribs and chicken, the menu has sides that include baked beans, corn on the cob, and potato salad. Following the meal, listen to a ranger talk and clear your throat for a campfire sing-along. Purchase tickets at Lodgepole Market, Wuksachi Lodge, or Wolverton Recreation Area's office. ⊠ *Wolverton Rd., 1½ mi northeast off Generals Hwy. (Rte. 198),Giant Forest* ☎ *559/565–4070 or 559/565–3301* ⊟ *AE, D, DC, MC, V* ☺ *No lunch. Closed early Sept.–mid-June.*

$$$ ✕ **Wuksachi Village Dining Room.** Huge windows run the length of the high-ceilinged dining room, and a large fireplace on the far wall warms body and soul. The diverse dinner menu—by far the best in the two parks—includes filet mignon, rainbow trout, and vegetarian pasta, in addition to the inescapable burgers. Wines are from California only, which isn't such a bad thing. Try the peach cobbler for dessert. The children's menu is economically priced. Breakfast and lunch also are served. ⊠ *Wuksachi Village, Giant Forest* ☎ *559/565–4070* ⚐ *Reservations essential* ⊟ *AE, D, DC, MC, V.*

OUTSIDE THE PARKS

$–$$ ✕ **Montecito-Sequoia Lodge.** This family-style restaurant in ☺ Sequoia National Forest serves soups, sandwiches, and burgers at lunch, and pasta, salads, fish, and steaks in the evening. ✉ *Generals Hwy. (Rte. 198), between Sequoia and Kings Canyon parks, 12 mi south of Grant Grove, Sequoia National Forest* ☎ *559/565–3909* ▭ *AE, D, MC, V* ⊘ *Closed mid-Oct.–May.*

¢ ✕ **Stony Creek Restaurant.** Although it once contained a family-style restaurant, this property in Sequoia National Forest now offers nonguests just dinnertime pizza. You can grab coffee, a prepackaged sandwich, or picnic supplies in the small market. ✉ *Generals Hwy. (Rte. 198), between Sequoia and Kings Canyon parks, 12 mi south of Grant Grove, Sequoia National Forest* ☎ *559/565–3909* ▭ *AE, D, MC, V* ⊘ *Closed mid-Oct.–May.*

PICNIC AREAS

Why not enjoy a leisurely lunch in the shade of some of the world's tallest trees? Just take special care to dispose of your food scraps properly, which the bears might not appreciate short-term but which aids their long-term survival.

✕ **Big Stump.** At the edge of a logged sequoia grove, some trees still stand at this site. Near the park's entrance, the area is paved and next to the road. It is the only picnic area in either park that is plowed in the wintertime. Restrooms, grills, and drinking water are available, and the area is entirely accessible. ✉ *Just inside Rte. 180, Big Stump entrance, Grant Grove.*

✕ **Columbine.** This shaded picnic area near the Giant Grove sequoias is relatively level. Tables, restrooms, drinking water, and grills are available. ✉ *Grant Tree Rd., just off Generals Hwy. (Rte. 198), ½ mi northwest of Grant Grove Visitor Center, Grant Grove.*

✕ **Crescent Meadow.** A mile or so past Moro Rock, this comparatively remote picnic area has meadow views and, quite handily, is by a lovely trail on which you can burn off those potato chips and cookies. Tables are under the giant sequoias, off the parking area. There are restrooms and drinking water. Fires are not allowed. ✉ *End of Moro Rock–Crescent Rd., 2.6 mi east off Generals Hwy. (Rte. 198), Giant Forest.*

✕ **Foothills Picnic Area.** Near the parking lot at the southern entrance of the park, this small area has tables on grass. Drinking water and restrooms are available. ✉ *Across from the Foothills Visitor Center, Foothills.*

✕ **Grizzly Falls.** This little gem is worth a pull-over, if not a picnic. From the small parking lot, take a very short trek into the woods to picnic tables and to the base of the delightful, 100-foot-plus falls. An outhouse is on-site, but grills are not, and water is unavailable. ✉ *Off Rte. 180, 2½ mi west of Cedar Grove entrance, Cedar Grove.*

DID YOU KNOW? Sequoia and Kings Canyon have a pronounced problem with pollution from the Central Valley, as you will see upon checking daily air-quality postings in the parks' visitors centers. "Unhealthful" might as well be written in ink, rather than chalk. Theoretically, you should be able to see the coastal mountain range from Moro Rock and spots along Generals Highway. If you can, quick—go buy lottery tickets. It's your lucky day. Maine's Acadia National Park also struggles with smog, which drifts up from New York, Boston, and other Eastern Seaboard cities.

✕ **Halstead Meadow.** An ongoing restoration project is bound to make this spot more scenic, although picnickers must ignore Generals Highway noise. Multimillion-dollar plans call for a bridge to cross the meadow; the picnic area could use more parking space, as the current pullouts are inadequate. Grills and restrooms are provided, but there's no drinking water. ✉ *Generals Hwy. (Rte. 198), 4 mi north of Lodgepole junction, Giant Forest.*

✕ **Hospital Rock.** Native Americans once ground acorns into meal at this site; outdoor exhibits tell the story. The picnic area's name, however, stems from a Caucasian hunter/trapper having been treated for a leg wound here in 1873, nearly a decade after the Potwisha tribe had left the area. Tables are on grass a short distance from the parking lot. Look up and you'll see imposing Moro Rock up the road—way up, as you'll soon find out if you are just entering. Grills, drinking water, and restrooms are available. ✉ *Generals Hwy. (Rte. 198), 6 mi north of Ash Mountain entrance, Foothills.*

✕ **Lodgepole Picnic Area.** Basic but centrally located, this spot is a candidate if you have just purchased food from the nearby deli, market, or snack bar. A handful of tables and an outhouse constitute stops along a dirt path; there is no water or grills. Traffic noise can be distracting. ⊠ *Generals Hwy. (Rte. 198), ¼ mi north the Lodgepole facilities' turnoff, Giant Forest.*

✕ **Pinewood Picnic Area.** Picnic in Giant Forest, in the vicinity of sequoias if not actually under them. Drinking water, restrooms, grills, and wheelchair-accessible spots are provided in this expansive, lovely setting that is near Sequoia National Park's most popular attractions. ⊠ *Generals Hwy. (Rte. 198), 2 mi north of Giant Forest Museum, halfway between Giant Forest Museum and General Sherman Tree, Giant Forest.*

✕ **Wolverton Meadow.** At a major trailhead to the backcountry, this is a great place to stop for lunch before a hike. The area sits in a mixed-conifer forest adjacent to parking. Drinking water, grills, and restrooms are available. ⊠ *Wolverton Rd., 1.5 mi northeast off Generals Hwy. (Rte. 198),Giant Forest.*

WHERE TO STAY

Hotel accommodations in Sequoia & Kings Canyon are limited, and although they are clean and comfortable, they tend to lack much in-room character. Keep in mind, however, that the extra money you spend on lodging here is offset by the time you save by being inside the parks. You won't be faced with a 60- to 90-minute commute from the less-expensive motels in Three Rivers and Fresno. Reserve as far in advance as you can, especially for summertime stays. If you are planning to camp, keep in mind that Lodgepole and Dorst Creek often are full; they also take reservations.

WHAT IT COSTS				
¢	$	$$	$$$	$$$$
HOTELS				
Under $70	$70–$120	$121–$175	$176–$250	Over $250

Hotel prices are for a double room in high season and do not include taxes, service charges, or resort fees.

IN THE PARKS

$$ ☒ **Cedar Grove Lodge.** Backpackers like to stay here on the eve of their long treks into the High Sierra wilderness, so bedtimes tend to be early and quiet. The lodge is not attractive, aside from the natural beauty that surrounds it, but it is the only indoor accommodation in this part of Kings Canyon National Park. Each room has two queen-size beds, and three have kitchenettes and patios. You can order trout, hamburgers, hot dogs, and sandwiches at the snack bar (¢–$) and take them to one of the picnic tables along the river's edge. **Pros:** a definite step up from camping in terms of comfort. **Cons:** impersonal; not everybody agrees it's clean enough. ⊠ *Kings Canyon Scenic Byway, 30 mi east of Grant Grove Village, Cedar Grove* ☎ *559/565–0100 front desk, 866/522–6966 reservations* ⊕ *www.sequoia-kingscanyon. com* ↩ *21 rooms* ⚿ *In-room: no phone, kitchen (some), no TV. In-hotel: laundry facilities, no-smoking rooms, Wi-Fi* ☐ *AE, D, MC, V* ⊗ *Closed mid-Oct.–mid-May* ⦶*EP.*

$–$$ ☒ **Grant Grove Cabins.** Some of the wood-paneled cabins here have heaters, electric lights, and private baths, but most have woodstoves, battery lamps, and shared baths. Those who do not mind roughing it even more might opt for the tent cabins. The Grant Grove Restaurant (¢–$$), a family-style coffee shop, serves American standards for breakfast, lunch, and dinner. In winter, only the cabins that have private baths remain open. **Pros:** comparatively inexpensive; good location. **Cons:** only one step above camping in some cases. ⊠ *Kings Canyon Scenic Byway in Grant Grove Village, Grant Grove* ☎ *559/335–5500 front desk, 866/522–6966 reservations* ⊕ *www.sequoia-kingscanyon. com* ↩ *36 cabins, 9 with bath; 19 tent cabins* ⚿ *In-room: no a/c, no phone, no TV. In-hotel: restaurant* ☐ *AE, D, MC, V* ⦶*EP.*

$$$ ☒ **John Muir Lodge.** This modern, timber-sided lodge is nestled in a wooded area in the hills above Grant Grove Village and offers year-round accommodations. The rooms and suites all have queen-size beds and private baths, and there is a comfortable common room where you can play cards and board games, or peruse a loaner book. Look above the stone fireplace at a giant painting of Muir himself, shown relaxing on a rock by a meadow. The inexpensive, family-style Grant Grove Restaurant is a three-minute walk away. This is a good motel in a beautiful forest setting. **Pros:** common room stays warm; it's far enough from the main road to be quiet. **Cons:** check-in is down in the village. ✉ *Kings Canyon Scenic Byway, ¼ mi north of Grant Grove Village, Grant Grove* ☎ *559/335–5500 front desk, 866/522–6966 reservations* ⊕ *www.sequoia-kingscanyon. com* ⊅ *24 rooms, 6 suites* ♨ *In-room: no a/c, no TV. In-hotel: Wi-Fi* ⊟ *AE, D, MC, V* ⦾*EP.*

$$–$$$ ⊡ **Silver City Resort.** High on the Mineral King Road, this
♨ privately owned resort has rustic cabins and Swiss-style chalets (which can accommodate up to eight people and are considerably more expensive than other units), all with at least a stove, refrigerator, and sink. While the more expensive chalets have full bathrooms and kitchens, the cabins (both "family" and "historical") share a central shower and bath; family cabins have a toilet and sink while historical cabins have no toilets at all. The spacious grounds contain several inviting hammocks and a babbling brook, and deer are likely to meander through at any time. The modestly priced on-site restaurant serves full meals Thursday through Monday only. Church services are conducted Sunday mornings on the patio, no alcohol is sold in the small store, and the generator is turned off before 10 PM— this is not a place that parties. Wi-Fi service is only available when the generator is on in the evening. **Pros:** Lovely setting; friendly staff. **Cons:** No electricity except in the evenings. ✉ *Mineral King Rd., 20 mi east of Hwy. 198, Mineral King* ☎ *559/561–3223 or 805/528–2730* ⊕ *www.silver cityresort.com* ⊅ *13 units, 8 with shared bath* ♨ *In-room: no a/c, no phone (some), kitchen, refrigerator (some), no TV, dial-up (some). In-hotel: restaurant, no-smoking rooms, Wi-Fi* ⊟ *MC, V* ⊗ *Closed mid-Oct.–late May* ⦾*EP.*

★ Fodor'sChoice ⊡ **Wuksachi Lodge.** The striking cedar-and-stone
$$$– main building is a fine example of how a man-made struc-
$$$$ ture can blend effectively with lovely mountain scenery. The lobby is small but offers a comfy setting—it has sort of a Ralph Lauren–esque rustic appeal. Guest rooms, which have modern amenities, are in three buildings up the hill a bit from the main lodge. Many of the rooms have spectacular views of the surrounding mountains. You can usually see deer roaming around the spacious and hilly grounds, which are 7,200 feet above sea level. The front desk can help you arrange any number of outdoor activities, including ski and snowshoe rental. Wi-Fi is available in the main lodge but not in guest rooms. **Pros:** best place to stay in the parks; wildlife much in evidence. **Cons:** rooms can be

small; the main lodge is a few minutes' walk away from guest rooms. ⊠ *Wuksachi Village, 2 mi north of the Lodgepole Visitor Center and 23 mi southeast of the Big Stump entrance, Giant Forest Box 89, Wuksachi Village, Sequoia National Park* ☎ *559/565–4070 front desk, 559/253–2199, 888/252–5757 reservations* ⊕ *www.visitsequoia.com* ⊲ *102 rooms* ⋄ *In-room: no a/c, refrigerator, dial-up. In-hotel: restaurant, bar, no-smoking rooms, Wi-Fi* ⊟ *AE, D, DC, MC, V* ⦿*EP.*

OUTSIDE THE PARKS

Significant stretches of the main roads—Generals Highway, Kings Canyon Scenic Byway, and Mineral King Road—are outside the two national parks' boundaries but within Sequoia National Forest and/or Giant Sequoia National Monument. Those stretches contain three properties, the most inviting of which is Montecito-Sequoia Lodge. *See* ⊲ *Chapter 8, What's Nearby, for lodging recommendations in Fresno, Three Rivers, and Visalia.*

$$ 🏚 **Kings Canyon Lodge.** About midway between Grant Grove and Cedar Grove on the Kings Canyon Scenic Byway, the region's oldest operating lodge has basic but comfortable rooms and cabins. Its dark bar also has a grill, and the gas pumps out front can come in handy. **Pros:** in some respects a better indoor option than the Cedar Grove Lodge; nice views. **Cons:** remote; right next to the road. ⊠ *Off Kings Canyon Scenic Byway, 12 mi northeast of Grant Grove Village and 18 mi west of Cedar Grove Village, Sequoia National Forest* ☎ *559/335–2405* ⊲ *3 rooms, 8 cabins* ⋄ *In-room: no a/c, no TV* ⊟ *MC, V* ⊘ *Closed mid-Oct.–late May* ⦿*EP.*

$$–$$$ 🏚 **Montecito-Sequoia Lodge.** Outdoor activities are what this year-round family resort is all about, including many that are geared toward teenagers and small children. Off Generals Highway in Sequoia National Forest, between Sequoia National Park and the western portion of Kings Canyon National Park, it's also centrally located. The lodge rooms are spare but clean, and all have private baths. Cabins, which can sleep up to eight people, have electricity and contain wood-burning stoves, but bathrooms are in shared buildings. **Pros:** friendly staff; great for kids; lots of fresh air and planned activities. **Cons:** can be noisy with all the activity; could be cleaner. ⊠ *63410 Generals Hwy., Sequoia National Forest* ☎ *559/565–3909* ⊕ *www.montecito*

CLOSE UP

The Greater Sequoia Region

As you are driving about the Sequoia and Kings Canyon region, you may start to wonder about all the boundaries you are crossing. Kings Canyon National Park, Sequoia National Park, Giant Sequoia National Monument, Sequoia National Forest—what does it all mean?

National parks must be recognized as such by an act of Congress, and within them are many protections for plant and animal life, as well as geological features. They are overseen by the National Park Service, part of the Department of the Interior.

National monuments can be declared by presidents without Congressional approval but generally protect one or two specific things (such as sequoia groves) rather than the gamut of protections in national parks. They can be run by the Department of the Interior or by the Department of Agriculture.

National forests are places where logging, grazing, and hunting can occur, with the idea being that federal oversight—by the Department of Agriculture—is geared toward keeping the forests' "resources" secure for future generations. These are places where environmentalists often square off against the government and private interests over matters such as whether animals should be placed on endangered-species lists.

Kings Canyon National Park has two parts, the small area around Grant Grove Village and a massive, mostly wilderness area, whose gateway is Cedar Grove Village. The total land area for Kings Canyon is 462,901 acres, or about 725 square mi.

Sequoia National Park is in one large piece, bordering the southern end of Kings Canyon National Park, and encompasses 404,051 acres (about 630 square mi).

Giant Sequoia National Monument is in two father far-flung portions. One surrounds Grant Grove Village, and the other, larger portion is directly south of Sequoia National Park. It covers 327,769 acres (about 510 square mi).

Sequoia National Forest fills in all the gaps of the areas listed above, its acreage totaling 1,144,235 (about 1,790 square mi). Parts of the national forest overlap with Giant Sequoia National Monument.

sequoia.com ⇨ *38 rooms, 13 cabins* ♿ *In-room: no a/c, no TV. In-hotel: restaurant, bar, 24-hour snack bar, no-smoking rooms* ▭ *AE, D, DC, MC, V* 🍽 *BP.*

7

$$–$$$ ☒ **Stony Creek Lodge.** Small and the recipient of some fairly harsh reviews in recent years, Stony Creek nevertheless is conveniently located just off Generals Highway between the two national parks, 15 mi south of Grant Grove. The rooms are basic and bland. Buy groceries in the small store downstairs, or order pizza in the evenings. **Pros:** nice setting; intimate. **Cons:** expensive for what you get; thin walls. ☒ *66659 Generals Hwy., Sequoia National Forest* ☎ *559/565–3909* ⊕ *www.sequoia-kingscanyon.com* ☞ *11 rooms* ☖ *In-room: no TV. In-hotel: Wi-Fi* ⊟ *AE, D, MC, V* ⊗ *Closed mid-Oct.–May* ⑩*CP.*

WHERE TO CAMP

Campgrounds in Sequoia and Kings Canyon are in wonderful settings, with lots of shade and nearby hiking possibilities. But beware that party-loving "locals" from Fresno and other Central Valley cities swarm up here on Friday and Saturday nights. Their boisterous banter and loud music can detract from the back-to-nature experience. On the Dorst and Lodgepole campgrounds accept reservations (up to five months in advance), and none has RV hookups. Those around Lodgepole and Grant Grove get quite busy in summer with vacationing families. Permits are required for backcountry camping.

WHAT IT COSTS				
¢	$	$$	$$$	$$$$
CAMPING				
Under $8	$8–$14	$15–$20	$21–$25	Over $25

Camping prices are for a campsites including a tent area, fire pit, bear-proof food-storage box, picnic table; potable water and pit toilets or restrooms will be nearby.

IN THE PARKS

$ ⛺ **Atwell Mill Campground.** Pitch your tent right amid sequoias in this amply shaded spot off lightly traveled Mineral King Road. It's quiet here, so you're likely to hear nothing other than the buzzing mosquitoes and nearby creek. At 6,650 feet, this tents-only campground is just south of the Western Divide. The Silver City Resort, which has a telephone and very limited supplies, is 1¼ mi farther down the poorly maintained road. Reservations are not accepted. ⊠ *Mineral King Rd., 20 mi east of Hwy. 198, Mineral King* ☎ *559/565–3341* ⊷ *21 tent sites* ⚇ *Pit toilets, drinking water, bear boxes, fire grates, picnic tables, public telephone* ⚇ *Reservations not accepted* ▭ *No credit cards* ☉ *May–Oct.*

$$ ⚇ **Azalea Campground.** Of the three campgrounds in the Grant Grove area (the others are Sunset and Crystal Springs), Azalea is the only one open year-round. It sits at 6,500 feet amid giant sequoias, yet is close to restaurants, stores, and other facilities. Some sites at Azalea are wheel-chair-accessible. The campground can accommodate RVs up to 30 feet. Although there is a charge to camp here from May through mid-October, off-season camping is free. ⊠ *Kings Canyon Scenic Byway, ¼ mi north of Grant Grove Village, Grant Grove* ☎ *559/565–3341* ⊷ *110 tent and RV sites* ⚇ *Flush toilets, drinking water, bear boxes, fire grates, picnic tables, public telephone, general store* ⚇ *Reservations not accepted* ▭ *No credit cards* ☉ *Open year-round.*

$$ ⚇ **Buckeye Flat Campground.** This tents-only campground is at the southern end of Sequoia National Park surrounded by oak trees and within earshot of the Middle Fork of the Kaweah River. It is much more remote than the nearby—and much larger—Potwisha Campground. Because of Buck-eye Flat's low elevation (2,800 feet), temperatures can be scorching here in summer. ⊠ *1 mi east of Generals Hwy., 6 mi north of Foothills Visitor Center, Foothills* ☎ *559/565–3341* ⊷ *28 tent sites* ⚇ *Flush toilets, drinking water, bear boxes, fire grates, picnic tables* ⚇ *Reservations not accepted* ▭ *No credit cards* ☉ *Apr.–late Sept.*

$$ ⚇ **Canyon View Campground.** The smallest and most primitive of four campgrounds near Cedar Grove, this one is near the start of the Don Cecil Trail, which leads to Lookout Point. The elevation of the camp is 4,600 feet along the Kings River. There are no wheelchair-accessible sites. ⊠ *Off Kings Canyon Scenic Byway, ½ mi east of Cedar Grove Village, Cedar Grove* ☎ *No phone* ⊷ *23 tent sites* ⚇ *Flush toilets, drinking water, bear boxes, fire grates, picnic tables,* ⚇ *Reservations not accepted* ▭ *No credit cards* ☉ *Late May–Oct.*

$ ⚇ **Cold Springs Campground.** Near the end of Mineral King Road, this tents-only campground sits up high at 7,500 feet. You must drive on a small side road over a bridge to get here, which adds to the remoteness. Trailheads, about 1 mi down the road, are gateways to the area's spectacular high country. Silver City Resort is 2 mi back. ⊠ *At end of Mineral King Rd., Mineral King* ☎ *559/565–3341* ☖ *Pit toilets, drinking water, bear boxes, picnic tables, ranger station* ⊅ *40 tent sites* ☖ *Reservations not accepted* ▭ *No credit cards* ☉ *May–Oct.*

$$ ⛰ **Crystal Springs Campground.** Near the Grant Grove Village and the enormous General Grant Tree, this campground has a nice, hilly feel to it—almost terraced. There are wheelchair-accessible sites here, as well as more than a dozen for groups. ⊠ *Off Generals Hwy. (Rte. 198), ¼ mi north of Grant Grove Visitor Center, Grant Grove* ☎ *No phone* ⊅ *36 tent and RV sites, 14 group sites* ☖ *Flush toilets, drinking water, bear boxes, fire grates, picnic tables, public telephone* ☖ *Reservations not accepted* ▭ *No credit cards* ☉ *Memorial Day–Labor Day.*

$$ ⛰ **Dorst Creek Campground.** This large campground, at 6,700 feet, is often visited by bears, so make sure your foods and fragrances are stowed securely in bear boxes—not in your tents or automobiles. The underrated John Muir Trail starts near the campground's far end. Reservations, made by mail or through the Web site, are essential in summer. There are accessible sites here. ⊠ *Generals Hwy. (Rte. 198), 8 mi north of Lodgepole Visitor Center, near Kings Canyon border, Giant Forest* ☎ *877/444–6777 or 800/365–2267* ⊕ *www.recreation.gov* ⊅ *204 tent and RV sites* ☖ *Flush toilets, dump station, drinking water, bear boxes, fire grates, picnic tables, public telephone, ranger station* ▭ *D, MC, V* ☉ *Memorial Day–Labor Day.*

$$ ⛰ **Lodgepole Campground.** Sequoia's largest campground is also the noisiest, though things do quiet down usually by 10 PM. Restrooms are nearby. Lodgepole and Dorst Creek (several miles to the west) are the two campgrounds within Sequoia that accept reservations (essential up to five months in advance for stays between mid-May and mid-October), but unlike Dorst Creek, the Lodgepole Campground is open year-round. ⊠ *Off Generals Hwy. beyond Lodgepole Village, Giant Forest* ☎ *559/565–3341 Ext. 2 information, 877/444–6777, 800/365–2267 reservations* ⊕ *www.recreation.gov* ⊅ *203 tent and RV sites* ☖ *Flush toilets, dump station, drinking water, guest laundry (summer only), showers (summer only), bear boxes, fire grates,* picnic tables, public telephone, ranger station, general store ▭ D, MC, V ☉ Open year-round.

$$ ⚠ **Moraine Campground.** Close to the Kings River and a short walk from Cedar Grove Village, this camp opens only to accommodate overflow from the Sentinel and Sheep Creek campgrounds. There are no accessible sites. ✉ *Kings Canyon Scenic Byway, ¼ mi east of Cedar Grove Village, Cedar Grove* ☎ *559/565–3341* ⤴ *120 tent and RV sites* ♿ *Flush toilets, drinking water, bear boxes, fire grates, picnic tables, ranger station* ⚠ *Reservations not accepted* ▭ No credit cards ☉ June–Sept.

$$ ⚠ **Potwisha Campground.** On the Marble Fork of the Kaweah River, this midsize campground with attractive surroundings sits at 2,100 feet—which means it gets no snow in winter and can be hotter in summer than campgrounds at higher elevations. RVs up to 30 feet long can camp here, although they are not permitted to trek on up Generals Highway to the Giant Forest area. Larger and less remote than the nearby Buckeye Flat Campground, this is the better option for families. ✉ *Generals Hwy., 4 mi north of Foothills Visitor Center, Foothills* ☎ *559/565–3341* ⤴ *42 tent and RV sites* ♿ *Flush toilets, dump station, drinking water, bear boxes, fire grates, picnic tables, public telephone, ranger station* ⚠ *Reservations not accepted* ▭ No credit cards ☉ Open year-round.

$$ ⚠ **Sentinel Campground.** Of the four campgrounds in the Cedar Grove area, Sentinel is open the longest and fills up fastest in the summer. Some sites are wheelchair-accessible, and the campground can accommodate RVs up to 30 feet. Within walking distance are the laundry facilities, restaurant, general store, and ranger station that constitute Cedar Grove Village. ✉ *Kings Canyon Scenic Byway, ¼ mi west of Cedar Grove Village, Cedar Grove* ☎ *559/565–3341* ⤴ *82 tent and RV sites* ♿ *Flush toilets, drinking water, bear boxes, fire grates, picnic tables, ranger station* ⚠ *Reservations not accepted* ▭ No credit cards ☉ Apr.–Oct.

★ Fodor'sChoice ⚠ **Sheep Creek Campground.** Of all the two parks'
$$ campgrounds, this is one of the prettiest. Tucked between Sheep Creek and the South Fork of the King River, it is a short stroll from Cedar Grove Village. ✉ *Off Kings Canyon Scenic Byway, 1 mi west of Cedar Grove Village, Cedar Grove* ☎ No phone ⤴ *111 tent and RV sites* ♿ *Flush toilets, drinking water, bear boxes, fire grates, picnic tables,*

CLOSE UP

Other California Parks

In addition to Yosemite, Sequoia, and Kings Canyon National Parks, the National Park Service oversees over 20 other parks in California. These are some of the more popular attractions:

■ **Cabrillo National Monument.** Juan Rodriguez Cabrillo was the first European explorer to set foot on the West Coast at or very near this spot in San Diego.

■ **Channel Islands National Park.** On these five islands not far from Santa Barbara, off California's Central Coast, diverse wildlife and vegetation are preserved.

■ **Death Valley National Park.** The country's lowest point in elevation can be found in this vast expanse west of Las Vegas. Temperatures here routinely top 115 degrees in summer.

■ **Devils Postpile National Monument.** The rock formations at this remote monument, accessible during the summer only by bus from Mammoth Ski Area, resemble stuck clumps of spaghetti.

■ **Joshua Tree National Park.** Find thousands of these unique trees and discover many good trails and camping possibilities in this large and popular park north of Palm Springs.

■ **Lassen Volcanic National Park.** The powerful geologic forces that created the Sierra Nevada can be explored here in Northern California. Mt. Lassen is a great summer hike destination.

■ **Lava Beds National Monument.** You're pretty much left on you own to explore dozens of subterranean holes in California's far north. Bring a powerful flashlight and a little courage.

■ **Muir Woods National Monument.** If you enjoy the sequoias of the Sierra parks, you are sure to like the coastal redwoods, too, of which there are many in this popular spot just north of San Francisco.

■ **Pinnacles National Monument.** Dramatic monoliths and spires from ancient volcanic activity make this monument, a few hours' drive south of the Bay Area, a special place.

■ **Redwood National Park.** Find more big coastal trees way up north in this park, which in a way is overshadowed by the nearby state parks that also feature redwoods.

---

ranger station ⚲ *Reservations not accepted* ▭ *No credit cards* ☽ *Late May–late Sept.*

$ ⌂ **South Fork Campground.** At 3,600 feet, this tiny campground is at the southernmost corner of Sequoia National Park. Do not think of staying here if you are nervous about being well off the beaten path. At the end of a dirt road, it best accommodates tent campers. A fee is only charged from May through Labor Day; in the off-season camping here is free. ✉ *End of South Fork Rd., 12 mi east of Generals Hwy. (Rte. 198),Foothills* 🕾 *No phone* ⇗ *10 tent sites* ⚬ *Pit toilets, running water (non-potable), bear boxes, fire grates, picnic tables* ⚱ *Reservations not accepted* 🚫 *No credit cards* ☉ *Open year-round.*

$$ ⚠ **Sunset Campground.** Many of the easiest trails through Grant Grove are adjacent to this large and gently hilly camp, near the giant sequoias at 6,500 feet. ✉ *Off Generals Hwy. (Rte. 198), near Grant Grove Visitor Center, Grant Grove* 🕾 *No phone* ⇗ *157 tent and RV sites* ⚬ *Flush toilets, drinking water, bear boxes, fire grates, picnic tables, public telephone* ⚱ *Reservations not accepted* 🚫 *No credit cards* ☉ *Late May–mid-Sept.*

OUTSIDE THE PARKS

¢ ⚠ **Big Meadows Campsites.** Sites at this camp at 7,600 feet elevation are scattered along Big Meadows Creek. The campsites have plenty of buffer room and the area is pretty, but facilities are limited. For example, there is no drinking water. RVs larger than 22 feet are not permitted. ✉ *Forest Rd. 14S11, 5 mi east off Generals Hwy. (Rte. 198), 7 mi southeast of Grant Grove, Sequoia National Forest* 🕾 *559/338–2251* ⇗ *30 tent and RV sites* ⚬ *Pit toilets, fire grates, picnic tables, no water* ⚱ *Reservations not accepted* 🚫 *No credit cards* ☉ *Late May–Oct.*

$ ⚠ **Hume Lake Campground.** Hume Lake is small and lovely, but gets busy in summer. The campground has many more sites for tents than RVs. It is at 5,200 feet elevation. RVs larger than 22 feet are not permitted. Reservations are accepted, but you must pay a $10 reservation fee. ✉ *Hume Lake Rd., 3 mi south of Kings Canyon Scenic Byway (Rte. 180), Sequoia National Forest* 🕾 *877/444–6777* ⊕ *www. reserveusa.com* ⇗ *60 tent sites, 14 RV sites* ⚬ *Flush toilets, drinking water, bear boxes, fire grates, picnic tables, public telephone, swimming (lake)* ⚱ *Reservations essential* 🚫 *AE, D, MC, V* ☉ *Late May–Oct.*

$ ⚠ **Landslide Campground.** On a creek that feeds nearby Hume Lake, this quiet camp is set at 5,800 feet and puts the rust in rustic. You almost need a four-wheel drive to get down here from the road, even though it's only a few hundred feet away. ✉ *Tenmile Rd., 12 mi northeast of Grant Grove*

7

CAMPING IN SEQUOIA/KINGS CANYON

Campground Name	Total # of Sites	# of RV sites	# of hook-ups	Drive-to sites	Hike-to sites	Flush toilets	Pit toilets	Drinking water	Showers	Fire grates/pits	Swimming	Boat access	Playground	Dump station	Ranger station	Public telephone	Reservations Possible	Daily fee per site	Dates open
Atwell Mill	21						Y	Y		Y						Y		$12	May-Oct
Azalea	110	110				Y		Y		Y						Y		$18	Y/R
Buckeye Flat	28					Y		Y		Y								$18	Apr-Sept
Canyon View	23					Y		Y		Y								$18	May-Oct
Cold Springs	40			31	9		Y	Y		Y					Y	Y		$12	May-Oct
Crystal Springs	36	36				Y		Y		Y				Y	Y	Y		$18	May-Sept
Dorst Creek	204	204				Y		Y		Y				Y	Y	Y	Y	$20	Jun-Sept
Lodgepole	203	203				Y		Y		Y					Y	Y	Y	$18-$20	Y/R
Moraine	120	120				Y		Y		Y					Y			$18	May-Oct

Y/R = year-round ** = Summer Only

Potwisha	42	42			Y		Y	Y					Y	Y	Y	$18	Y/R
Sentinel	82	82			Y		Y	Y							Y	$18	Apr-Oct
Sheep Creek	111	111			Y		Y	Y						Y	Y	$18	May-Nov
South Fork	10					Y		Y								$12**	Y/R
Sunset	157	157			Y		Y	Y					Y		Y	$18	May-Sept
Big Meadows	21					Y	Y	Y					Y		Y	$12	May-Oct
Hume Lake	110	110			Y		Y	Y					Y		Y	$18	Y/R
Landslide	28				Y		Y	Y								$18	Apr-Sept
Princess	23				Y	Y	Y	Y								$18	May-Oct
Stony Creek	40		31		Y		Y	Y						Y	Y	$12	May-Oct
Tenmile	36	36	9		Y		Y	Y					Y		Y	$18	May-Sept

Y/R = year-round   ** = Summer Only

off Hume Lake Rd. from Rte. 180, Sequoia National Forest ☎ *559/338–2251* ⇔ *9 tent sites* ⚄ *Pit toilets, drinking water, fire grates, picnic tables* ⚗ *Reservations not accepted* ▭ *No credit cards* ☉ *Late May–Oct.*

$ ⚠ **Princess Campground.** This camp is at 6,000 feet in Sequoia National Forest, near Hume Lake. There's a fee to use the nearby by unaffiliated dump station, which is the only one in the area. RVs larger than 25 feet are not recommended. Reservations are accepted (and are strongly recommended for August), but there's a $10 reservation fee. ✉ *Rte. 180, 6 mi north of Grant Grove entrance, Sequoia National Forest* ☎ *877/444–6777* ⊕ *www.reserveusa.com* ⇔ *50 tent sites, 40 RV sites* ⚄ *Pit toilets, drinking water, fire grates, picnic tables* ▭ *AE, D, MC, V* ☉ *Late May–late Sept.*

$ ⚠ **Stony Creek Campground.** Along a creek at 6,400 feet, this campground is between Sequoia and Kings Canyon parks. It is pretty close to the road, but also within walking distance of Stony Creek Lodge, which has showers and a general store. Reservations are accepted (and necessary), but you will have to pay a $10 reservation fee. ✉ *Generals Hwy. (Rte. 198), 13 mi south of Grant Grove, Sequoia National Forest* ☎ *877/444–6777* ⊕ *www.reserveusa.com* ⇔ *49 tent and RV sites* ⚄ *Flush toilets, drinking water, fire grates, picnic tables, public telephone* ⚗ *Reservations essential* ▭ *AE, D, MC, V* ☉ *Late May–Oct.*

¢ ⚠ **Tenmile Campground.** Above Hume Lake at 5,800 feet, this tiny camp is rustic for its lack of facilities. There is no drinking water. ✉ *Tenmile Rd., 5 mi northeast of Grant Grove, off Hume Lake Rd. from Rte. 180, Sequoia National Forest* ☎ *559/338–2251* ⇔ *13 tent and RV sites* ⚄ *Pit toilets, fire grates, picnic tables* ⚗ *Reservations not accepted* ☉ *Late May–Oct.*

What's Nearby

WORD OF MOUTH

"Mono Lake is well worth exploring. Go to the nature center (the turn is just north of town, a bit past the Mono Inn) and walk the boardwalk to the water's edge. Signs note the changing levels of the lake over the years—it is finally on its way to recovery. You will see an amazing number of birds on the water from the observation platform."

—Enzian

Updated
by Reed
Parsell

VAST GRANITE PEAKS AND GIANT SEQUOIAS are among the mind-boggling natural wonders of the Southern Sierra, many of which are protected in Yosemite, Sequoia, and Kings Canyon national parks. Outside the parks, pristine lakes, superb skiing, rolling hills, and small towns complete the picture of the Southern Sierra. Heading up Highway 395, on the Sierra's eastern side, you'll be rewarded with outstanding vistas of dramatic mountain peaks, including Mt. Whitney, the highest point in the contiguous United States, and Mono Lake, a vast but slowly vanishing expanse of deep blue—one of the most-photographed natural attractions in California.

GATEWAYS TO YOSEMITE NATIONAL PARK

Marking the southern end of the Sierra's gold-bearing mother lode, **Mariposa** is the last moderate-sized town before you enter Yosemite on Route 140. In addition to a mining museum, Mariposa has numerous shops, restaurants, and service stations. Motels and restaurants dot both sides of Route 41 as it cuts through the town of **Oakhurst,** a boomtown during the Gold Rush that is now a magnet for fast-food restaurants and chain stores. Oakhurst has a population of about 13,000 and sits 15 mi south of the park. Stroll Washington Street and see Old West storefronts with second-story porches and 19th-century hotels. The tiny town of **Lee Vining** is home to the eerily beautiful, salty Mono Lake, where millions of migratory birds nest. You'll pass through Lee Vining if you're coming to Yosemite through the eastern entrance (which is closed in winter). Visit **Mammoth Lakes,** about 40 mi southeast of Yosemite's Tioga Pass entrance, for excellent skiing and snowboarding in winter, with fishing, mountain biking, hiking, and horseback riding in summer. Nine deep-blue lakes form the Mammoth Lakes Basin, and another hundred dot the surrounding countryside. Devils Postpile National Monument sits at the base of Mammoth Mountain.

GATEWAYS TO SEQUOIA & KINGS CANYON NATIONAL PARKS

In the foothills of the Sierra along the Kaweah River, **Three Rivers** is a leafy hamlet whose livelihood depends largely on tourism from Sequoia and Kings Canyon. Close to Sequoia's Ash Mountain and Lookout Point (Mineral King) entrances, this is a good spot to find a room when park lodgings are full. **Visalia,** a city of 93,000, lies 46 mi east of Sequoia and 55 mi west of Kings Canyon on the edge of the San Joaquin Valley. Its vibrant downtown contains several good restaurants and B&Bs. Closest to Kings Canyon's Big Stump entrance, **Sanger** lies on the Kings River where it emerges from the foothills, about 40 minutes from the park. The agricultural community calls itself "the Nation's Christmas Tree City" and celebrates the holiday each year with a caravan to the General Grant Tree. **Fresno,** the main gateway to the Southern Sierra region, is about 55 mi west of Kings Canyon and about 65 mi southwest of Yosemite. California's sixth-largest city is sprawling and unglamorous, but it has all the amenities you'd expect of a major crossroads.

THREE RIVERS

8 mi south of Ash Mountain/Foothills entrance to Sequoia National Park on Hwy. 198.

In the foothills of the Sierra along the Kaweah River, this sparsely populated, serpentine hamlet serves as the main gateway town to Sequoia and Kings Canyon national parks. Its livelihood depends largely on tourism from the parks, courtesy of two markets, a few service stations, banks, a post office, and several lodgings, which are good spots to find a room when park accommodations are full.

WHERE TO EAT

$$–$$$ ✕**Gateway Restaurant & Lodge.** The patio of this raucous roadhouse overlooks the roaring Kaweah River as it plunges out of the high country, and though the food is nothing special, the location makes up for it. Standouts include baby back ribs and eggplant parmigiana; there's also a cocktail lounge, and guest rooms are available for overnight visitors. Breakfast isn't served weekdays; dinner reservations are essential on weekends. ✉*45978 Sierra Dr.* ☎*559/561–4133* ▭*AE, D, MC, V.*

$ ✕**We Three Bakery.** This friendly, popular-with-the-locals spot packs lunches for trips into the nearby national parks; the restaurant is also open for breakfast. ✉*43688 Sierra Dr.* ⊕*www.wethreerestaurant.com* ☎*559/561–4761* ▭*MC, V.*

WHERE TO STAY

$–$$ ▦**Buckeye Tree Lodge.** Every room at this two-story motel has a patio facing a sun-dappled grassy lawn, right on the banks of the Kaweah River. Accommodations are simple and well kept, and the lodge sits a mere quarter mile from the park gate. Book well in advance for the summer. The

8

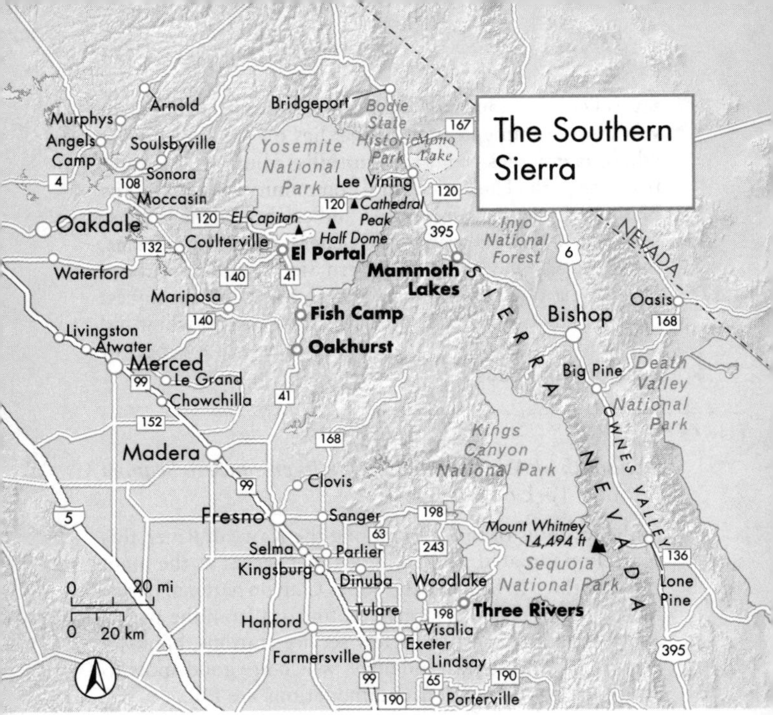

jointly owned **Sequoia Village Inn** (☎*559/561–3652*), across the highway, was extensively renovated in 2006 and is another good option; accommodation options there are cottages, cabins, and chalets. **Pros:** scenic setting; clean, popular. **Cons:** rooms could use a renovation. ✉*46000 Sierra Dr., Hwy. 198* ☎*559/561–5900* 🌐*www.buckeyetree.com* *11 rooms, 1 cottage* *In-room: Wi-Fi. In-hotel: pool, some pets allowed, no-smoking rooms* *AE, D, DC, MC, V* *CP.*

$–$$ **Lazy J Ranch Motel.** Surrounded by 12 acres of green lawns and a split-rail fence, the Lazy J is a modest, well-kept compound of freestanding cottages near the banks of the Kaweah River. A few hundred feet off Highway 198, it's also very quiet and has an inviting pool as its centerpiece. Some rooms have gas fireplaces; all have coffeemakers. **Pros:** friendly service, rustic, spacious. **Cons:** on the far side of town from the national park. ✉*39625 Sierra Dr., Hwy. 198,* ☎*559/561–4449 or 888/315–2378* 🌐*www.bvilazyj.com* *18 rooms, 5 cottages, 2 2-bedroom houses* *In-room: kitchen (some), refrigerator. In-hotel: pool, laundry facilities, some pets allowed (fee), no-smoking rooms* *AE, D, MC, V* *CP.*

$–$$ ⛄**Sequoia Motel.** An old-fashioned, single-story, mom-and-pop motel, the Sequoia stands out with such extra touches as country-style quilts and mismatched Americana furnishings that lend a retro charm to the meticulously clean rooms. There are also one- and two-bedroom cottages with full kitchens. **Pros:** cute property; friendly service. **Cons:** some guests say it could be cleaner. ⌧*43000 Sierra Dr., Hwy. 198, Box 145* ☎*559/561–4453* ⊕*www.sequoiamotel. com* ⇱*11 rooms, 3 cottages* ⌂*In-room: no phone, kitchen (some), VCR (some), Wi-Fi. In-hotel: pool, laundry facilities, no-smoking rooms* ⊟*AE, D, MC, V* ⦿*EP.*

$–$$ ⛄**Sierra Lodge.** If you're on a budget, this vintage-1960s cinder-block motel has the cheapest rooms in town. They're in passable shape, but nothing special—though some have patios, wood-burning fireplaces, and good mountain views. Outside there's a large deck with plastic flowers on it. ⌧*43175 Sierra Dr.* ☎*559/561–3681 or 888/575–2555* ⊕*www.sierra-lodge.com* ⇱*17 rooms, 5 suites* ⌂*In-room: kitchen (some), refrigerator, Wi-Fi. In-hotel: pool, no-smoking rooms, some pets allowed (fee)* ⊟*AE, D, DC, MC, V* ⦿*CP.*

SPORTS & THE OUTDOORS

Kaweah White Water Adventures (☎*559/561–1000 or 800/229–8658* ⊕*www.kaweah-whitewater.com*) guides two-hour and full-day rafting trips in spring and early summer, with some Class III rapids; longer trips may include some Class IV.

For hourly horseback rides or riding lessons, contact **Wood 'n' Horse Training Stables** (⌧*42846 North Fork Dr., Three Rivers,* ☎*559/561–4268* ⊕*www.wdnhorse.com*).

OFF THE BEATEN PATH. **Hume Lake,** built by loggers in the early 1900s, is now the site of several church-affiliated camps, a gas station, and a public campground. Just outside Kings Canyon's borders, the small lake has views of the mountains in the distance. ⌧*Hume Lake Rd., off Kings Canyon Hwy., 8 mi northeast of Grant Grove, .*

MID-CENTRAL VALLEY

FROM VISALIA TO FRESNO

The Mid-Central Valley extends over three counties—Tulare, Kings, and Fresno. From Visalia, Highway 198 winds east 35 mi to Generals Highway, which passes through Sequoia and Kings Canyon national parks. From Fresno, Highway 180 snakes east 55 mi to Sequoia and Kings Canyon while Highway 41 leads north 95 mi to Yosemite National Park.

VISALIA

35 mi west of Sequoia and Kings Canyon National Parks on Hwy. 198

Visalia's combination of a reliable agricultural economy and civic pride has yielded perhaps the most vibrant downtown in the Central Valley. A clear day's view of the Sierra from Main Street is spectacular, if sadly rare due to smog and dust, and even Sunday night can find the streets busy with pedestrians.

Founded in 1852, the town contains many historic homes; ask for a free guide at the **visitor center** (⊠*220 N. Santa Fe St.* ☎*559/734–5876* ☉*Mon. 10–5, Tues.–Fri. 8:30–5*).

The **Chinese Cultural Center,** housed in a pagoda-style building, mounts exhibits about Asian art and culture. ⊠*500 S. Akers Rd., at Hwy. 198,* ☎*559/625–4545* ☜*Free* ☉*Wed.– Sun. 11–6.*

☾ In oak-shaded **Mooney Grove Park** you can picnic alongside duck ponds, rent a boat for a ride around the lagoon, and view a replica of the famous *End of the Trail* statue. The original, designed by James Earl Fraser for the 1915 Panama-Pacific International Exposition, is now in the Cowboy Hall of Fame in Oklahoma. ⊠*27000 S. Mooney Blvd., 5 mi south of downtown* ☎*559/733–6291* ☜*$6 per car, free in winter (dates vary)* ☉*Late May–early Sept., weekdays 8–7, weekends 8 AM–9 PM; early Sept.–Oct. and Mar.–late May, Mon., Thurs., and Fri. 8–5, weekends 8–7; Nov.–Feb., Thurs.–Mon. 8–5.*

The indoor-outdoor **Tulare County Museum** contains several re-created environments from the pioneer era. Also on display are Yokuts tribal artifacts (basketry, arrowheads, clamshell-necklace currency) as well as saddles, guns, dolls, quilts, and gowns. At this writing, a $1.45 million replacement building was expected to open in 2009. ⊠*Mooney Grove Park, 27000 S. Mooney Blvd., 5 mi south of downtown* ☎*559/733–6616* ☜*Free with park entrance fee of $6* ☉*Weekdays 10–4, weekends 1–4.*

Trails at the 324-acre **Kaweah Oaks Preserve,** a wildlife sanctuary off the main road to Sequoia National Park, lead past majestic valley oak, sycamore, cottonwood, and willow trees. Among the 134 bird species you might spot are hawks, hummingbirds, and great blue herons. Lizards, coyotes, and cottontails also live here. ✛*Follow Hwy. 198 for 7 mi east of Visalia, turn north on Rd. 182, and proceed ½ mi to gate on left side* ☎*559/738–0211* ⊕*www.sequoia riverlands.org* ⊠*Free* ☉*Daily sunrise–sunset.*

WHERE TO EAT

$$–$$$ ✕**Café 225.** This downtown favorite combines high ceilings and warm yellow walls with soft chatter and butcher-papered tables to create an elegance that's relaxed enough for kids. The basic menu of pastas and grilled items is highlighted with unusual treats, such as *scusami* (calzone with melting Gorgonzola and tomato, basil, and garlic). ⊠*225 W. Main St.* ☎*559/733–2967* ⊕*www.cafe225.com* ▤*AE, D, DC, MC, V* ☉*Closed Sun.*

$–$$ ✕**Henry Salazar's.** Traditional Mexican food with a contemporary twist is served at this restaurant that uses fresh ingredients from local farms. Bring your appetite if you expect to finish the Burrito Fantastico, a large flour tortilla stuffed with your choice of meat, beans, and chili sauce, and smothered with melted Monterey Jack cheese. Another signature dish is grilled salmon with lemon-butter sauce. Colorfully painted walls, soft reflections from candles in wall niches, and color-coordinated tablecloths and napkins make the atmosphere cozy and restful. ⊠*123 W. Main St.* ☎*559/741–7060* ▤*AE, D, MC, V.*

★ **Fodor's**Choice ✕**The Vintage Press.** Built in 1966, the Vintage
$$–$$$ Press is the best restaurant in the Central Valley. Cut-glass doors and bar fixtures decorate the artfully designed rooms. The California–Continental cuisine includes dishes such as crispy veal sweetbreads with a port-wine sauce, and a bacon-wrapped filet mignon stuffed with mushrooms. The chocolate Grand Marnier cake is a standout among the homemade desserts and ice creams. The wine list has more than 900 selections. ⊠*216 N. Willis St.* ☎*559/733–3033* ⊕*www.thevintagepress.com* ▤*AE, DC, MC, V.*

WHERE TO STAY

$$ ▦**Ben Maddox House.** Housed in a building dating to 1876, this homey B&B offers the best of all worlds: plush beds, a cool swimming pool, and excellent service remind you you're on vacation; private bathrooms and dining tables

8

on the sunny porch make the surroundings homey and comfortable. All rooms have Wi-Fi access. **Pros:** modern-day comforts in a 19th-century home; renowned full breakfasts. **Cons:** it can be hot and stinky outside. ⊠*601 N. Encina St.* ☎*559/739–0721 or 800/401–9800* ⊕*www.benmaddoxhouse.com* ⬧*3 rooms* ⬧*In-room: Internet, Wi-Fi. In-hotel: pool, no-smoking rooms* ⊟*AE, D, MC, V* ⦿*BP.*

$ 🖼**The Spalding House.** This restored colonial-revival B&B is decked out with antiques, Oriental rugs, handcrafted woodwork, and glass doors. The house, built in 1901, has suites with separate sitting rooms and private baths. The quiet neighborhood, also home to the Ben Maddox House, offers a place for one of life's simple pleasures: an evening walk on lovely, tree-lined streets. **Pros:** warm feel; old-time atmosphere; great place for a twilight stroll. **Cons:** only three rooms. ⊠*631 N. Encina St.* ☎*559/739–7877* ⊕*www.thespaldinghouse.com* ⬧*3 suites* ⬧*In-room: no phone, no TV. In-hotel: no-smoking rooms* ⊟*AE, MC, V* ⦿*BP.*

FRESNO

55 mi west of Sequoia & Kings Canyon National Parks via Highway 180, 95 mi south of Yosemite National Park via Highway 41

Sprawling Fresno, with more than 486,000 people, is the center of the richest agricultural county in the United States. Cotton, grapes, and tomatoes are among the major crops; poultry and milk are also important. About 75 ethnic groups, including Armenians, Laotians, and Indians, call Fresno home. The city has a vibrant arts scene, several public parks, and an abundance of low-price restaurants. The Tower District—with its chic restaurants, coffeehouses, and boutiques—is the trendy spot. Pulitzer Prize–winning playwright and novelist William Saroyan (*The Time of Your Life, The Human Comedy*) was born here in 1908.

☾ **Roeding Park.** This tree-shaded expanse is a place of respite on hot summer days; it has picnic areas, playgrounds, tennis courts, horseshoe pits, and a zoo.

The most striking exhibit at **Chaffee Zoological Gardens** (☎*559/498–2671* ⊕*www.chaffeezoo.org* 🎫*$7* ☻*Feb.–Oct., daily 9–4; Nov.–Jan., daily 10–3*) is the tropical rain forest, where you'll encounter exotic birds along the paths and bridges. Elsewhere on the grounds you'll find tigers, grizzly bears, sea lions, tule elk, camels, elephants, and hooting siamangs. Also here, are a high-tech reptile house and a petting zoo.

A train, little race cars, paddleboats, and other rides for kids are among the amusements that operate March through November at **Playland** (☎559/233–3980 ☉Wed.–Fri. 11–5, weekends 10–6).

Children can explore attractions with fairy-tale themes at **Rotary Storyland** (☎559/264–2235 ☉Weekdays 11–5, weekends 10–6), which is also open March through November. ⊠Olive and Belmont Aves. ☎559/498–1551 ☎$1 per vehicle at park entrance, Playland rides require tokens, Storyland $4.

☾ **Fresno Metropolitan Museum.** The museum, whose delayed renovation project was completed in late 2008, mounts art, history, and hands-on science exhibits, many of them quite innovative. The William Saroyan History Gallery presents a riveting introduction in words and pictures to the author's life and times. ⊠1515 Van Ness Ave. ☎559/441–1444 ⊕www.fresnomet.org ☎$8 ☉Tues., Wed., and Fri.–Sun. 11–5.

Legion of Valor Museum. This is a real find for military-history buffs of all ages. It has German bayonets and daggers, a Japanese Nambu pistol, a Gatling gun, and an extensive collection of Japanese, German, and American uniforms. The staff is extremely enthusiastic. ⊠2425 Fresno St. ☎559/498–0510 ⊕www.legionofvalor.com ☎Free ☉Mon.–Sat. 10–3.

Meux Home Museum. The restored 1889 Victorian displays furnishings typical of early Fresno. Guided tours proceed from the front parlor to the backyard carriage house. ⊠Tulare and R Sts. ☎559/233–8007 ⊕www.meux.mus. ca.us ☎$5 ☉Fri.–Sun. noon–3:30.

Fresno Art Museum. Exhibits here include American, Mexican, and French art; highlights of the permanent collection include pre-Columbian works and graphic art from the postimpressionist period. The 152-seat Bonner Auditorium is the site of lectures, films, and concerts. ⊠Radio Park, 2233 N. 1st St. ☎559/441–4221 ⊕www.fresnoart museum.org ☎$4; free Sun. ☉Tues., Wed., and Fri.–Sun. 11–5, Thurs. 11–8.

★ **Woodward Park.** The Central Valley's largest urban park has 300 acres of jogging trails, picnic areas, and play-grounds in the northern reaches of the city. It's especially pretty in spring, when plum and cherry trees, magnolias, and camellias bloom. Outdoor concerts take place in summer. The **Shinzen Friendship Garden** has a teahouse, a koi pond, arched bridges, a waterfall, and Japanese art. ✉*Audubon Dr. and Friant Rd.* ☎*559/621–2900* ✎*$3 per car Feb.–Oct.; additional $3 for Shinzen Garden* ☉*Apr.–Oct., daily 7 AM–10 PM; Nov.–Mar., daily 7–7.*

☾ **Forestiere Underground Gardens.** Sicilian immigrant Baldasare
★ Forestiere spent four decades (1906–46) carving out the subterranean realm of rooms, tunnels, grottoes, alcoves, and arched passageways that once extended for more than 10 acres between Highway 99 and busy, mall-pocked Shaw Avenue. Only a fraction of Forestiere's prodigious output is on view, but you can tour his underground living quarters, including bedrooms (one with a fireplace), the kitchen, living room, and bath, as well as a fishpond and auto tunnel. Skylights allow exotic full-grown fruit trees, including one that bears seven kinds of citrus as a result of grafting, to flourish more than 20 feet belowground. The gardens were extensively renovated in 2007. ✉*5021 W. Shaw Ave., 2 blocks east of Hwy. 99* ☎*559/271–0734* ⊕*www.under groundgardens.info* ✎*$12* ☉*Tours weekends 11–2 year-round; also Fri. in summer. Call for other tour times.*

Kearney Mansion Museum. The drive along palm-lined Kearney Boulevard is one of the best reasons to visit this mansion that stands in shaded 225-acre **Kearney Park.** The century-old home of M. Theo Kearney, Fresno's onetime "raisin king," is accessible only by taking a guided 45-minute tour. ✉*7160 W. Kearney Blvd., 6 mi west of Fresno* ☎*559/441–0862* ✎*Museum $5; park entry $4 (waived for museum visitors)* ☉*Park 7 AM–10 PM; museum tours Fri.–Sun. at 1, 2, and 3.*

OFF THE BEATEN PATH. **Along the Blossom Trail, roughly halfway between Fresno and Visalia, the colorful handiwork of local quilters is on display at the Mennonite Quilt Center (** ✉*1012 G St., take Manning Ave. exit off Hwy. 99 and head east 12 mi, Reedley* ☎*559/638–3560*). **The center is open weekdays 10–5 and Saturday 10–4, but try to visit on Monday (except holidays) between 8 and noon, when two dozen quilters stitch, patch, and chat over coffee. Prime viewing time—with the largest number of** quilts—is in February and March, before the center's early-April auction. Ask a docent to take you to the locked upstairs room, where most of the quilts hang; she'll explain the fine points of patterns such as the Log Cabin Romance, the Dahlia, and the Snowball-Star. Admission is free.

WHERE TO EAT

$ ✕**Guadalajara.** Authentic Mexican food served in a friendly atmosphere draws locals to this eatery. On the site of what had been El Rosal, Guadalajara has two other restaurants in greater Fresno. ⊠*5730 N. 1st St.* ☎*559/437–9614* ⊟*AE, D, MC, V* ⊘*Closed Sun.*

$ ✕**Irene's Café Dining.** Downtown workers pack this Tower District restaurant at lunchtime. Handmade, half-pound burgers are the most popular, and most filling, items on the menu. Other popular dishes include the smoked ham and melted Swiss cheese sandwich served on a hard roll, and fresh salads. For breakfast, homemade granola, huge buttermilk pancakes, and the Denver omelet (with ham, onions, and green peppers) will fill up even those with the heartiest of appetites. ⊠*747 E. Olive Ave.* ☎*559/237–9919* ⊕*www.tower2000.com* ⊟*AE, D, MC, V.*

$$ ✕**La Rocca's Ristorante Italiano.** The sauces that top these pasta and meat dishes will make your taste buds sing. The rich tomato sauce, which comes with or without meat, is fresh and tangy. The marsala sauce—served on either chicken or veal—is rich but not overpowering. Typical red-sauce dishes such as spaghetti, rigatoni, and lasagna are offered here, but you'll also be happily surprised with more adventurous offerings such as the bow-tie pasta with cream, peas, bacon, tomato sauce, and olive oil. Pizzas also are served. ⊠*6735 N. 1st St.* ☎*559/431–1278* ⊟*AE, MC, V* ⊘*No lunch weekends.*

$$–$$$ ✕**Tahoe Joe's.** This restaurant is known for its steaks—rib eye, strip, or filet mignon. Other selections include the slow-roasted prime rib, center-cut pork chops, and chicken breast served with a whiskey-peppercorn sauce. The baked potato that accompanies almost every dish is loaded table-side with your choice of butter, sour cream, chives, and bacon bits. Tahoe Joe's has two Fresno locations. ⊠*7006 N. Cedar Ave.* ☎*559/299–9740* ; ⊠ *2700 W. Shaw Ave.,* ☎*559/277–8028* ⊕*www.tahoejoes.com* ⬧*Reservations not accepted* ⊟*AE, D, MC, V* ⊘*No lunch.*

8

WHERE TO STAY

$$–$$$ 🖼 **Piccadilly Inn Shaw.** This two-story property has 7½ attractively landscaped acres and a big swimming pool. The sizeable rooms have king- and queen-size beds, robes, ironing boards, and coffeemakers; some have fireplaces and wireless Internet access. **Pros:** big rooms; nice pool; best lodging option in town. **Cons:** some visitors complain of a smell; some rooms are showing wear; neighborhood is somewhat sketchy. ⊠*2305 W. Shaw Ave.,* ☎*559/226–3850* ⊕*www.piccadillyinn.com* ⇔*194 rooms, 5 suites* ⟐*In-room: refrigerator, Internet, Wi-Fi. In-hotel: restaurant, pool, gym, laundry facilities, laundry service, no-smoking rooms* ⊟*AE, D, DC, MC, V.*

$–$$ 🖼 **La Quinta Inn.** Rooms are ample at this basic three-story motel near downtown. Most rooms have large desks that prove helpful for business travelers. **Pros:** comfortable, predictable, near key sites. **Cons:** somewhat drab, hard beds. ⊠*2926 Tulare St.* ☎*559/442–1110 or 866/725–1661* ⊕*www.lq.com* ⇔*129 rooms* ⟐*In-room: refrigerator (some), Internet. In-hotel: pool, gym, no-smoking rooms* ⊟*AE, D, DC, MC, V* ⦿*CP.*

SPORTS & THE OUTDOORS

Kings River Expeditions (⊠*211 N. Van Ness Ave.* ☎*559/233– 4881 or 800/846–3674* ⊕*www.kingsriver.com*) arranges one- and two-day white-water rafting trips on the Kings River. **Wild Water Adventures** (⊠*11413 E. Shaw Ave., Clovis* ☎*559/299–9453 or 800/564–9453* ⊕*www.wildwater.net* ⛱*$26, $17 after 3* PM), a 52-acre water park about 10 mi east of Fresno, is open from late May to early September.

SOUTH OF YOSEMITE

FROM OAKHURST TO EL PORTAL

Several gateway towns to the south and west of Yosemite National Park, most within an hour's drive of Yosemite Valley, have food, lodging, and other services. Highway 140 heads east from the San Joaquin Valley to El Portal and Yosemite's west entrance. Highway 41 heads north from Fresno to Oakhurst and Fish Camp to Yosemite's south entrance.

OAKHURST

40 mi north of Fresno and 23 mi south of Yosemite National Park's south entrance on Hwy. 41.

Motels, restaurants, gas stations, and small businesses line both sides of Highway 41 as it cuts through Oakhurst. This is the last sizeable community before Yosemite and a good spot to find provisions. There are two major grocery stores near the intersection of highways 41 and 49. Three miles north of town, then 6 mi east, honky-tonky Bass Lake is a popular spot in summer with motorboaters, Jet Skiers, and families looking to cool off in the reservoir.

A couple of miles south outside the park's south entrance, the **Yosemite Mountain Sugar Pine Railroad** has a narrow-gauge steam train that chugs through the forest. It follows 4 mi of the route the Madera Sugar Pine Lumber Company cut through the forest in 1899 to harvest timber. The steam train, as well as Jenny railcars, run year-round on fluctuating schedules; call for details. On Saturday (and Wednesday in summer), the Moonlight Special dinner excursion (reservations essential) includes a picnic with toe-tappin' music by the Sugar Pine Singers, followed by a sunset steam-train ride. ⊠ *56001 Rte. 41, Fish Camp* ☎ *559/683–7273* ⊕ *www.ymsprr.com* ☒ *$17.50 steam train; Jenny railcar $13.50; Moonlight Special $46 (adults only)* ☉ *Mar.–Oct., 10–2 daily; extended hrs in summer*

WHERE TO EAT

★ Fodor'sChoice ✕**Erna's Elderberry House.** Austrian-born Erna
$$$$ Kubin-Clanin, the grande dame of Château du Sureau, has created a culinary oasis, stunning for its elegance, gorgeous setting, and impeccable service. Crimson walls and dark beams accent the dining room's high ceilings, and arched windows reflect the glow of candles. The seasonal six-course prix-fixe dinner can be paired with superb wines, a must-do for oenophiles. When the waitstaff places all the plates on the table in perfect synchronicity, you know this will be a meal to remember. Premeal drinks are served in the former wine cellar. ⊠*48688 Victoria La.* ☎*559/683–6800* ⊕*www.elderberryhouse.com* ⚱*Reservations essential* ☐*AE, D, MC, V* ☉*No lunch Mon.–Sat.*

$–$$ ✕**Yosemite Fork Mountain House.** Bypass Oakhurst's greasy spoons and instead head to this family restaurant, 3 mi north of the Highway 49/Highway 41 intersection, with an open-beam ceiling and a canoe in the rafters. Portions are huge. Expect standard American fare: bacon and eggs at breakfast, sandwiches at lunch, and pastas and steaks at dinner. ⊠*Hwy. 41, at Bass Lake turnoff* ☎*559/683–5191* ⚭*Reservations not accepted* ⊟*D, MC, V.*

WHERE TO STAY

$$–$$$ 🏨**Best Western Yosemite Gateway Inn.** Oakhurst's best motel
☾ has carefully tended landscaping and rooms with attractive dark-wood American colonial–style furniture and slightly kitsch hand-painted wall murals of Yosemite. Kids love choosing between the two pools. **Pros:** pretty close to Yosemite; clean; comfortable. **Cons:** chain property; some walls may seem thin. ⊠*40530 Hwy. 41* ☎*559/683–2378 or 888/256–8042* ⊕*www.yosemitegatewayinn.com* ⇗*121 rooms, 16 suites* ⚭*In-room: refrigerator, Internet. In-hotel: restaurant, bar, pools, laundry facilities, no-smoking rooms* ⊟*AE, D, MC, V.*

★ **Fodor**ʾsChoice 🏨**Château du Sureau.** This romantic inn, adjacent
$$$$ to Erna's Elderberry House, is straight out of one of Grimm's fairy tales. From the moment you drive through the wrought-iron gates and up to the enchanting castle, you feel pampered. Every room is impeccably styled with European antiques, sumptuous fabrics, fresh-cut flowers, and oversize soaking tubs. Fall asleep by the glow of a crackling fire amid feather-light goose-down pillows and Italian linens, awaken to a hearty European breakfast in the dining room, then relax with a game of chess in the grand salon beneath an exquisite mural—or play chess on the giant board amid tall pine trees off the impeccably landscaped garden trail. Cable TV is available by request only. In 2006 the Château added a stunning spa. **Pros:** luxurious, spectacular property. **Cons:** you'll need to take out a second mortgage to stay here. ⊠*48688 Victoria La.* ☎*559/683–6860* ⊕*www.elderberryhouse.com* ⇗*10 rooms, 1 villa* ⚭*In-room: Internet, Wi-Fi. In-hotel: restaurant, bar, pool, spa, laundry service, no kids under 8, no-smoking rooms* ⊟*AE, MC, V* ❑*BP.*

$$–$$$ 🏨**Homestead Cottages.** If you're looking for peace and quiet,
★ this is the place. Serenity is the order of the day at this secluded getaway in Ahwahnee, 6 mi west of Oakhurst. On 160 acres of rolling hills that once held a Miwok village, these cottages have gas fireplaces, living rooms, fully equipped kitchens, and queen-size beds; the largest sleeps six. The cottages, hand-built by the owners out of real adobe bricks, are stocked with soft robes, oversize towels,

and paperback books. **Pros:** remote; quiet; friendly ov
Cons: remote; some urbanites might find it *too* qu.
✉*41110 Rd. 600, 2½ mi off Hwy. 49, Ahwahnee*
☎*559/683–0495 or 800/483–0495* ⊕*www.homestead
cottages.com* ⤶*5 cottages, 1 loft* ⚷*In-room: no phone,
kitchen. In-hotel: no-smoking rooms* ▤*AE, D, MC, V.*

SPORTS & THE OUTDOORS
Bass Lake Water Sports & Marina (✉*Bass Lake Reservoir,*
☎*559/642–3565*), 3 mi north and 6 mi east of Oakhurst,
rents ski boats, patio boats, and fishing boats. In summer
the noisy reservoir gets packed shortly after it opens at
8 AM. There's also a restaurant and snack bar.

MAMMOTH AREA

A jewel in the vast eastern Sierra Nevada, the Mammoth
Lakes area lies just east of the Sierra crest, on the back side
of Yosemite and the Ansel Adams Wilderness. It's a place of
rugged beauty, where giant sawtooth mountains drop into
the vast deserts of the Great Basin. In winter, 11,053-foot-
high Mammoth Mountain provides the finest skiing and
snowboarding in California—sometimes as late as June or
even July. Once the snows melt, Mammoth transforms itself
into a warm-weather playground, with fishing, mountain
biking, golfing, hiking, and horseback riding. Nine deep-
blue lakes are spread through the Mammoth Lakes Basin,
and another 100 lakes dot the surrounding countryside.
Crater-pocked Mammoth Mountain hasn't had a major
eruption for 50,000 years, but the region is alive with hot
springs, mud pots, fumaroles, and steam vents.

8

MAMMOTH LAKES

*30 mi south of eastern edge of Yosemite National Park
on U.S. 395.*

Much of the architecture in Mammoth Lakes (elevation
7,800 feet) is of the faux-alpine variety. You'll find increasingly sophisticated dining and lodging options here. International real-estate developers joined forces with Mammoth
Mountain Ski Area and have worked hard to transform the
once sleepy town into a chic ski destination. The Mammoth
Mountain Village is the epicenter of all the recent devel-
opment. Winter is high season at Mammoth; in summer
room rates plummet. Highway 203 heads west from U.S.
395, becoming Main Street as it passes through the town of

minute walk from ostpile National ranger station takes :ologic formation of smooth, vertical basalt columns sculpted by volcanic and glacial forces. A short but steep trail winds to the top of the 60-foot-high rocky cliff, where you'll find a bird's-eye view of the columns. A fairly easy 2-mi hike past the Postpile leads to the monument's second scenic wonder, **Rainbow Falls,** where a branch of the San Joaquin River plunges more than 100 feet over a lava ledge. When the water hits the pool below, sunlight turns the mist into a spray of color. Walk down a bit from the top of the falls for the best view.

Devils Postpile National Monument is only accessible from June or July through late October. To get here, you must take the shuttle bus from the Adventure Center at the Mammoth Mountain Main Lodge gondola building. The shuttle departs approximately every 20 to 30 minutes, generally from 7 AM to 7 PM, with the last ride out of Red's Valley (the area surrounding Devils Postpile) at 7:30. The shuttle stops running by the end of September. ⊠ *Hwy. 203, 13 mi west of Mammoth Lakes* ☎ *760/934–2289, 760/924–5502 shuttle-bus information* ⊕ *www.nps.gov/depo*

🎟 *$7 per person, not to exceed $20 per carload* ⊗ *Shuttle mid-June–mid-Sept., daily.*

Hot Creek Geological Site/ Hot Creek Fish Hatchery. Forged by an ancient volcanic eruption, the Hot Creek Geological Site is a landscape of boiling hot springs, fumaroles, and occasional geysers about 10 mi southeast of the town of Mammoth Lakes. You can soak in hot springs (at your own risk, bathing suits mandatory) or look down from the parking area into the canyon to view the steaming volcanic features, a very cool sight indeed. Fly-fishing for trout is popular upstream from the springs. En route to the geologic site is the outdoor Hot Creek Fish Hatchery, the breeding ponds for many of the fish (typically 3 to 5 million annually) with which the state stocks eastern Sierra lakes and rivers. In recent years, budget cuts have drastically reduced these numbers, but locals have formed foundations to keep the hatchery going. For more details, take the worthwhile self-guided tour. ⊠ *Hot Creek Hatchery Rd., east of U.S. 395* ☎ *760/924–5500 for geological site, 760/934–2664 for hatchery* 🎟 *Free* ⊗ *Site daily sunrise–sunset; hatchery June–Oct., daily 8–4, depending on snowfall.*

Mammoth Lakes, and later Minaret Road (which makes a right turn) as it continues west to the Mammoth Mountain ski area and Devils Postpile National Monument.

The lakes of the **Mammoth Lakes Basin,** reached by Lake Mary Road off Highway 203 southwest of town, are popular for fishing and boating in summer. First comes Twin Lakes, at the far end of which is Twin Falls, where water cascades 300 feet over a shelf of volcanic rock. Also popular are Lake Mary, the largest lake in the basin; Lake Mamie; and Lake George. Horseshoe Lake is the only lake in which you can swim.

The glacier-carved sawtooth spires of the Minarets, the remains of an ancient lava flow, are best viewed from the **Minaret Vista,** off Highway 203 west of Mammoth Lakes.

★ Fodor'sChoice Even if you don't ski, ride the **Panorama Gondola** ☾ to see Mammoth Mountain, the aptly named dormant volcano that gives Mammoth Lakes its name. Gondolas serve skiers in winter and mountain bikers and sightseers in summer. The high-speed, eight-passenger gondolas whisk you from the chalet to the summit, where you can read about the area's volcanic history and take in top-of-the-world views. Standing high above the tree line atop this dormant volcano, you can look west 150 mi across the state to the Coastal Range; to the east are the highest peaks of Nevada and the Great Basin beyond. You won't find a better view of the Sierra High Country without climbing. Remember, though, that the air is thin at the 11,053-foot summit; carry water, and don't overexert yourself. The boarding area is at the Main Lodge. ⊠*Off Hwy. 203* ☏*760/934–2571 Ext. 2400 information, Ext. 3850 gondola station* ☏*$18 in summer* ☾*July 4–Oct., daily 9–4:30; Nov.–July 3, daily 8:30–4.*

The overwhelming popularity of Mammoth Mountain has generated a real-estate boom, and a huge new complex of shops, restaurants, and luxury accommodations, called the **Village at Mammoth,** has become the town's tourist center. Parking can be tricky. There's a lot across the street on Minaret Road; pay attention to time limits.

WHERE TO EAT

$$ ✕**Alpenrose.** Hearty portions of classic Swiss-inspired dishes such as Wiener schnitzel, rib-eye steak au poivre, and cheese fondue are served at cozy booths beneath alpine murals. There's also a good selection of reasonably priced wines.

If you're on a budget, come before 6:30 PM for the early-bird special. ⊠*343 Old Mammoth Rd.* ☎*760/934–3077* ⚑*Reservations essential* ⊟*AE, D, MC, V* ☉*No lunch Mon.–Sat. in winter.*

$–$$ ✕**Burgers.** Don't even think about coming to this bustling restaurant unless you're hungry. Burgers is known, appropriately enough, for its burgers and sandwiches, and everything comes in mountainous portions. At lunch try the sourdough patty melt, at dinner the pork ribs; salads are great all day. The seasoned french fries are delicious. ⊠*6118 Minaret Rd., across from the Village* ☎*760/934–6622* ⊟*MC, V* ☉*Closed 2 wks in May and 4–6 wks in Oct.–Nov.*

¢–$ ✕**Hot Chicks Rotisserie.** Owned by the chef of Convict Lake Restaurant—so you know it's got to be good—Hot Chicks makes rotisserie chicken to eat in or take out, as well as pulled-pork sandwiches and grilled tri-tip steak. Best of all, a family of four can eat for $30. ⊠*452 Old Mammoth Rd.* ☎*760/934–4900* ⚑*Reservations not accepted* ⊟*MC, V.*

$$–$$$$ ✕**The Mogul.** The Mogul has been around for a long time. It's the place to go when you want a straightforward steak and salad bar. The only catch is that the waiters cook your steak—and the result depends on the waiter's experience. But generally you can't go wrong. And kids love it. The knotty-pine-panel walls lend a woodsy touch and a taste of Mammoth before all the development. ⊠*Mammoth Tavern Rd. off Old Mammoth Rd.* ☎*760/934–3039* ⊟*AE, D, MC, V* ☉*No lunch.*

$$$ ✕**Petra's Bistro & Wine Bar.** Other restaurateurs speak highly of Petra's as the most convivial restaurant in town. Its lovely ambience—quiet, dark, and warm—complements the carefully prepared meat main dishes and seasonal sides, and the more than two dozen California wines from behind the bar. The service is top-notch. Downstairs, the Clocktower Cellar bar provides a late-night, rowdy alternative—or chaser. ⊠*6080 Minaret Rd.* ☎*760/934–3500* ⚑*Reservations essential* ⊟*AE, D, DC, MC, V* ☉*No lunch.*

✕**Restaurant at Convict Lake.** Tucked in a tiny valley ringed by mile-high peaks, Convict Lake is one of the most spectacular spots in the eastern Sierra. Thank heaven the food lives up to the view. The chef's specialties include beef Wellington, rack of lamb, and pan-seared local trout, all beautifully prepared. The woodsy room has a vaulted knotty-pine ceiling and a copper-chimney fireplace that roars on cold nights. Natural light abounds there in the daytime, but if it's summer, opt instead for outdoor dining under the white-barked aspens. Service is so good that if you forget your glasses, the waiter will provide a pair. The wine list is exceptional for its reasonably priced European and California varietals. ⊠*2 mi off U.S. 395, 4 mi south of Mammoth Lakes* ☎*760/934–3803* ⚑*Reservations essential* ⊟*AE, D, MC, V* ☉*No lunch early Sept.–July 4.*

$$$– **✕Restaurant LuLu.** LuLu imports the sunny, sensual, and
$$$$ assertive flavors of Provençal cooking—think olive tap-
★ enade, aioli, and lemony vinaigrettes—to Mammoth Lakes. At this outpost of the famous San Francisco restaurant, the formula remains the same: small plates of southern French cooking served family-style in a spare, modern, and sexy dining room. Standouts include rotisserie meats, succulent roasted mussels, homemade gnocchi, and a fantastic wine list, with 50 vintages available in 2-ounce pours. Outside, the sidewalk café includes a fire pit where kids will love do-it-themselves s'mores. LuLu's only drawback is price, but if you can swing it, it's worth every penny. The waiters wear jeans, so you can, too. ⊠*Village at Mammoth, 1111 Forest Trail, Unit 201* ☎*760/924–8781* ⚑*Reservations essential* ⊟*AE, D, MC, V.*

$ **✕Side Door Café.** Half wine bar, half café, this is a laid-back spot for an easy lunch or a long, lingering afternoon. The café serves grilled panini sandwiches, sweet and savory crepes, and espresso. At the wine bar, order cheese plates and charcuterie platters, designed to pair with the 25 wines (fewer in summertime) available by the glass. If you're lucky, a winemaker will show up and hold court at the bar. ⊠*Village at Mammoth, 1111 Forest Trail, Unit 229* ☎*760/934–5200* ⊟*AE, D, MC, V.*

$–$$ **✕The Stove.** A longtime family favorite for down-to-earth,
☺ folksy cooking, the Stove is the kind of place you take the family to fill up before a long car ride. The omelets, pancakes, huevos rancheros, and meat loaf won't win any awards, but they're tasty. The room is cute, with gingham curtains and pinewood booths, and service is friendly. Breakfast and lunch are the best bets here. ⊠*644 Old Mammoth Rd.* ☎*760/934–2821* ⚑*Reservations not accepted* ⊟*AE, MC, V.*

WHERE TO STAY

$$-$$$ ⓦ**Alpenhof Lodge.** The owners of the Alpenhof lucked out when developers built the fancy-schmancy Village at Mammoth right across the street from their mom-and-pop motel. The place remains a simple, mid-budget motel, with basic comforts and a few niceties like attractive pine furniture. Rooms are dark and the foam pillows thin, but the damask bedspreads are pretty and the low-pile carpeting clean, and best of all you can walk to restaurants and shops. Downstairs there's a lively, fun pub; if you want quiet, request a room that's not above it. Some rooms have fireplaces and kitchens. In winter the Village Gondola is across the street, a major plus for skiers. **Pros:** convenient for skiers; good price. **Cons:** could use an update; rooms above the pub can be noisy. ⊠*6080 Minaret Rd., Box 1157* ☎*760/934–6330 or 800/828–0371* ⊕*www.alpenhof-lodge.com* ⇆*54 rooms, 3 cabins* ⌂*In-room: no a/c, kitchen (some), refrigerator (some). In-hotel: restaurant, bar, pool, laundry facilities, no-smoking rooms* ⊟*AE, D, MC, V.*

$$ ⓦ**Cinnamon Bear Inn Bed & Breakfast.** In a business district off Main Street, this bed-and-breakfast feels more like a small motel, with nicely decorated rooms, many with four-poster beds. Suites have pull-out sofas, good for families; some have full kitchens. The exterior is weathered, but not at all derelict. For skiers looking for an alternative to a motel, this is a solid choice. Year-round, it's comparatively quiet due to its being a block from the main drag. Rates include a made-to-order breakfast and wine and cheese in the afternoon. **Pros:** quiet; affordable; friendly. **Cons:** a bit tricky to find; limited parking. ⊠*113 Center St.* ⌂*Box 3338, 93546* ☎*760/934–2873 or 800/845–2873* ⊕*www. cinnamonbearinn.com* ⇆*22 rooms* ⌂*In-room: no a/c, kitchen (some), Wi-Fi. In-hotel: bar, no-smoking rooms* ⊟*AE, D, DC, MC, V* ⓦ*BP.*

$$$– ⓦ**Convict Lake Resort.** The lake on which this resort stands
$$$$ (about 10 minutes south of Mammoth Lakes) was named for an 1871 gunfight between local vigilantes and six escaped prisoners. Cabins here range from rustic to modern, and come with fully equipped kitchens (including coffee-makers and premium coffee). The least fancy feel like upgraded fishing cabins; the nicest have Jacuzzi tubs and other creature comforts. Regardless of what room you book, the valley here is so drop-dead gorgeous, chances are you'll want to spend all your time outdoors. **Pros:** great views; tranquil atmosphere; tons of wildlife; clean rooms.

Cons: quarters can be tight. ⊠*2 mi off U.S. 395* ⌂*HCR-79 Box 204, 93546* ☎*760/934-3800 or 800/992-2260* ⊕*www.convictlake.com* ⌁*27 cabins, 3 houses* ⌂*In-room: no a/c, no phone, kitchen, DVD. In-hotel: restaurant, bicycles, Internet terminal, some pets allowed* ⊟*AE, D, MC, V.*

$$$–
$$$$ ⊺**Double Eagle Resort & Spa.** You won't find a better spa retreat in the eastern Sierra than the Double Eagle. Dwarfed by towering, craggy peaks, the resort is in a spectacularly beautiful spot along a creek, near June Lake, 20 minutes north of Mammoth Lakes. Accommodations are in comfortable knotty-pine two-bedroom cabins that sleep up to six, or in cabin suites with efficiency kitchens; all come fully equipped with modern amenities. If you don't want to cook, the Eagles Landing Restaurant ($$–$$$) serves three meals a day, but the quality is erratic. Spa services and treatments are available for nonguests by reservation. The small, uncrowded June Mountain Ski Area is 1.5 mi away. **Pros:** pretty setting; generous breakfast; good for families. **Cons:** expensive. ⊠*5587 Hwy. 158, Box 736, June Lake* ☎*760/648-7004 or 877/648-7004* ⊕*www. doubleeagleresort.com* ⌁*16 2-bedroom cabins, 16 cabin suites, 1 3-bedroom cabin* ⌂*In-room: no a/c, kitchen (some), refrigerator, Internet. In-hotel: restaurant, bar, pool, gym, spa, some pets allowed, no-smoking rooms* ⊟*AE, D, MC, V.*

$$–$$$ ⊺**Holiday Inn Mammoth Lakes.** In a town known for Carter-era condo units, this stands out as being the only modern, mid-price hotel, with fresh looking decor. Rooms and public areas are sparkling clean, and extras include voice mail, irons, microwaves, and refrigerators. Families enjoy the special "kids' suites," which have bunk beds and video games. There's also a year-round indoor pool. The place looks decidedly prefab and the maids spray too much air freshener, but for up-to-date amenities and services, you'll be hard pressed to find better in this price range. **Pros:** great price; clean rooms; chain dependability. **Cons:** nothing fancy. ⊠*3236 Main St.* ☎*760/924-1234 or 866/924-1234* ⊕*www.holidayatmammoth.com* ⌁*71 rooms, 3 suites* ⌂*In-room: kitchen (some), refrigerator, Internet, Wi-Fi. In-hotel: restaurant, bar, pool, laundry facilities, no-smoking rooms* ⊟*AE, D, DC, MC, V.*

$$$–
$$$$ ⊺**Juniper Springs Lodge.** Tops for slope-side comfort, these condominium-style units have full kitchens and ski-in, ski-

out access to the mountain. Extras include gas fireplaces, balconies, and stereos with CD players; the heated outdoor pool—surrounded by a heated deck—is open year-round. If you like to be near nightlife, you'll do better at the Village, but if you don't mind having to drive to go out for the evening, this is a great spot. In summer fewer people stay here, although package deals and lower prices provide incentive. Skiers: the lifts on this side of the mountain close in mid-April; for springtime ski-in, ski-out access, stay at the Mammoth Mountain Inn. **Pros:** bargain during summer; direct access to the slopes; good views. **Cons:** no nightlife within walking distance; no a/c; some complaints about service. ⊠*4000 Meridian Blvd.* ☎*Box 2129, 93546* ☎*760/924–1102 or 800/626–6684* ⊕*www.mammoth mountain.com* ⤳*10 studios, 99 1-bedroom, 92 2-bedroom, 3 3-bedroom* ☖*In-room: no a/c, kitchen, refrigerator, Internet. In-hotel: restaurant, room service, bar, golf course, pool, bicycles, concierge, laundry facilities, no-smoking rooms* ⊟*AE, MC, V.*

$$$– 🏨**Mammoth Mountain Inn.** If you want to be within walking
$$$$ distance of the Mammoth Mountain Main Lodge, this is the place. In summer the proximity to the gondola means you can hike and mountain bike to your heart's delight. The accommodations, which vary in size, include standard hotel rooms and condo units. The inn, ski lodge, and other summit facilities are likely to be razed and rebuilt within a decade, bringing more of a 21st-century ski resort feel to what's been a quaint 1950s-born resort. Meanwhile, the inn has done a respectable job with continual refurbishing. **Pros:** great location; big rooms; a traditional place to stay. **Cons:** can be crowded in ski season; won't be around for many more years. ⊠*Minaret Rd., 4 mi west of Mammoth Lakes* ☎*Box 353, 93546* ☎*760/934–2581 or 800/626–6684* ⊕*www.mammothmountain.com* ⤳*124 rooms, 91 condos* ☖*In-room: no a/c, kitchen (some), refrigerator (some), Internet (some). In-hotel: Wi-Fi, 2 restaurants, bar, pool, laundry facilities, no-smoking rooms* ⊟*AE, MC, V.*

★ **Fodor's**Choice 🏨**Tamarack Lodge Resort & Lakefront Restaurant.**
$$–$$$ Tucked away on the edge of the John Muir Wilderness Area, where cross-country ski trails loop through the woods, this original 1924 lodge looks like something out of a snow globe, and the lake it borders is serenely beautiful. Rooms in the charming main lodge have spartan furnishings, and in old-fashioned style, some share a bathroom.

For more privacy, opt for one of the cabins, which range from rustic to downright cushy; many have fireplaces, kitchens, or wood-burning stoves. In warm months, fishing, canoeing, hiking, and mountain biking are right outside. The small and romantic Lakefront Restaurant ($$$) serves outstanding contemporary French-inspired dinners, with an emphasis on game, in a candlelit dining room. Reservations are essential. **Pros:** rustic but not run-down; tons of nearby outdoor activities. **Cons:** thin walls; some main lodge rooms have shared bathrooms. ⊠*Lake Mary Rd., off Hwy. 203* ⌂*Box 69, 93546* ☎*760/934–2442 or 800/626–6684* ⊕*www.tamaracklodge.com* ♺*11 rooms, 35 cabins* ⌂*In-room: no a/c, kitchen (some), no TV. In-hotel: restaurant, bar, Wi-Fi, no-smoking rooms* ▭*AE, MC, V.*

$$$$ ▦**Village at Mammoth.** At the epicenter of Mammoth's burgeoning dining and nightlife scene, this cluster of four-story timber-and-stone condo buildings nods to Alpine style, with exposed timbers and peaked roofs. Units have gas fireplaces, kitchens or kitchenettes, daily maid service, high-speed Internet access, DVD players, slate-tile bathroom floors, and comfortable furnishings. The decor is a bit sterile, but there are high-end details like granite counters. And you won't have to drive anywhere: the buildings are connected by a ground-floor pedestrian mall, with shops, restaurants, bars, and—best of all—a gondola (November through mid-April only) that whisks you right from the Village to the mountain. **Pros:** central location; clean, big rooms; lots of good restaurants nearby. **Cons:** pricey; can be noisy outside. ⊠*100 Canyon Blvd.* ⌂*Box 3459, 93546* ☎*760/934–1982 or 800/626–6684* ⊕*www. mammothmountain.com* ♺*277 units* ⌂*In-room: no a/c, kitchen (some), Internet. In-hotel: pool, gym, laundry facilities, parking (no fee), no-smoking rooms* ▭*AE, MC, V.*

WHERE TO CAMP

$$ ⛰**Convict Lake Campground.** Ten minutes south of Mammoth, this campground near the Convict Lake Resort is run by the U.S. Forest Service. It's open May to October, and sites are available on a first-come, first-served basis. They're extremely popular. One look at the scenery and you'll understand why. ⊠*2 mi off U.S. 395* ☎*760/924–5500* ⊕*www.fs.fed.us/r5/ inyo* ♺*88 campsites* ⌂*Flush toilets, dump station, drinking water, showers, fire pits, general store.*

8

$$ ⚲ **Lake Mary Campground.** There are few sites as beautiful as this lakeside campground at 8,900 feet, open June to September. If it's full, which it often is, try the adjacent Coldwater campground. You can catch trout in tourmaline Lake Mary, the biggest lake in the region. There's a general store nearby. ✉ *Lake Mary Loop Dr., off Hwy. 203* ☎ *760/924–5500* ⊕ *www.fs.fed.us/r5/inyo* ⌘ *48 sites (tent or RV)* ⚬ *Flush toilets, drinking water, fire grates, picnic tables.*

$$ ⚲ **Minaret Falls Campground.** This is one of several campgrounds along Minaret Road, past the entrance gate to Devils Postpile National Monument. At 7,700 feet, it's close to many trails in the high country above Mammoth Lakes, including the Pacific Crest Trail. In addition to the campground fee, you'll have to pay $7 per person to the Forest Service for access to the area, but they cap the maximum at $20 per carload. ✉ *Off Minaret Rd., Hwy. 203, 6 mi beyond Inyo National Forest entrance station* ☎ *760/924–5500* ⊕ *www.fs.fed.us/r5/inyo* ⌘ *27 sites (tent or RV)* ⚬ *Pit toilets, drinking water, grills, picnic tables* ▭ *No credit cards* ⊘ *June–Sept.*

SPORTS & THE OUTDOORS

For information on winter conditions around Mammoth, call the **Snow Report** (☎ 760/934–7669 or 888/766–9778). The **U.S. Forest Service ranger station** (☎ 760/924–5500) can provide general information year-round.

BICYCLING

Mammoth Mountain Bike Park (✉ *Mammoth Mountain Ski Area* ☎ *760/934–3706* ⊕ *www.mammothmountain. com*) opens when the snow melts, usually by July, with 70-plus mi of single-track trails—from mellow to super-challenging. Chairlifts and shuttles provide trail access, and rentals are available. Various shops around town also rent bikes and provide trail maps, if you don't want to ascend the mountain.

DOGSLEDDING

Mammoth Dog Teams (✉ *Kennels Hwy. 203, 4 mi east of Mammoth Lakes* ☎ *760/934–6270* ⊕ *www.mammoth dogteams.com*) operates rides through the forest on sleds pulled by teams of 10 dogs. Options range from 25-minute rides to overnight excursions; book three to seven days in advance. In summer you can tour the kennels (at 10, 1, and 3) and learn about the dogs; call ahead.

FISHING

Crowley Lake is the top trout-fishing spot in the area; Convict Lake, June Lake, and the lakes of the Mammoth Basin are other prime spots. One of the best trout rivers is the San Joaquin, near Devils Postpile. Hot Creek, a designated Wild Trout Stream, is renowned for fly-fishing (catch-and-release only). The fishing season runs from the last Saturday in April until the end of October. To maximize your time on the water, get tips from local anglers, or better yet, book a guided fishing trip with **Sierra Drifters Guide Service** (☎760/935–4250 ⊕www.sierradrifters.com).

Kittredge Sports (⊠3218 Main St., at Forest Trail ☎760/934–7566 ⊕www.kittredgesports.com) rents rods and reels and also conducts guided trips.

GOLF

Because it's nestled right up against the forest, you might see deer and bears on the fairways on the picture-perfect 18-hole **Sierra Star Golf Course** (⊠2001 Sierra Star Pkwy.93546 ☎760/924–2200 ⊕www.mammothmountain.com), California's highest-elevation golf course (take it slow!). Greens fees run $84 to $129.

The 9-hole course at **Snowcreek Resort** (⊠Old Mammoth Rd. ☎760/934–6633 ⊕www.snowcreekresort.com) sits in a meadow with drop-dead gorgeous, wide-open vistas of the mountains. Nine-hole play costs $35 and includes a cart; 18 holes run $55.

HIKING

Hiking in Mammoth is stellar, especially along the trails that wind through the pristine alpine scenery around the Lakes Basin. Carry lots of water; and remember, you're above 8,000-foot elevation, and the air is thin. Stop at the **U.S. Forest Service ranger station** (⊠Hwy. 203 ☎760/924–5500 ⊕www.fs.fed.us/r5/inyo), on your right just before the town of Mammoth Lakes, for a Mammoth area trail map and permits for backpacking in wilderness areas.

HORSEBACK RIDING

Stables around Mammoth are typically open from June through September. **Mammoth Lakes Pack Outfit** (⊠Lake Mary Rd., between Twin Lakes and Lake Mary ☎760/934–2434 or 888/475–8747 ⊕www.mammothpack.com) runs day and overnight horseback trips, or will shuttle you to the high country. **McGee Creek Pack Station** (☎760/935–4324 or 800/854–7407 ⊕www.mcgeecreekpackstation.com)

customizes pack trips or will shuttle you to camp alone. Operated by the folks at McGee Creek, **Sierra Meadows Ranch** (⊠*Sherwin Creek Rd., off Old Mammoth Rd.* ☎*760/934–6161*) conducts horseback and wagon rides that range from one-hour to all-day excursions.

HOT-AIR BALLOONING

The balloons of **Mammoth Balloon Adventures** (☎*760/937–8787* ⊕*www.mammothballoonadventures.com*) glide over the countryside in the morning from spring until fall, weather permitting.

EAST OF YOSEMITE NATIONAL PARK

FROM LEE VINING TO BRIDGEPORT

The area to the east of Yosemite National Park includes some ruggedly handsome, albeit desolate, terrain, most notably around Mono Lake. The area is best visited by car, as distances are great and public transportation is negligible. U.S. 395 is the main north–south road on the eastern side of the Sierra Nevada, at the western edge of the Great Basin. It's one of California's most beautiful highways; plan to snap pictures at roadside pullouts.

LEE VINING

20 mi east of Tuolumne Meadows via Hwy. 120 to U.S. 395; 30 mi north of Mammoth Lakes on U.S. 395.

Tiny Lee Vining is known primarily as the eastern gateway to Yosemite National Park (open only in summer) and the location of vast and desolate Mono Lake. Pick up supplies at the general store year-round, or stop here for lunch or dinner before or after a drive through the high country. In winter the town is all but deserted, except for the ice climbers who come to scale frozen waterfalls. You can meet these hearty souls at Nicely's restaurant, where the climbers congregate for breakfast around 8 on winter mornings.

If you want to try your hand at the ice climbing, contact **Sierra Mountain Guides** (☎*760/648–1122 or 877/423–2546* ⊕*www.themountainguide.com*).

★ Eerie tufa towers—calcium carbonate formations that often resemble castle turrets—rise from impressive **Mono Lake.** Since the 1940s, the city of Los Angeles has diverted water from streams that feed the lake, lowering its water level and exposing the tufa. Court victories by environmentalists in the 1990s forced a reduction of the diversions, and the lake has since risen about 9 feet. From April through August, millions of migratory birds nest in and around Mono Lake. The best place to view the tufa is at the south end of the lake along the mile-long **South Tufa Trail.** To reach it, drive 5 mi south from Lee Vining on U.S. 395, then 5 mi east on Highway 120. There's a $3 fee. You can swim (or float) in the salty water at Navy Beach near the South Tufa Trail or take a kayak or canoe trip for close-up views of the tufa (check with rangers for boating restrictions during bird-nesting season). You can rent kayaks in Mammoth Lakes.

The sensational **Scenic Area Visitor Center** (⊠ *U.S. 395* ☏ *760/647–3044*) is open daily from June through September (Sunday through Thursday 8–5, Friday and Saturday 8–7), and the rest of the year Thursday through Monday 9–4. Its hilltop, sweeping views of Mono Lake, along with its interactive exhibits inside, make this one of California's best visitor centers. Rangers and naturalists lead walking tours of the tufa daily in summer and on weekends (sometimes on cross-country skis) in winter. In town, the Mono Lake Committee Information Center & Bookstore (⊠ *U.S. 395 and 3rd St.* ☏ *760/647–6595* ⊕ *www.monolake.org*) has more information about this beautiful area.

EN ROUTE. Heading south from Lee Vining, U.S. 395 intersects the June Lake Loop (⊠ *Hwy. 158 W*). This gorgeous 17-mi drive follows an old glacial canyon past Grant, June, Gull, and other lakes before reconnecting with U.S. 395 on its way to Mammoth Lakes. The loop is especially colorful in fall.

WHERE TO EAT

¢ ✕**Mono Cone.** Get soft-serve ice cream, burgers, and fries at this hopping shack in the middle of Lee Vining, but be prepared to do what's rare in these uncrowded parts: wait in line. There's some indoor seating, but unless the clouds are leaking, take your food to nearby (and quiet) Hess Park, whose views of Mono Lake make it one of the best picnic spots in eastern California. It has a playground and tennis court, too. ⊠ *51508 U.S. 39593541* ☏ *760/647–6606* ⊟ *No credit cards.*

$–$$ ✕**Nicely's.** For-sale artworks decorate the walls of this vintage-1965 diner. The country cooking isn't fancy— think blueberry pancakes for breakfast and chicken-fried steak for dinner—but it's a good spot for families with kids and unfussy eaters looking for a square meal, the kind of place where the waitress walks up with a pot of coffee and asks, "Ya want a warm-up, hon?" ⊠*U.S. 395 and 4th St.93541* ☎*760/647-6477* ⊟*MC, V* ⊘*Closed Tues. and Wed. in winter.*

$-$$ ✕**Tioga Gas Mart & Whoa Nelli Deli.** Near the eastern entrance
★ to Yosemite, Whoa Nelli serves some of Mono County's best food, including lobster taquitos, pizzas, and enormous slices of multilayered cakes. But what makes it special is that it's in a gas station—possibly the only one in America where you can order cocktails (a pitcher of mango margaritas, anyone?)—and outside there's a full-size trapeze where you can take lessons (by reservation).This wacky spot is well off the noisy road and has plenty of shaded outdoor tables with views of Mono Lake; bands play here on summer evenings, and locals love it, too. ⊠*Hwy. 120 and U.S. 395* ☎*760/647–1088* ⊟*AE, MC, V* ⊘*Closed mid-Nov.–mid-Apr.*

WHERE TO STAY

$-$$ ▦**Tioga Lodge.** The lodge, across the highway from the lake, centers around a 19th-century building that has been by turns a store, a saloon, a tollbooth, and a boardinghouse. Surrounding the rustic lodge are modest, attached, weathered-wooden cottages, tucked beneath towering cottonwoods on a grassy hillside. The simple, country-cute rooms have cozy furnishings that—thank heaven—manage not to be tacky. Alas, everything is close to the noisy road, but the views of Mono Lake compensate. Be sure to ask about summer boat tours. **Pros:** its nine-table Hammond Station Restaurant is quite pleasant. **Cons:** close to the road. ⊠*54411 U.S. 395* ☐*Box 580 93541* ☎*760/647–6423 or 888/647–6423* ⊕*www.tiogalodgeatmonolake.com* ➤*14 rooms* ⌂*In-room: no a/c, no phone, no TV, refrigerator (some). In-hotel: restaurant, no-smoking rooms* ⊟*AE, D, MC, V* ⊘*Closed Nov.–Apr.*

$$ ▦**Lake View Lodge.** Lovely landscaping, which includes several inviting and shaded places to sit, is what sets this clean motel apart from its handful of competitors in town. It's also up and off the highway by a few hundred feet, which means it's peaceful as well as pretty. Open morning and early afternoon, a stand-alone coffee shop adds to the appeal. The cottages lack the main building's lake views; some have kitchens and can sleep up to six. **Pros:** attractive, clean; friendly staff. **Cons:** could use updating. ⊠*51285 U.S. 395* ☎*760/647–6543 or 800/990–6614* ⊕*www.lake viewlodgeyosemite.com* ↪*76 rooms, 12 cottages* ⚭*In-room: no a/c, refrigerator (some), Wi-Fi. In-hotel: no-smoking rooms* ⊟*AE, D, MC, V.*

BODIE STATE HISTORIC PARK

23 mi northeast of Lee Vining via U.S. 395 to Hwy. 270 (last 3 mi are unpaved).

★ Fodor's Choice Old shacks and shops, abandoned mine shafts,
☯ a Methodist church, the mining village of Rattlesnake Gulch, and the remains of a small Chinatown are among the sights at fascinating **Bodie Ghost Town.** The town, at an elevation of 8,200 feet, boomed from about 1878 to 1881, as gold prospectors, having worked the best of the western Sierra mines, headed to the high desert on the eastern slopes. Bodie was a mean place—the booze flowed freely, shootings were commonplace, and licentiousness reigned. Evidence of the town's wild past survives today at an excellent museum, and you can tour an old stamp mill and a ridge that contains many mine sites. Bodie, unlike Calico in Southern California near Barstow, is a genuine ghost town, its status proudly stated as "arrested decay." No food, drink, or lodging is available in Bodie. Though the park stays open in winter, snow may close Highway 270. Still, it's a fantastic time to visit: rent cross-country skis in Mammoth Lakes, drive north, ski in, and have the park to yourself. ⊠*Museum: Main and Green Sts.* ☎*760/647–6445* ⊕*www.bodie.net* 🎫*Park $3, museum free* ☉*Park: late May–early Sept., daily 8–7; early Sept.–late May, daily 8–4. Museum: late May–early Sept., daily 9–6; early Sept.–late May, hrs vary.*

WHERE TO STAY & EAT

$$–$$$ ✕**Bridgeport Inn.** The dining room at this Victorian-era inn looks like it was decorated by the owner's grandmother, with sweetheart-rose wallpaper and lace, but it's a reasonable choice for a sit-down hot lunch. Locals swear by the prime rib at dinner. The soups are homemade; there are no surprises on the plain-old American menu. The inn rents 10 rooms upstairs (with shared bath) for $50 to $80 that are nicely appointed and have a sort of retro appeal, but thin walls make earplugs a good idea. Six other rooms, including a suite with furniture rescued from Bodie, are available, too. **Pros:** has an authentic, old-timey Western feel; restaurant is popular. **Cons:** thin walls; not much to do in town. ✉*205 Main St.* ☎*760/932–7380* 🖃*D, MC, V* ⊗*Closed Dec.–Feb.*

$$–$$$ 🏨**Cain House.** Lovely details such as country quilts and Victorian oak antiques (some from Bodie) lend a homey warmth to this sweet little B&B, Bridgeport's top choice for lodging. Every room is different, with styles ranging from white wicker to dark wood, but all are carefully tended. In the afternoon there's wine and cheese, and in the morning a full hot breakfast. Cain House is partnered with the neighboring Silver Maple Inn. **Pros:** lots of character; within easy driving distance of many wonderful things. **Cons:** anything worth seeing requires getting in your car. ✉*340 Main St.* ☎*760/932–7383* ⊕ *www.silver mapleinn.com* ⟿*7 rooms* ♿*In-room: refrigerator (some). In-hotel: tennis court, no elevator, no-smoking rooms* 🖃*AE, D, MC, V* ⊗*Closed Nov.–Apr.* ⊠*BP.*

$ 🏨**Silver Maple Inn.** Next to the Mono County Courthouse (1880), this single-story 1930s-era motel has lush, shady lawns with mature trees, perfect for a picnic or game of hide-and-seek with the kids. The rooms are barely modern, with thin foam pillows, but they're clean and well maintained, and the service is friendly, which you can't say about all the motels in town. For anglers, there are fish-cleaning and -freezing facilities and barbecue pits in which to cook your catch. **Pros:** good for families; helpful staff. **Cons:** you'll be spending the night in Bridgeport, not in the mountains. ✉*310 Main St.* ☎*760/932–7383* ⊕*www.silvermaple inn.com* ⟿*20 rooms* ♿*In-room: no a/c, refrigerator (some), Wi-Fi. In-hotel: no elevator, some pets allowed, no-smoking rooms* 🖃*AE, D, MC, V* ⊗*Closed Nov.–Mar.*

Travel Smart
Yosemite,
Sequoia &
Kings Canyon

WORD OF MOUTH

"Sequoia and Kings Canyon were in the same area [as Yosemite], so decided to include them. It takes about and hour and a half to go from Yosemite to Fresno and then another hour and a half to get to Grant's Grove. We were flying in and out of Fresno, so that worked for us."

—Maj

GETTING HERE & AROUND

We're proud of our Web site: Fodors.com is a great place to begin any journey. Scan Travel Wire for suggested itineraries, travel deals, restaurant and hotel openings, and other up-to-the-minute info. Check out Booking to research prices and book plane tickets, hotel rooms, rental cars, and vacation packages. Head to Talk for on-the-ground pointers from travelers who frequent our message boards. You can also link to loads of other travel-related resources.

Most people drive to these national parks. Los Angeles is roughly four hours from Sequoia (202 mi), while San Francisco is about four hours from Yosemite (195 mi). Fresno is 90 mi from Yosemite Valley and 55 mi from Kings Canyon National Park. Amtrak can get you to Yosemite fairly efficiently; it's a good option for single travelers who are interested only in Yosemite Valley. Within the parks, main roads are in good to excellent shape, although speeds in excess of 40 MPH pose a danger to wildlife. Side roads, such as those to remote campgrounds, can be pretty bad.

▌ BY AIR

If you are coming from out of state to see one of these parks, chances are other California attractions also are on your itinerary. In that case, you might as well fly to Los Angeles (or the satellite airports Burbank, John Wayne, Long Beach, and Ontario) or to San Francisco (or nearby airports Oakland and Sacramento), depending on whether you are focusing on Southern or Northern California. You will end up driving everywhere—just like the natives.

Airlines & Airports **Airline and Airport Links.com** (⊕*www.airlineand airportlinks.com*) has links to many of the world's airlines and airports.

Airline-Security Issues **Transportation Security Administration** (⊕*www.tsa.gov*) has answers for almost every question that might come up.

AIRPORTS

Fresno Yosemite International Airport (FYI) is the nearest airport to all three national parks. Neither of Nevada's major airport options, Reno and Las Vegas, makes any sense as a base destination unless you intend to spend time in those cities. The best strategy is to fly into Los Angeles or San Francisco and rent a vehicle.

Airport Information **Fresno Yosemite International Airport** (✉*5175 E. Clinton Ave., Fresno* ☎*559/621–4500 or 559/498–4095* ⊕*www.flyfresno.org*).

FLIGHTS

Alaska, Allegiant, American, Delta, Frontier, Horizon, Mexicana, United, United Express, and US Airways fly to Fresno. Most of the daily flights are from Los Angeles and San Francisco, while a few others come from Dallas, Denver, and Las Vegas.

Airline Contacts Alaska Airlines (☎800/426-0333 ⊕ www.alaskaair.com). **Allegiant Airlines** (☎702/505-8888 ⊕ www.allegiantair.com). **American Airlines** (☎800/433-7300 ⊕ www.aa.com). **Delta Airlines** (☎800/221-1212 ⊕ www.delta.com). **Horizon Air** (☎800/547-9308 ⊕ www.horizonair.com). **Mexicana Airlines** (☎800/531-7921 www.mexicana.com). **United Airlines/United Express** (☎800/241-6522 ⊕ www.united.com). **US Airways** (☎800/428-4322 ⊕ www.usairways.com).

▌BY CAR

Unless you are content with taking Amtrak and the Route 140 public bus, YARTS, to Yosemite Valley, you will need a car to explore Yosemite National Park. It is possible to see the major sites in Sequoia via a shuttle service from Visalia, but service is limited and operates only in the summer. You're better off driving. Kings Canyon is not served by any public transportation.

The route to Yosemite from San Francisco is pretty much due east, if you enter the park on Highway 120. From Los Angeles, count on a six-hour trip: north to Fresno on Interstate 5 and Highway 99, then a diagonal on Highway 41 to the park's south entrance.

Six hours also is a reasonable estimate to drive from the Bay Area to Grant Grove Village in Kings Canyon National Park. The quickest route is to work your way to Fresno, then head east on Highway 180. From Los Angeles, drive north to Visalia, then head east on Highway 198 through Three Rivers to the south entrance of Sequoia National Park.

The only plausible way to drive from the Eastern Sierra to any of the parks is on spectacularly scenic Tioga Road. Turn west off Highway 395 at Lee Vining, but you can only do so when Tioga Pass is open—roughly from early June through mid-October.

GASOLINE

There's no fuel available in Yosemite Valley, Sequoia, or Kings Canyon. Outside all the parks' entrances, however, you will have no trouble finding places to fuel up. The problem will be coming up with the necessary scratch: Expect pay at least 50¢ more per gallon than you would in California's Gold Country or Central Valley.

AUTOMOBILE SERVICE STATIONS

In Yosemite, Crane Flat, Tuolumne Meadows, and Wawona have gas pumps. Yosemite Village contains a garage, but it performs only basic repairs and does not sell gas.

There is no gasoline in either Sequoia or Kings Canyon, although there are pumps at Stony Creek Lodge, between the two parks on Generals Highway. If you're traveling in Kings Canyon, you can find gas at Hume Lake; if traveling in Sequoia, fuel up in Three Rivers. Cans of emergency gasoline are available at Lodgepole Market and Grant Grove Market. For emergency repairs, towing, lock-outs, or jump starts, your best bet is to call AAA or a service station in a neighboring town.

Yosemite Area Service Stations **Lit'l Joe's Automotive** (✉ *40326 Greenwood Way, Oakhurst* ☎ *559/683–3446*). **Wesley's Auto Repair** (✉ *4397 Ben Hur Rd., Mariposa* ☎ *209/742–2243*). **A-1 Auto Repair** (✉ *59 Sierra Park Rd., Mammoth Lakes* ☎ *760/934–7870*).

Sequoia & Kings Canyon Area Service Stations **Hume Lake Christian Camps Gas Station** (✉ *Hume Lake Rd., off Rte. 180, 11 mi east of Grant Grove* ☎ *559/335–2000 Ext. 279*). **Pat O'Connell's Service** (✉ *41500 Sierra Dr., Three Rivers* ☎ *559/561–4776*). **Three Rivers Chevron** (✉ *41907 Sierra Dr., Three Rivers* ☎ *559/561–3835*).

PARKING

In Yosemite Valley, park at either the Valley Village or Curry Village all-day lots, then walk, ride a bicycle, or take the free shuttle bus to other Valley attractions. Elsewhere in the Valley, especially on summer weekends, roadside parking spots can be hard to find. Outside the Valley, you should have no serious problems, although small parking lots or pull-offs at the most popular trailheads (for example, the North Dome Trail at Porcupine Creek off Tioga Road) can overflow.

The most important parking issue in Sequoia National Park is at the General Sherman Tree, where you might have to circle the large lot a few times to find a space, and after you have secured one, you still must walk a quarter-mile (with a 400-foot drop in elevation) to get to the tree.

RENTAL CARS

The car-rental outlets closest to the Southern Sierra are at Fresno–Yosemite International Airport, where the national chains have outlets. If you're traveling to Mammoth Lakes and the eastern Sierra in winter, the closest agencies are in Reno. In 2008, renting a compact car at Fresno's airport cost just under $200 per week, with rates for luxury sedans and large SUVs hovering around the $500 mark. The rates you can get in Fresno are not significantly different from those available at the Bay Area and Los Angeles area airports.

Contacts **Alamo** (☎ *800/462–5266* ⊕ *www.alamo.com*). **Avis** (☎ *800/462–5266* ⊕ *www.avis.com*). **Budget** (☎ *800/527–0700* ⊕ *www.budget.com*). **Hertz** (☎ *800/654–3131* ⊕ *www.hertz.com*). **National** (☎ *800/227–7368* ⊕ *www.nationalcar.com*).

RENTAL CAR INSURANCE

Everyone who rents a car wonders whether the insurance that the rental companies offer is worth the expense. No one—including us—has a simple answer. If you own a car, your personal auto insurance may cover a rental to some degree, though not all policies protect you abroad; always read your policy's fine print. If you don't have auto insurance, then seriously consider buying the collision- or loss-damage waiver (CDW or LDW) from the car-rental company, which eliminates your liability for damage to the car. Some credit cards offer CDW coverage, but it's usually supplemental to your own insurance and rarely covers SUVs, minivans, luxury models, and the like. If your coverage is secondary, you may still be liable for loss-of-use costs from the car-rental company. But no credit-card insurance is valid unless you use that card for *all* transactions, from reserving to paying the final bill. It's sometimes cheaper to buy insurance as part of your general travel insurance policy.

ROADSIDE EMERGENCIES

Dial ☎ 911 to report accidents on the road and to reach the police, the California Highway Patrol (CHP), or the fire department. On some rural highways and on most interstates, look for emergency phones on the side of the road. In Los Angeles, the Metro Freeway Service Patrol provides assistance to stranded motorists under non-emergency conditions. Call ☎ 399 on your cell phone to reach them 24 hours a day.

ROAD CONDITIONS

Although Yosemite is extremely popular and most visitors drive there, any traffic slowdowns you encounter most likely will be attributable to road construction or accidents, not volume-triggered congestion. Posted speed limits that can be as fast as 45 MPH on Tioga Road, Wawona Road, and Generals Highway, but 40 MPH is a better maximum speed because it gives drivers more time to react to the many animals that can cross at any time, but especially at dawn and dusk. Go even slower if you'd like—the scenery certainly war-

rants it—but be sure to use the many pullouts so speedier cars can get by. The side roads, such as those that branch off a mile or two to campgrounds or trailheads, can be veritable minefields for flat tires, containing potholes that might more appropriately be described as craters. The 6-mi "paved" road off Generals Highway to Crystal Cave in Sequoia National park is a good example.

From November through March, rain on the coast can mean heavy snow in the mountains. Carry tire chains, and know how to put them on. The places you are most likely to need them are on Route 120 as it approaches Yosemite from the northwest, and on Route 180 as it approaches Kings Canyon from Fresno; chains also can be required on Generals Highway, which connects Kings Canyon and Sequoia. Always check road conditions before you leave. Traffic in national parks in summer can be heavy, and there are sometimes travel restrictions.

Contacts **California Road Conditions** (☎*800/427–7623* ⊕*www.dot.ca.gov/cgi-bin/roads.cgi*). **Sequoia–Kings Canyon Road and Weather Information** (☎*559/565–3341*). **Yosemite Area Road and Weather Conditions** (☎*209/372–0200*).

▌ BY PUBLIC TRANSPORTATION

The Central Valley city of Visalia, in a partnership with the National Park Service, operates Sequoia Shuttle, a service that operates from Memorial Day weekend through Labor Day weekend. For $15 round-trip, a fee that includes park admission, you can ride from Visalia or Three Rivers (there are several pickup points in each town) to the Giant Forest Museum in Sequoia National Park. Five runs are made daily; reservations are required. Once you arrive at the museum, you can use the two in-park shuttle routes: One stops at the General Sherman Tree, Lodgepole, and Wuksachi Lodge; the other goes to and from Moro Rock and Crescent Meadow. Those interior buses run every 15 to 20 minutes, and they are free for all park visitors, not just those who have taken the bus from Visalia and Three Rivers.

Amtrak sometimes offers packages in the summer that include transportation from Los Angeles, Sacramento, or San Francisco and lodging in Visalia and in the park as well as park entry fees.

For visitors to Yosemite who are traveling alone and are interested primarily in the Yosemite Valley attractions, Amtrak offers competitive rates—roughly $60 round-trip from Los Angeles, Sacramento, or San Francisco in 2008's peak summer season. The railway's San Joaquin line drops you off at Merced, where a bus operated by Yosemite Area Regional Transportation System—everybody calls it YARTS—will get you to the Valley in another 2½ hours.

Park visitors who stay outside Yosemite along Route 140 can save money and avoid stressful driving by taking YARTS, which can get

you to the Valley as early as 7:28 AM (expect to see lots of rangers on this route). The last bus leaves Yosemite Lodge at 8:20 PM. Rates are based on how far you are going. In 2008, round-trips from Merced were $36, from Mariposa $24, and from El Portal $14. Whereas that YARTS run is year-round, the bus it runs between Mammoth Lakes and Yosemite Valley—one round-trip daily, $60—goes over Tioga Pass and subsequently usually operates only from early June through September. All YARTS riders are admitted free to Yosemite National Park.

In the Valley, you can use the free shuttle system that has 21 stops—from Yosemite Lodge to Happy Isles and every major site in between—and runs from 9 AM (earlier in the summer) to 10 PM. year-round. Buses come every 10 to 20 minutes. During the summer, a separate free shuttle can take you to the El Capitan area, in the valley's western side. In winter, a shuttle runs between Yosemite Valley and Badger Pass Ski Area. *For details about bus tours you can take from the Valley to Glacier Point and Tuolumne Meadows, see ⇨Chapter 3.*

Contacts Amtrak (☎ 800/872-7245 ⊕ www. amtrak.com). **Sequoia Shuttle** (☎ 559/713-4300 ⊕ www. sequoiashuttle.com). **YARTS** (☎ 877/989-2787 ⊕ www.yarts. com). **Yosemite National Park Transit** (☎ 209/372-1240 ⊕ www. nps.gov/yose).

ESSENTIALS

■ ACCESSIBILITY

Yosemite's facilities are continually being upgraded to make them more accessible. Portions of three popular Valley floor trails—"A Changing Yosemite" Interpretive Trail, Lower Yosemite Falls, and Mirror Lake—are wheelchair-accessible, though some assistance may be required. The Valley Visitor Center is fully accessible, as are the shuttle buses around the Valley. A sign-language interpreter is available for ranger programs if you call ahead. For complete details, pick up the park's accessibility brochure at any visitor center or entrance; you can also read the text on the National Park Service Web site (see Visitor Information, *below*). Visitors with respiratory difficulties should take note of the park's high elevations—the Valley floor is approximately 4,000 feet above sea level, but Tuolumne Meadows and parts of the high country are higher than 8,000 feet.

In Sequoia and Kings Canyon, all of the visitor centers, the Giant Forest Museum, and Big Trees Trail are wheelchair-accessible, as are some short ranger-led walks and talks. The General Sherman Tree can be reached via a paved, level trail near a parking area. None of the caves is accessible, and wilderness areas must be reached by horseback or on foot. Some picnic tables are extended to accommodate wheelchairs. Many of the major sites are in the 6,000-foot range, and thin air at high elevations can cause respiratory distress for people with breathing difficulties. Carry oxygen if necessary. Contact the park's main number for more information.

All three parks have campgrounds that include accessible sites. Reserve these as far in advance as possible.

■ ADMISSION FEES

For Yosemite, vehicle admission fee is $20 per car and is valid for seven days. For the combination of Sequoia and Kings Canyon, the fee is $20 total. For either park, individuals arriving by bus, or on foot, bicycle, motorcycle, or horseback pay $10 for a seven-day pass.

A one-year pass for Yosemite is $40, while one for Sequoia and Kings Canyon is $30. A 12-month "America the Beautiful—National Parks and Federal Recreational Lands Pass" is $80 and gets you (and your family) into all federal recreation sites that charge entrance fees. Seniors (ages 62 and older) can purchase the annual pass for $10. People with lifetime disabilities are entitled to an "Access Pass," which is free.

■ COMMUNICATIONS

INTERNET

In Yosemite, you can access the Web in Yosemite Lodge's lobby area if you are a guest and have the password; otherwise, you can ask at the front desk for the password, for a which a fee may apply. The situation is similar at the Ahwahnee, though guests should be able to get Wi-Fi in their rooms.

At Kings Canyon and Sequoia, you can tap into free Wi-Fi in the lobbies of the John Muir and Wuksachi lodges.

PHONES

The area code in Yosemite is 209, and in Sequoia/Kings Canyon it is 559.

In Yosemite, there are public telephones at park entrance stations, visitor centers, all restaurants and lodging facilities in the park, gas stations, and in Yosemite Village. Most cell phones seem to work just fine in the Valley; at higher and more remote locations, the odds diminish.

In Sequoia/Kings Canyon, public telephones may be found at the park entrance stations, visitor centers, ranger stations, some trailheads, and at all restaurants and lodging facilities in the park. Cell phones are not as likely to work here as they are in Yosemite, even from points on Generals Highway, where the Central Valley is visible—or theoretically within eyesight, through all the smog.

▌ EMERGENCIES

In an emergency, call 911 from any park phone.

In Yosemite, you call the Yosemite Medical Clinic, which provides 24-hour emergency care.

In Sequoia/Kings Canyon, there is no medical clinic, but rangers at the Cedar Grove, Foothills, Grant Grove, and Lodgepole visitor centers and the Mineral King ranger station are trained in first aid. Contact a ranger station or visitor center for police matters. For nonemergencies, call the parks' main number.

Emergency Services **Emergency services** (☎ *911*). **Yosemite Medical Clinic** (✉ *Yosemite Village,Yosemite National Park* ☎ *209/372–4637*).

▌ HOURS OF OPERATION

Yosemite is open daily, 24 hours a day. All entrances are open at all hours, except for Hetch Hetchy Entrance, open roughly dawn to dusk.

Sequoia and Kings Canyon are open daily 24 hours.

All three parks are in the Pacific time zone.

▌ LOST AND FOUND

To inquire about items lost or found in Yosemite's restaurants, hotels, lounges, shuttles, or tour buses, contact the Delaware North Corporation. For items lost or found in other areas of the park, contact the park's lost and found number.

In Sequoia & Kings Canyon, report lost items or turn in found items at any visitor center or ranger station. Items are held at a central location and are handled by park rangers. For more information, call park headquarters.

Contacts **Delaware North Corporation** (☎209/372–4357 ✐ yoselost@dncinc.com). **Yosemite National Park** (☎209/379–1001 ✐ yose_web_manager@nps.gov). **Sequoia & Kings Canyon National Parks** (☎559/565–3181).

▌ MAIL

Yosemite Post Offices **Curry Village Post Office** (✉*Curry Village, Yosemite National Park* ☎209/372–4475 ⊘*Closed Labor Day–Memorial Day*). **El Portal Post Office** (✉*5508 Foresta Rd., El Portal* ☎209/379–2311). **Yosemite Main Post Office** (✉*Yosemite Village, Yosemite National Park* ☎209/372–4475). **Wawona Post Office** (✉*Rte. 41, Wawona ,Yosemite National Park* ☎209/375–6574). **Yosemite Lodge Post Office** (✉*Yosemite Village,Yosemite National Park* ☎209/372–4853).

Sequoia & Kings Canyon Post Offices **Kings Canyon National Park Branch** (✉*86724 Rte. 180, Grant Grove Village, Grant Grove, Kings Canyon National Park* ☎559/335–2499). **Sequoia National Park Branch** (✉*Lodgepole Village, Giant Forest, Sequoia National Park* ☎559/565–3468). **Three Rivers Main Post Office** (✉*40857 Sierra Dr., Three Rivers* ☎559/561–4261).

▌ MONEY

Food and camping supplies are not that much more expensive in the parks than they are in the Central Valley and other parts of California. You will, however, pay about twice the normal going rate for ice.

Within and near the parks, gasoline is about 50¢ more per gallon than elsewhere in a state that has the Lower 48's highest gas prices.

In Yosemite, there are ATMs inside the stores at Yosemite Village, Curry Village, Wawona, and Tuolumne Meadows, as well as in the lobby of Yosemite Lodge, and outside the Art Activity Center.

In Sequoia and Kings Canyon, there are ATMs at the Grant Grove Gift Shop and the Lodgepole Market. The nearest banks are in Visalia and Three Rivers.

Banks Near Yosemite **Yosemite Bank** (✉*Hwy. 140 at Hwy. 49 North, Mariposa* ☎209/966–5444).

Banks Near Sequoia & Kings Canyon **Bank of America** (✉*212 E. Main St., Visalia* ☎559/635–3160). **Bank of the Sierra** (✉*40884 Sierra Dr., Three Rivers* ☎559/561–5910). **Grant Grove Village Gift Shop** (✉*Grant Grove Village, Grant Grove, Kings Canyon National Park*). **Lodgepole Market** (✉*Next to Lodgepole Visitor Center, Giant Forest, Sequoia National Park*).

CREDIT CARDS

Throughout this guide, the following abbreviations are used: **AE,** American Express; **D,** Discover; **DC,** Diners Club; **MC,** MasterCard; and **V,** Visa.

Reporting Lost Cards **American Express** (☎800/528–4800 ⊕www.americanexpress.com). **MasterCard** (☎800/627–8372 ⊕www.mastercard.com). **Visa** (☎800/847–2911⊕www.visa.com).

▌ PERMITS

If you plan to camp in the Yosemite backcountry, you must have a wilderness permit. Availability of permits, which are free, depends upon trailhead quotas. It's best to make a reservation, especially if you will be visiting from May through September. You can reserve two days to 24 weeks in advance by phone, mail, or e-mail; a $5 per person processing fee is charged if and when your reservations are confirmed. In your request, include your name, address, daytime phone, the number of people in your party, trip date, alternative dates, starting and ending trailheads, and a brief itinerary. Without a reservation, you may still get a free permit on a first-come, first-served basis at wilderness permit offices at Big Oak Flat, Hetch Hetchy, Tuolumne, Wawona, the Wilderness Center, and Yosemite Valley in summer; fall through spring, visit the Valley Visitor Center.

If you plan to camp in the Sequoia or Kings Canyon backcountry, your group must have a backcountry camping permit, which costs $15 for hikers or $30 for stock users (horseback riders, etc.). One permit covers the entire group. Availability of permits depends upon trailhead quotas. Advance reservations are accepted by mail, fax, or e-mail for a $15 processing fee, beginning March 1, and must be made at least three weeks in advance. Without a reservation, you may still get a permit on a first-come, first-served basis starting at 1 PM the day before you plan to hike. For more information on backcountry camping or

travel with pack animals (horses, mules, burros, or llamas), contact Sequoia & Kings Canyon's Wilderness Permit Office.

Yosemite Contacts **Wilderness Permits** (✉ *Box 545, Yosemite 95389* ☎ *209/372-0740* ⊕ *www.nps. gov/yose/wilderness/permits.htm*).

Sequoia & Kings Canyon Contacts **Wilderness Permit Office** (☎ *530/565-3761*). **Wilderness Permit Reservations** (✉ *HCR 89 Box 60, Three Rivers 93271* ☎ *559/575-3766* 📠 *559/565-4239* ⊕ *www.nps.gov/seki/planyourvisit/ wilderness_permits.htm*).

▌ RESTROOMS

In Yosemite, public restrooms are at visitor centers; all restaurants and lodging facilities in the park; at the Village Store, the Vernal Falls footbridge, Yosemite Falls, Tuolumne Meadows, and Glacier Point; and at the Swinging Bridge, Cathedral Beach, Sentinel Beach, Church Bowl, and El Capitan picnic areas. ▌TIP→ **Yosemite's best restrooms are those behind the golf shop at Wawona, and the worst (flush variety) are at the Crane Flat gas and convenience store.**

In Sequoia & Kings Canyon, public restrooms may be found at all visitor centers and campgrounds. Additional locations include Big Stump, Columbine, Grizzly Falls, Hospital Rock, Wolverton, Crescent Meadow, Giant Forest Museum, and Crystal Cave.

▌ SAFETY

Regardless of which outdoor activities you pursue or your level of skill, safety must come first. Remember: Know your limits. And try never to hike alone.

Many trails in the three parks are remote and sparsely traveled. In the 8,000-feet-plus altitudes of the High Sierra, oxygen is noticeably scarcer than it is at sea level. Hikers, bikers, and riders should carry emergency supplies. Proper equipment includes a flashlight, a compass, waterproof matches, a first-aid kit, a knife, a cell phone with an extra battery (although you may have to climb atop a mountain ridge to find a signal), and a light plastic tarp for shelter. Backcountry skiers should add a repair kit, a blanket, an avalanche beacon, and a lightweight shovel to their lists. Always bring extra food and water, as dehydration is a common occurrence at high altitudes. Never drink from streams or lakes unless you boil the water first or purify it with tablets. Giardia, an intestinal parasite, may be present.

Always check the condition of roads and trails, and get the latest weather reports before setting out. In summer, take precautions against heat stroke or exhaustion by resting frequently in shaded areas; in winter, take precautions against hypothermia by layering clothing. Ultimately, proper planning, common sense, and good physical conditioning are the strongest safeguards against the elements.

ALTITUDE

You may feel dizzy and weak and find yourself breathing heavily—signs that the thin mountain air isn't giving you your accustomed dose of oxygen. Take it easy and rest often for a few days until you're acclimatized. Throughout your stay, drink plenty of water and watch your alcohol consumption. If you experience severe headaches and nausea, see a doctor. It is easy to go too high, too fast. The remedy for altitude-related discomfort is to go down quickly, into heavier air. Other altitude-related problems include dehydration and overexposure to the sun because of thin air.

EXPOSURE

Altitude, severe cold temperatures, and sometimes windy weather in the High Sierra can often combine to create intense and dangerous outdoor conditions. In winter, exposure to wind and cold can quickly bring on hypothermia or frostbite. Protect yourself by dressing in layers, so you don't become overheated and then chilled. Any time of year, the region's clear air and high elevation make sunburn a particular risk. Always wear sunscreen, even when skies are overcast.

ANIMALS

One of the most wonderful parts of the Sierra Nevada and high wilderness areas is the abundant wildlife. And although a deer that's not too close is indeed a Kodak moment, an encounter with a bear or mountain lion is not. To avoid such a dangerous situation while hiking, make plenty of noise and keep small children between adults. While camping, be sure to store all food, utensils, and anything with fragrant smells in a bear canister or bear box. (In all three parks, it's routine to hear about bears that break into cars that contain food. Rangers will fine you if they see or strongly suspect there is food in your parked car.) If you come across a bear or mountain lion, do not run. For bears, back away quietly; for lions, make yourself look as big as possible. In either case, be prepared to fend off the animal with rocks, sticks, and so on. In the unlikely event a bear attacks, play dead. If a mountain lion attacks, fight for your life.

When in the wilderness, give all animals their space and never attempt to feed any of them. If you want to take a photograph, use a zoom lens rather than try to sneak closer. This is particularly important for winter visitors. Approaching an animal can cause it stress and affect its ability to survive the sometimes brutal climate. In all cases, remember the animals have the right-of-way; this is their home, and you are the visitor.

TAXES

Sales tax in California varies from about 7.25% to 8.5% and applies to all purchases except for food purchased in a grocery store; food consumed in a restaurant is taxed but take-out food purchases are not. Hotel taxes vary widely by region, from 10% to 15%.

TIPPING

Most service workers in California are fairly well paid compared to those in the rest of the country, and extravagant tipping is not the rule here. You may feel more pressure to tip generously at the Ahwahnee, which has a pronounced upscale vibe.

VISITOR INFORMATION

Contacts **Delaware North Companies Parks & Resorts** (☎559/565–4070 or 888/252–5757 ⊕www.visitsequoia.com) operates the lodgings and visitor services in Sequoia, and some in Kings Canyon. **Kings Canyon Park Services** (☎559/335–5500 or 888/564–7775 ⊕www.sequoia-kingscanyon.com) operates some park services, including lodging.**Sequoia and Kings Canyon National Parks** (☎559/565–3341 or 559/565–3134 ⊕www.nps.gov/seki). **Sequoia Natural History Association** (☎559/565–3759 ⊕www.sequoiahistory.org) operates Crystal Cave and the Pear Lake Ski Hut, and provides educational materials and programs. **Yosemite National Park** (☎209/372–0200 ⊕www.nps.gov/yose).

INDEX

NOTES

NOTES

NOTES

NOTES

NOTES

NOTES

NOTES

ABOUT OUR WRITER

An itinerant upbringing, which included living in Illinois, Colorado, and Australia, and a college semester in France, helped instill the traveling spirit in Reed Parsell. After a few short stints as a general assignment reporter for small newspapers in the Great Plains and graduate studies at Pennsylvania State University, Reed began dabbling in travel writing.

For more than 20 years he has been putting fingers to keyboard describing destinations throughout the United States and in much of the world. His stories and photographs have appeared in dozens of newspapers. Since 1994, he has been a copy editor and travel writer for the *Sacramento Bee*, and the weekly stories he writes for the state capital's daily usually are about Northern California attractions.

Researching Fodor's In Focus guide to Yellowstone and Sequoia/Kings Canyon national parks took Reed into the Sierra Nevada mountain range several times, exposing him more intimately to the countless wonders of the three national parks. For his many overnight absences from home, he wishes to thank the patience of his loving wife, Kari, who happily was able to spend a few days with him in Sequoia and Yosemite. Reed also wishes to thank Michael Nalepa and Douglas Stallings, two Fodor's editors who have helped Reed find a delightful way to keep traveling and get paid for the privilege.